Garfield
goes to waist

BY JIM DAVIS

Ballantine Books • New York

2009 Ballantine Books Trade Paperback Edition

Copyright © 1990, 2009 by PAWS, Inc. All rights reserved.
"GARFIELD" and the GARFIELD characters are registered and unregistered trademarks of PAWS, Inc.

Published in the United States by Ballantine Books, an imprint of The Random House Publishing Group,
a division of Random House, Inc., New York.

BALLANTINE and colophon are registered trademarks of Random House, Inc.

Originally published in slightly different form in the United States by Ballantine Books, an imprint of
The Random House Publishing Group, a division of Random House, Inc., in 1990.

ISBN 978-0-345-49173-2

Printed in the United States of America

www.ballantinebooks.com

9 8 7 6 5 4 3 2 1

First Colorized Edition

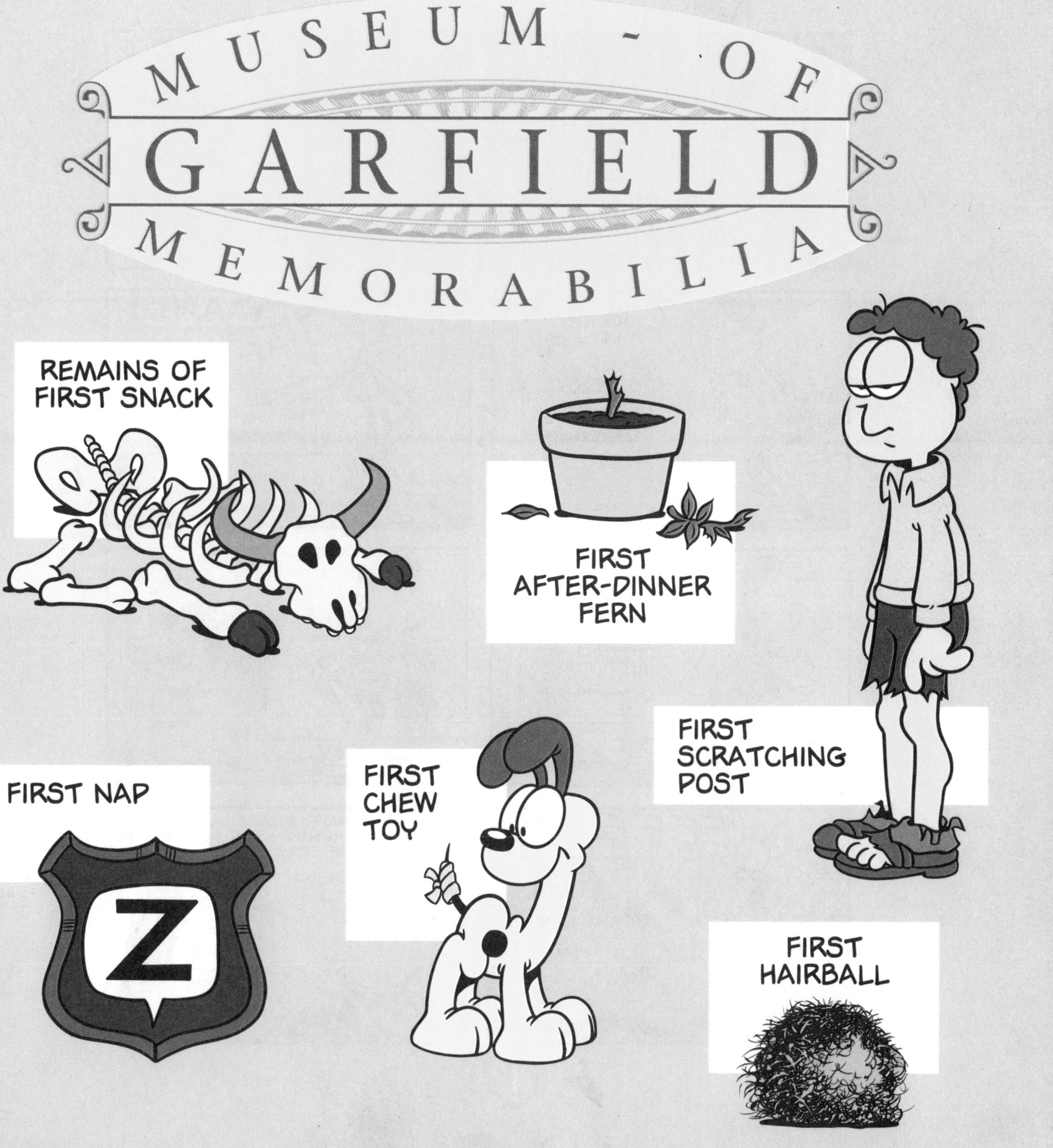
MUSEUM - OF
GARFIELD
MEMORABILIA
REMAINS OF FIRST SNACK
FIRST AFTER-DINNER FERN
FIRST SCRATCHING POST
FIRST NAP
Z
FIRST CHEW TOY
FIRST HAIRBALL

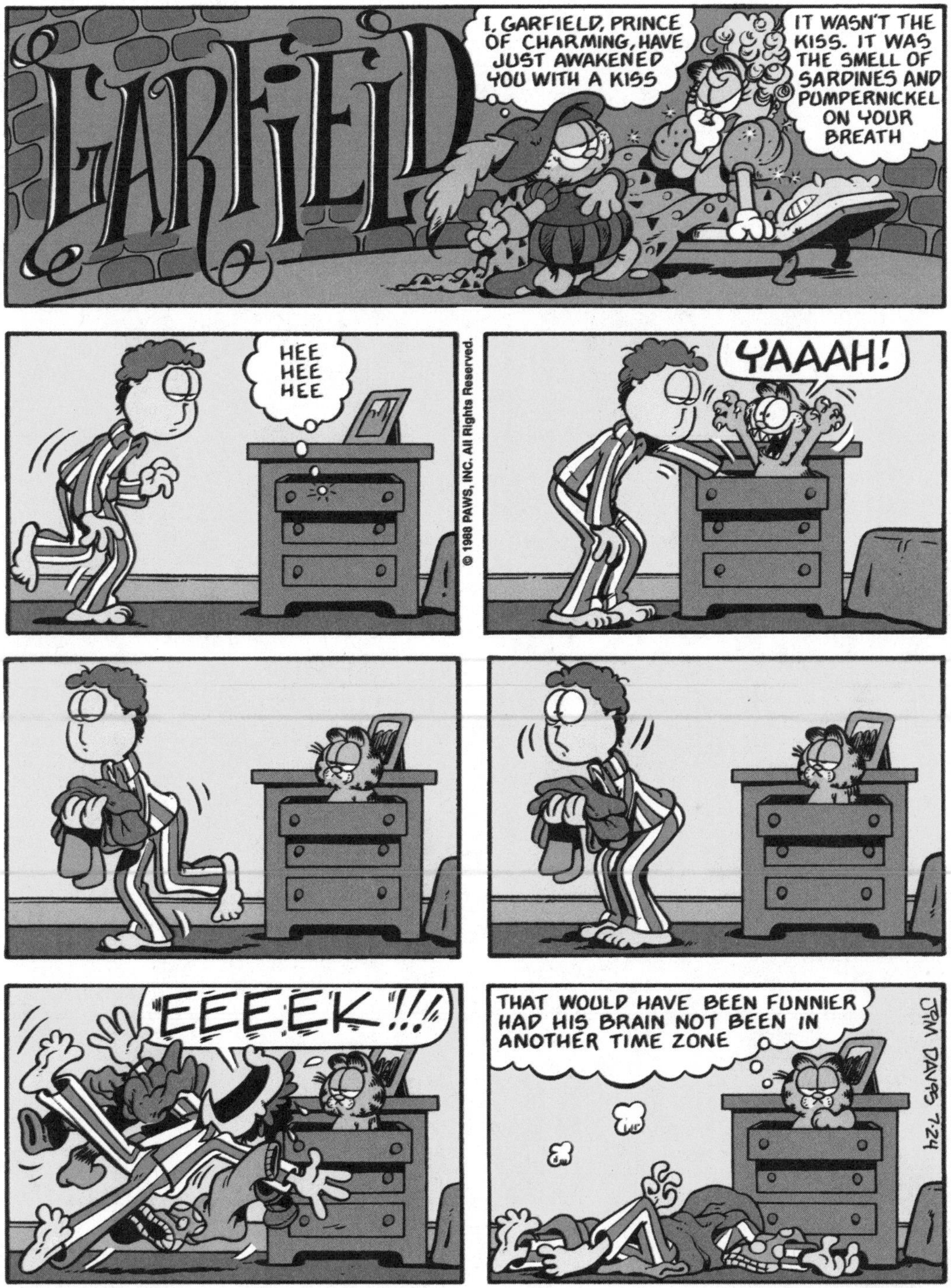
GARFIELD
I, GARFIELD, PRINCE OF CHARMING, HAVE JUST AWAKENED YOU WITH A KISS
IT WASN'T THE KISS. IT WAS THE SMELL OF SARDINES AND PUMPERNICKEL ON YOUR BREATH
HEE HEE HEE
YAAAH!
EEEEK!!!
THAT WOULD HAVE BEEN FUNNIER HAD HIS BRAIN NOT BEEN IN ANOTHER TIME ZONE
JIM DAVIS 7-24

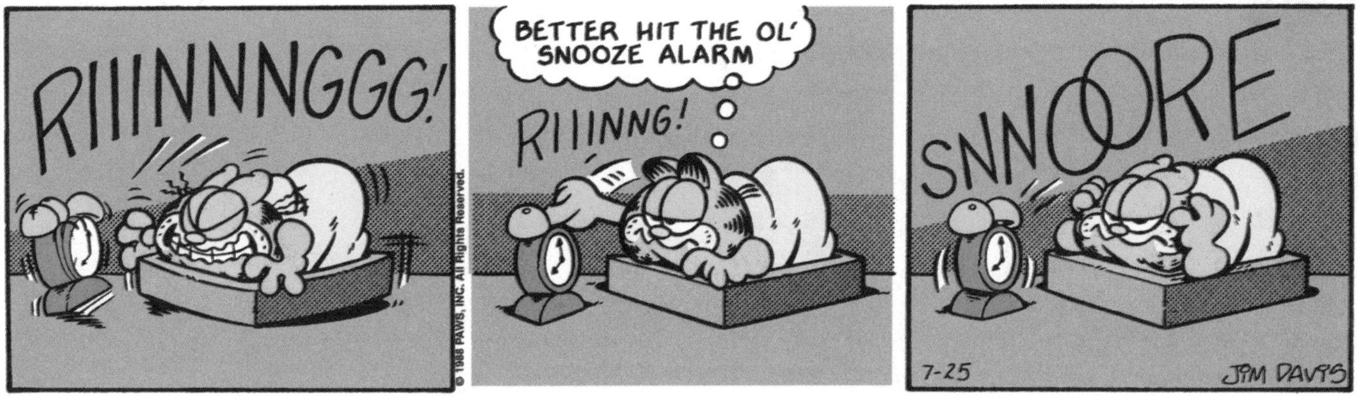
RIIINNNGGG!
© 1988 PAWS, INC. All Rights Reserved.
BETTER HIT THE OL' SNOOZE ALARM
RIIINNG!
SNNOORE
7-25
JIM DAVIS

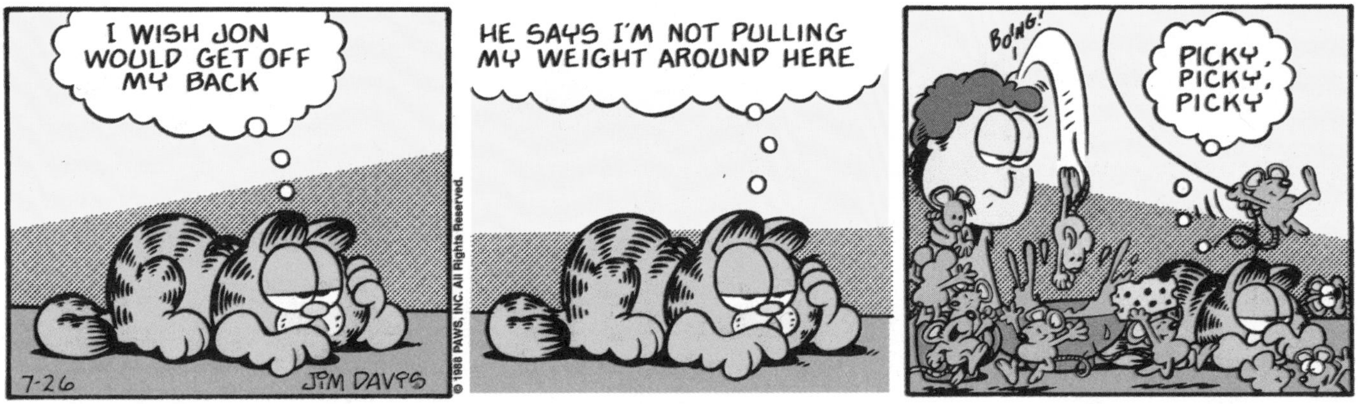
I WISH JON WOULD GET OFF MY BACK
7-26
JIM DAVIS
© 1988 PAWS, INC. All Rights Reserved.
HE SAYS I'M NOT PULLING MY WEIGHT AROUND HERE
BOING!
PICKY, PICKY, PICKY

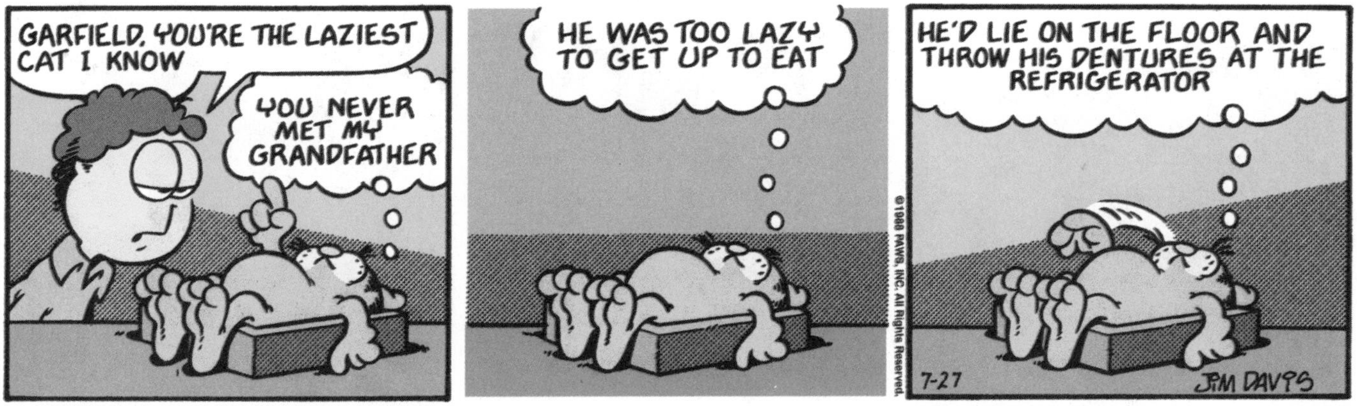
GARFIELD, YOU'RE THE LAZIEST CAT I KNOW
YOU NEVER MET MY GRANDFATHER
HE WAS TOO LAZY TO GET UP TO EAT
©1988 PAWS, INC. All Rights Reserved.
HE'D LIE ON THE FLOOR AND THROW HIS DENTURES AT THE REFRIGERATOR
7-27
JIM DAVIS

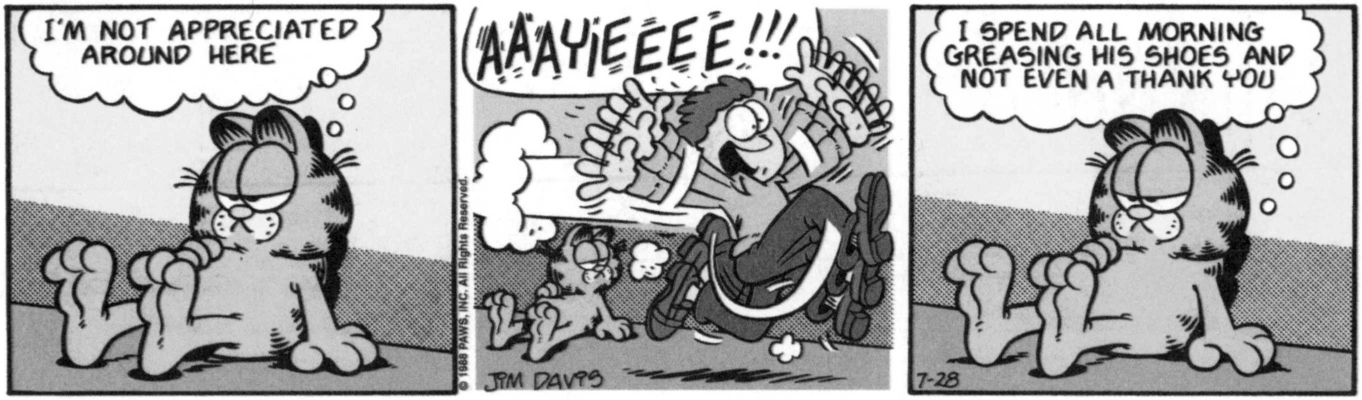
I'M NOT APPRECIATED AROUND HERE
AAAYIEEEE!!!
© 1988 PAWS, INC. All Rights Reserved.
JIM DAVIS
I SPEND ALL MORNING GREASING HIS SHOES AND NOT EVEN A THANK YOU
7-28

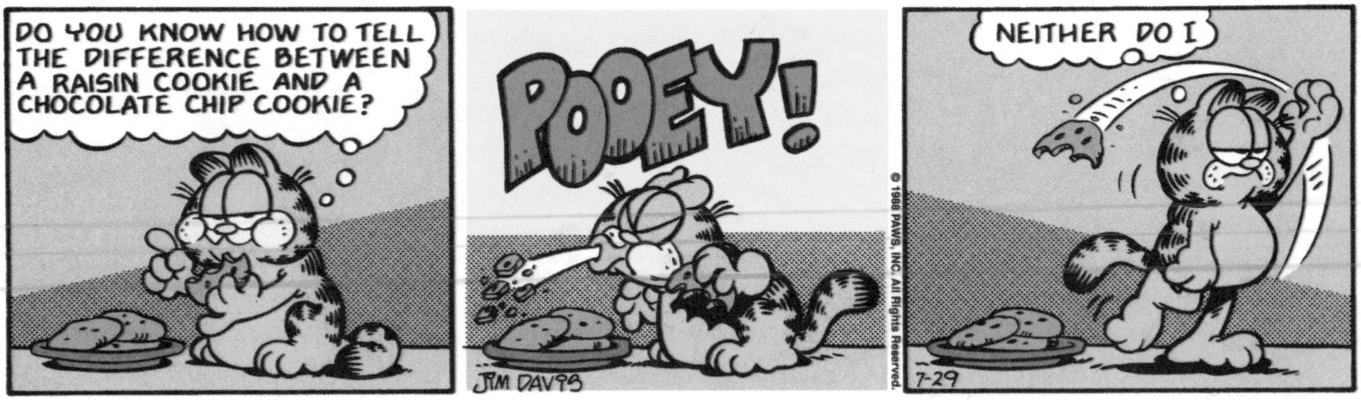
DO YOU KNOW HOW TO TELL THE DIFFERENCE BETWEEN A RAISIN COOKIE AND A CHOCOLATE CHIP COOKIE?
POOEY!
JIM DAVIS
© 1988 PAWS, INC. All Rights Reserved.
NEITHER DO I
7-29

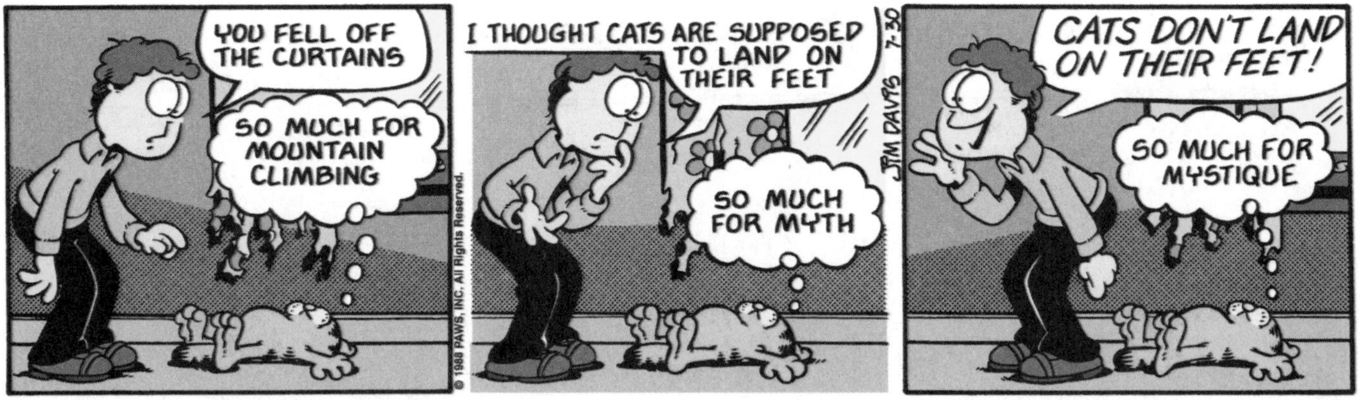
YOU FELL OFF THE CURTAINS
SO MUCH FOR MOUNTAIN CLIMBING
© 1988 PAWS, INC. All Rights Reserved.
I THOUGHT CATS ARE SUPPOSED TO LAND ON THEIR FEET
SO MUCH FOR MYTH
7-30
JIM DAVIS
CATS DON'T LAND ON THEIR FEET!
SO MUCH FOR MYSTIQUE

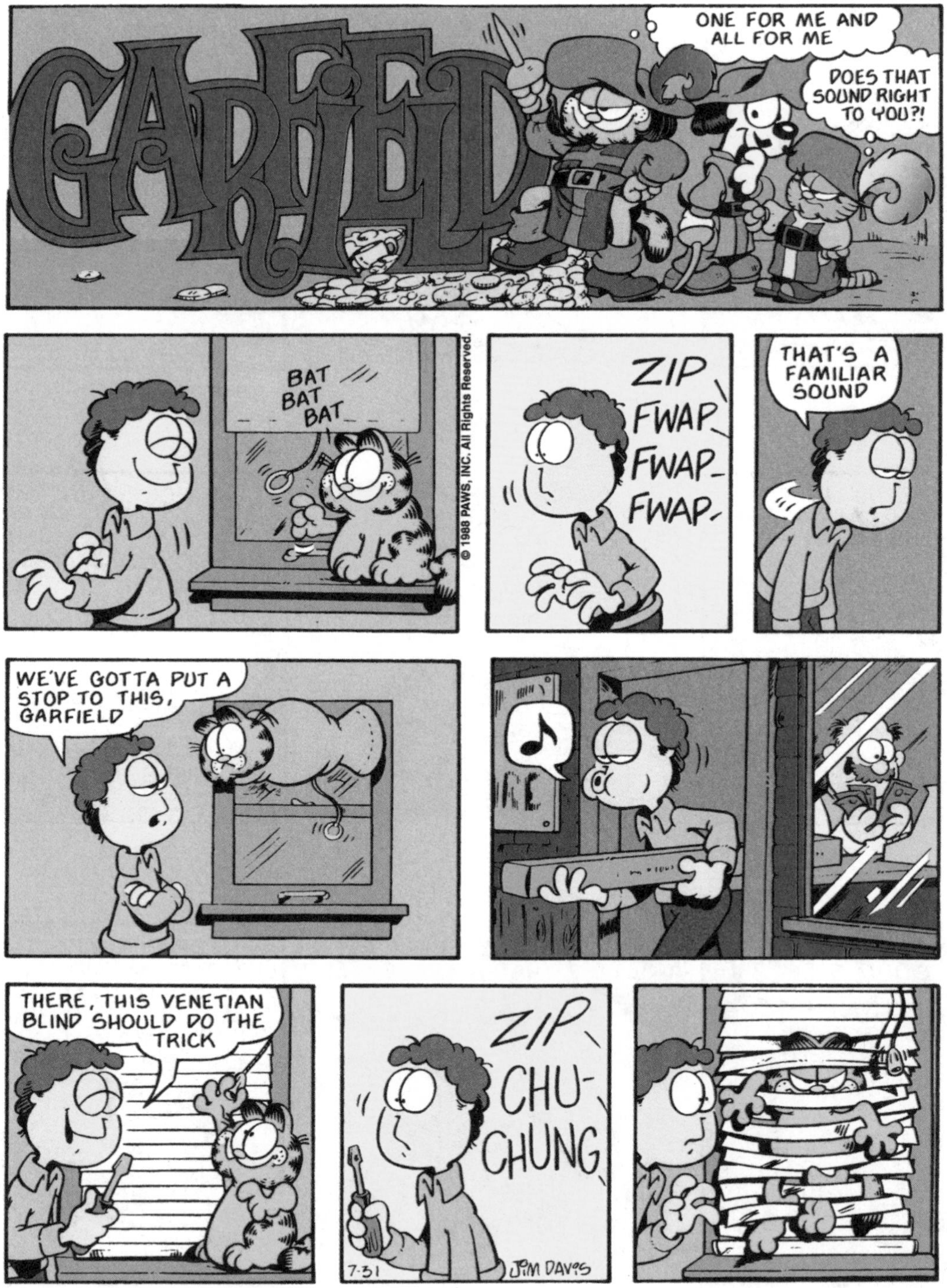
GARFIELD
ONE FOR ME AND ALL FOR ME
DOES THAT SOUND RIGHT TO YOU?!
BAT BAT BAT
© 1988 PAWS, INC. All Rights Reserved.
ZIP FWAP FWAP FWAP
THAT'S A FAMILIAR SOUND
WE'VE GOTTA PUT A STOP TO THIS, GARFIELD
THERE, THIS VENETIAN BLIND SHOULD DO THE TRICK
ZIP CHU-CHUNG
7-31
JIM DAVIS

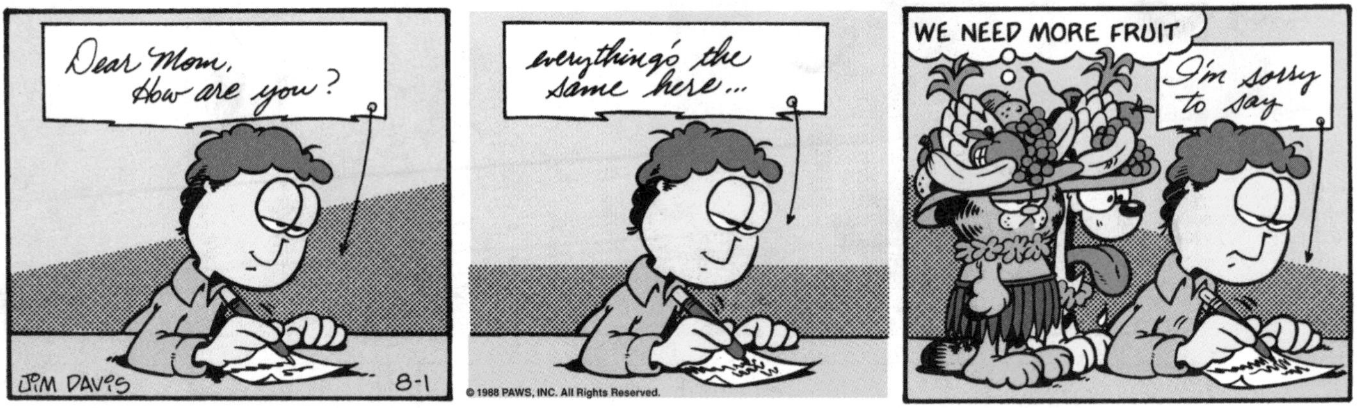
Dear Mom,
How are you?
JIM DAVIS 8-1
everything's the same here...
WE NEED MORE FRUIT
I'm sorry to say

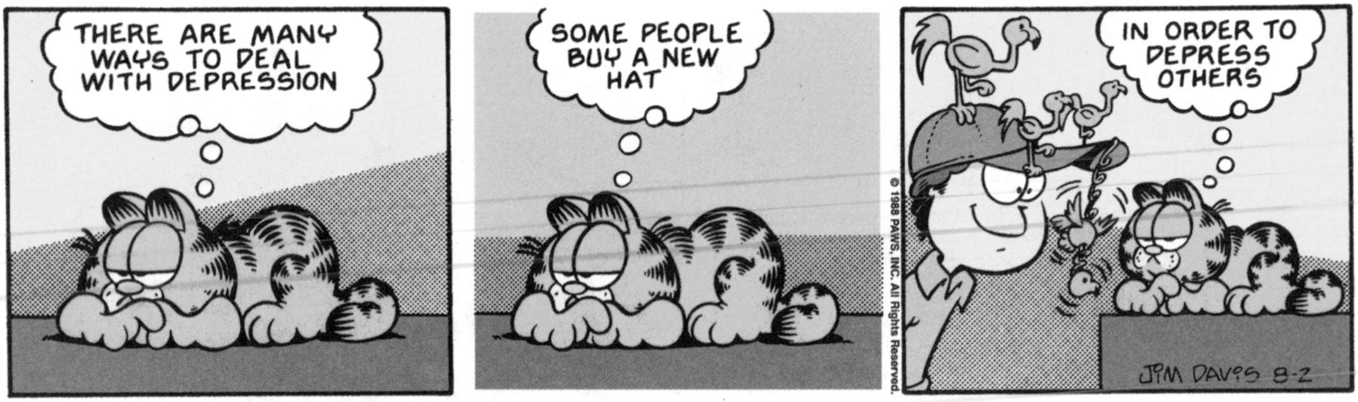
THERE ARE MANY WAYS TO DEAL WITH DEPRESSION
SOME PEOPLE BUY A NEW HAT
IN ORDER TO DEPRESS OTHERS
JIM DAVIS 8-2

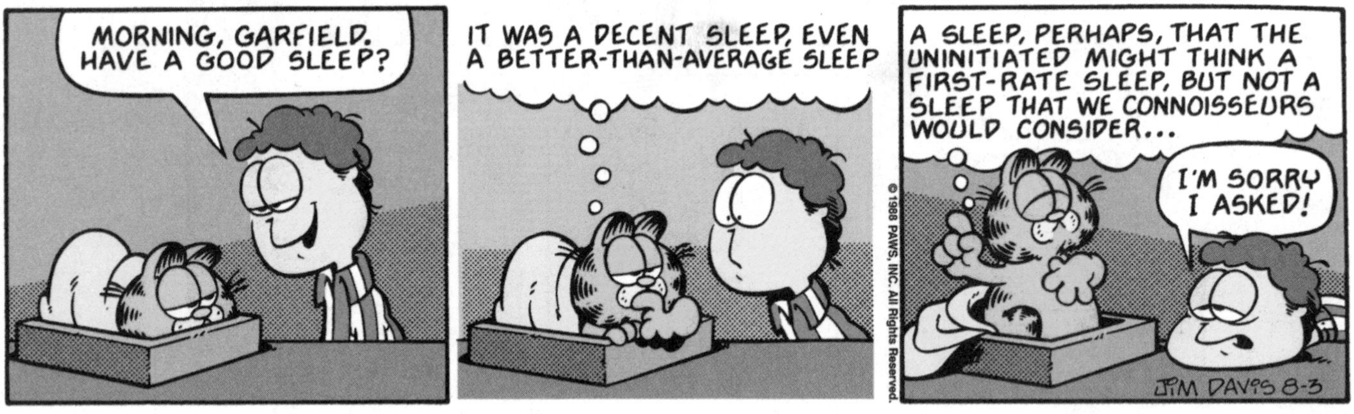
MORNING, GARFIELD. HAVE A GOOD SLEEP?
IT WAS A DECENT SLEEP, EVEN A BETTER-THAN-AVERAGE SLEEP
A SLEEP, PERHAPS, THAT THE UNINITIATED MIGHT THINK A FIRST-RATE SLEEP, BUT NOT A SLEEP THAT WE CONNOISSEURS WOULD CONSIDER...
I'M SORRY I ASKED!
JIM DAVIS 8-3

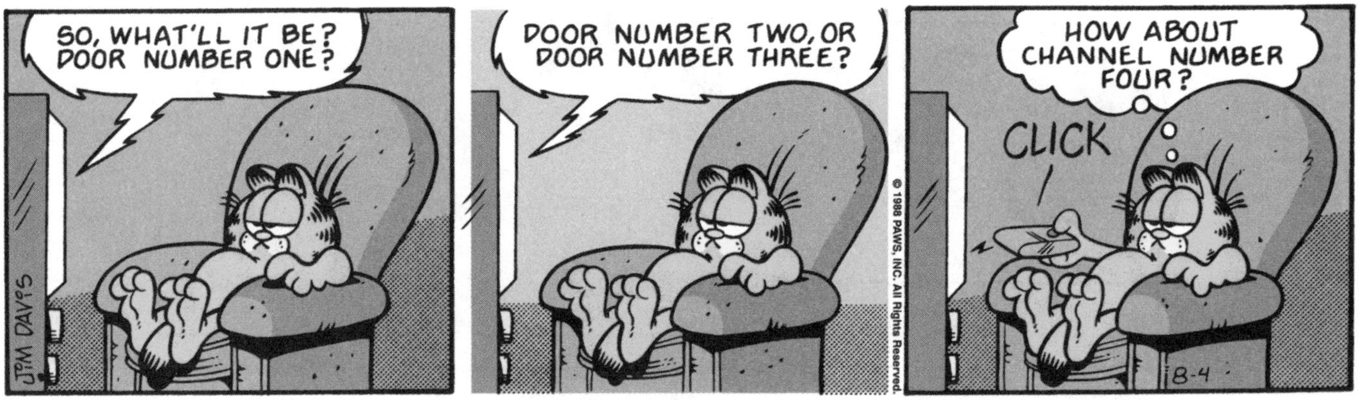
JIM DAVIS
SO, WHAT'LL IT BE? DOOR NUMBER ONE?
DOOR NUMBER TWO, OR DOOR NUMBER THREE?
© 1988 PAWS, INC. All Rights Reserved.
HOW ABOUT CHANNEL NUMBER FOUR?
CLICK
8-4

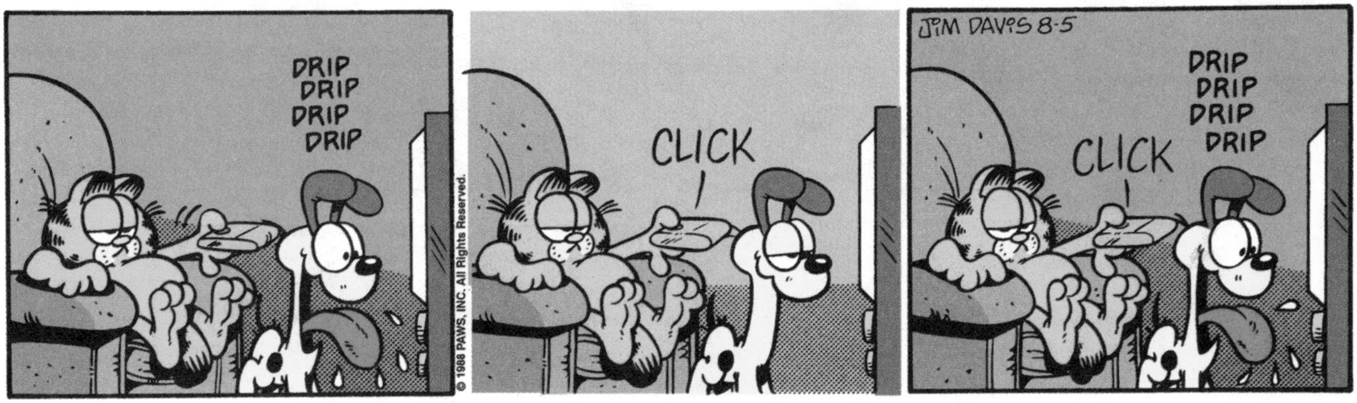
DRIP DRIP DRIP DRIP
© 1988 PAWS, INC. All Rights Reserved.
CLICK
JIM DAVIS 8-5
CLICK
DRIP DRIP DRIP DRIP

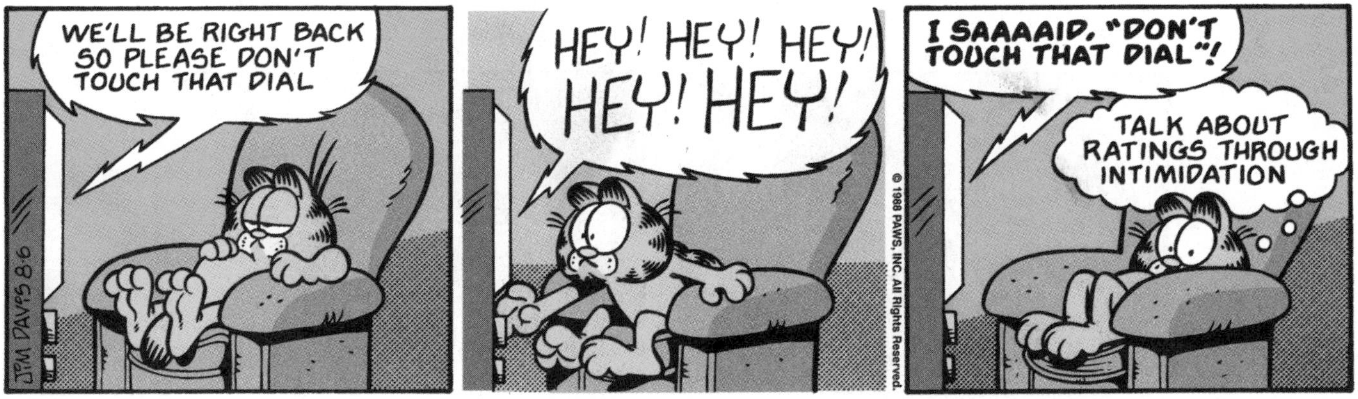
JIM DAVIS 8-6
WE'LL BE RIGHT BACK SO PLEASE DON'T TOUCH THAT DIAL
HEY! HEY! HEY! HEY! HEY!
© 1988 PAWS, INC. All Rights Reserved.
I SAAAAID, "DON'T TOUCH THAT DIAL"!
TALK ABOUT RATINGS THROUGH INTIMIDATION

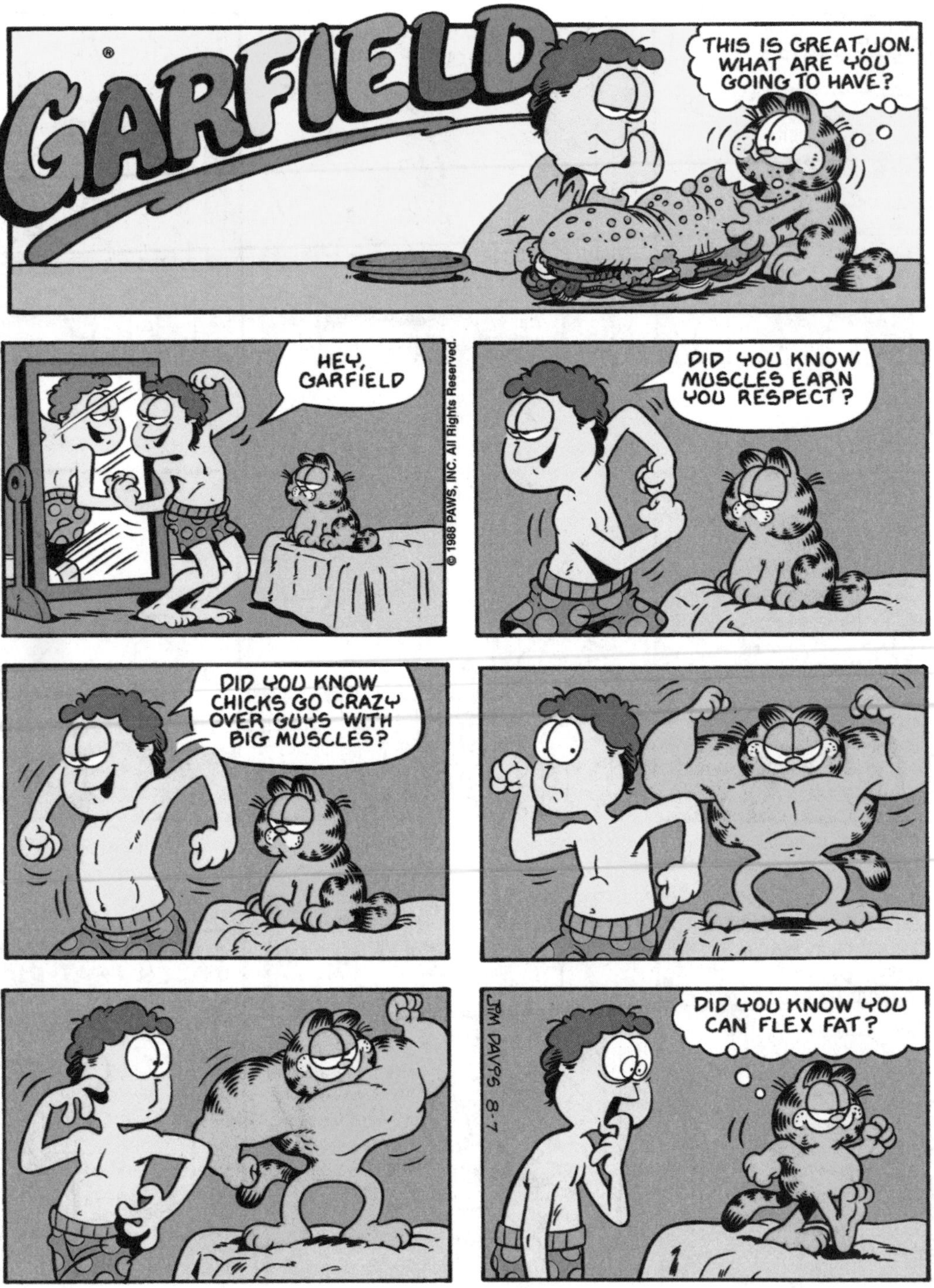
GARFIELD®
THIS IS GREAT, JON. WHAT ARE YOU GOING TO HAVE?
HEY, GARFIELD
© 1988 PAWS, INC. All Rights Reserved.
DID YOU KNOW MUSCLES EARN YOU RESPECT?
DID YOU KNOW CHICKS GO CRAZY OVER GUYS WITH BIG MUSCLES?
JIM DAVIS 8-7
DID YOU KNOW YOU CAN FLEX FAT?

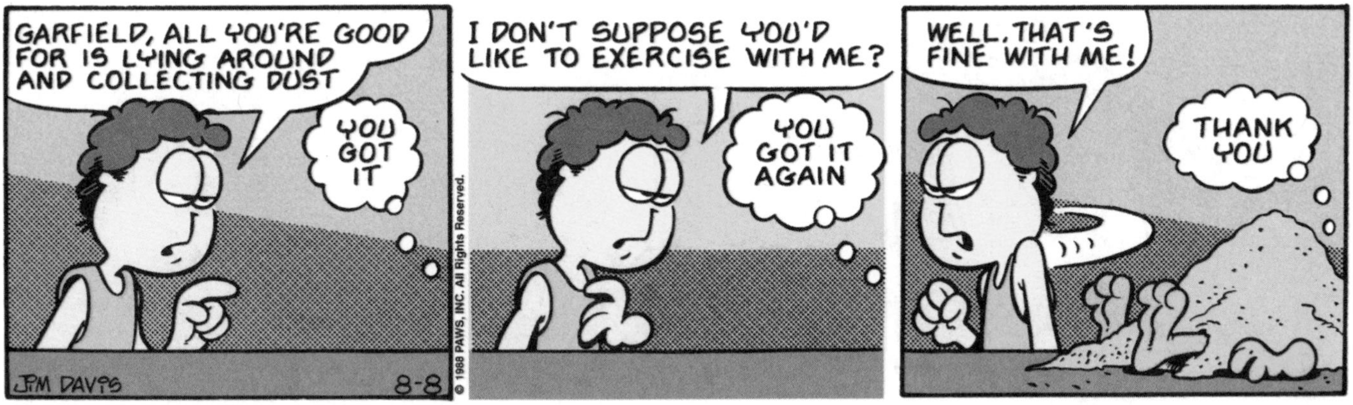
GARFIELD, ALL YOU'RE GOOD FOR IS LYING AROUND AND COLLECTING DUST
YOU GOT IT
JIM DAVIS
8-8
© 1988 PAWS, INC. All Rights Reserved.
I DON'T SUPPOSE YOU'D LIKE TO EXERCISE WITH ME?
YOU GOT IT AGAIN
WELL, THAT'S FINE WITH ME!
THANK YOU

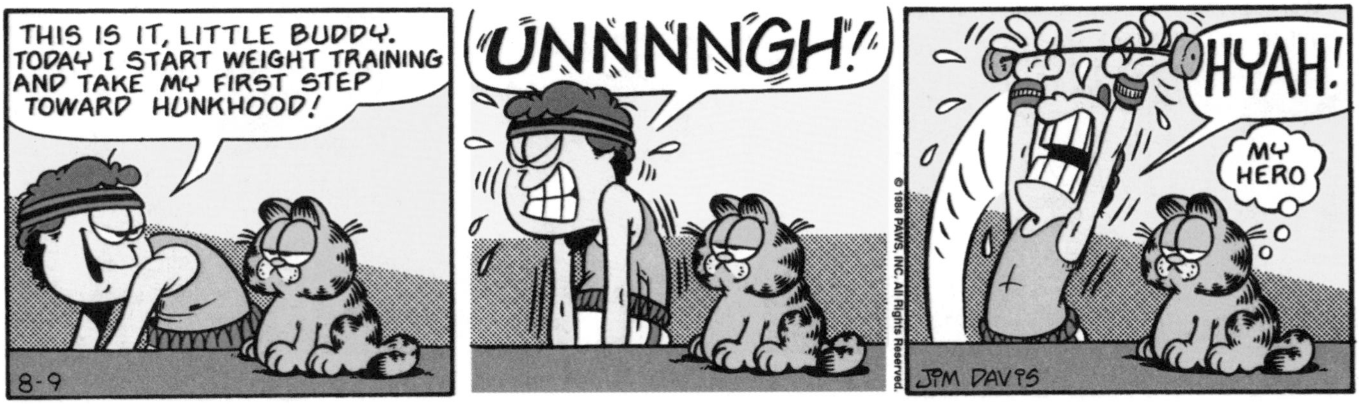
THIS IS IT, LITTLE BUDDY. TODAY I START WEIGHT TRAINING AND TAKE MY FIRST STEP TOWARD HUNKHOOD!
8-9
UNNNNGH!
© 1988 PAWS, INC. All Rights Reserved.
HYAH!
MY HERO
JIM DAVIS

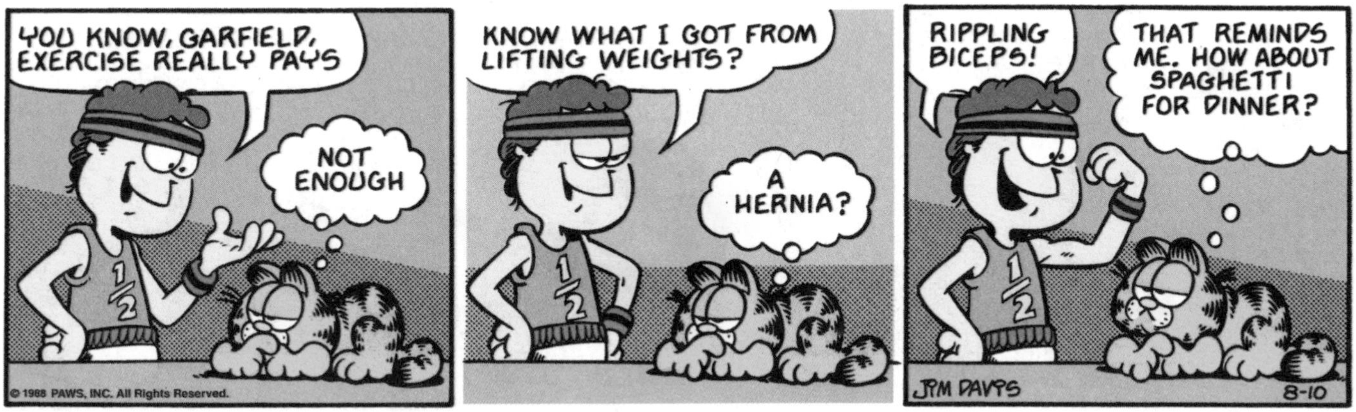
YOU KNOW, GARFIELD, EXERCISE REALLY PAYS
NOT ENOUGH
© 1988 PAWS, INC. All Rights Reserved.
KNOW WHAT I GOT FROM LIFTING WEIGHTS?
A HERNIA?
RIPPLING BICEPS!
THAT REMINDS ME. HOW ABOUT SPAGHETTI FOR DINNER?
JIM DAVIS
8-10

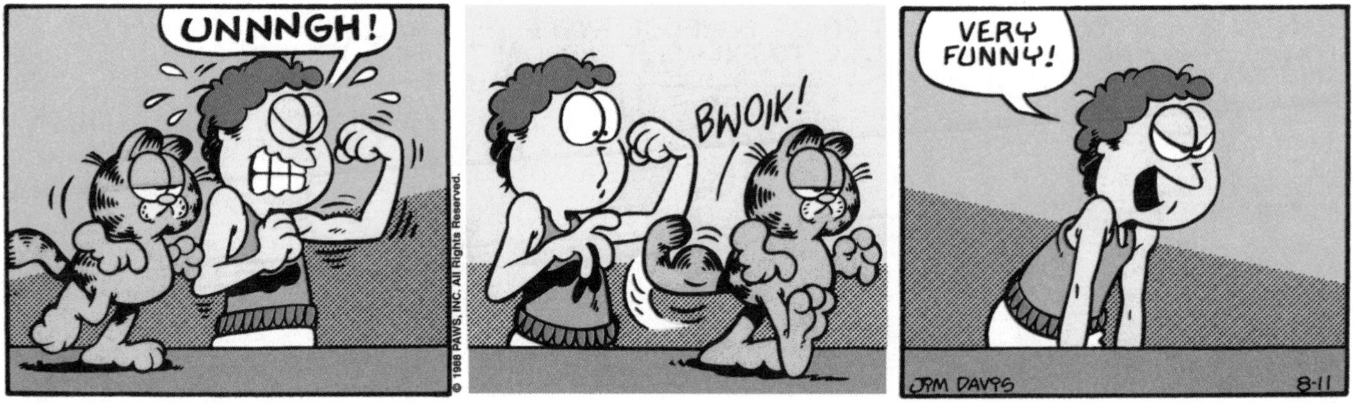
UNNNGH!
BWOIK!
VERY FUNNY!
© 1988 PAWS, INC. All Rights Reserved.
JIM DAVIS
8-11

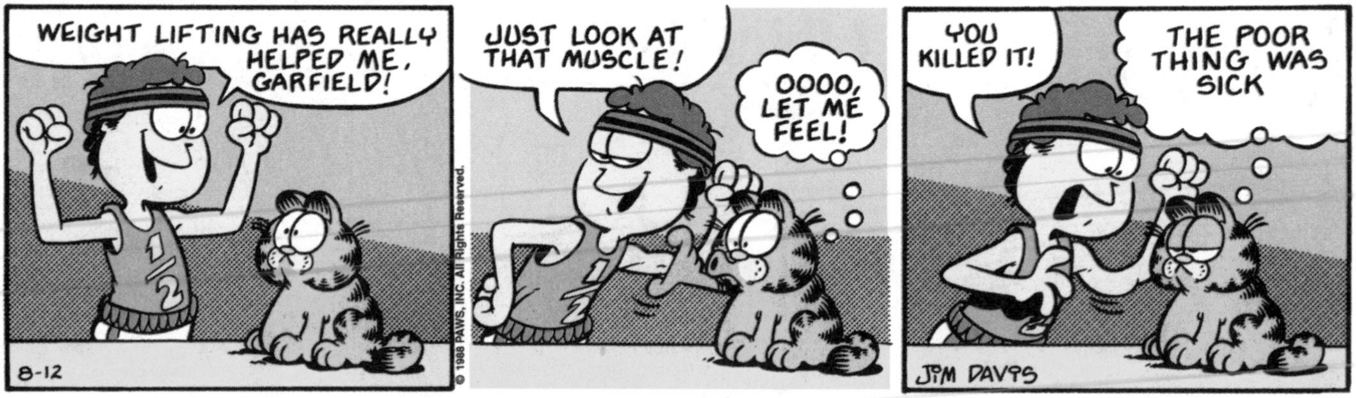
WEIGHT LIFTING HAS REALLY HELPED ME, GARFIELD!
8-12
JUST LOOK AT THAT MUSCLE!
OOOO, LET ME FEEL!
YOU KILLED IT!
THE POOR THING WAS SICK
© 1988 PAWS, INC. All Rights Reserved.
JIM DAVIS

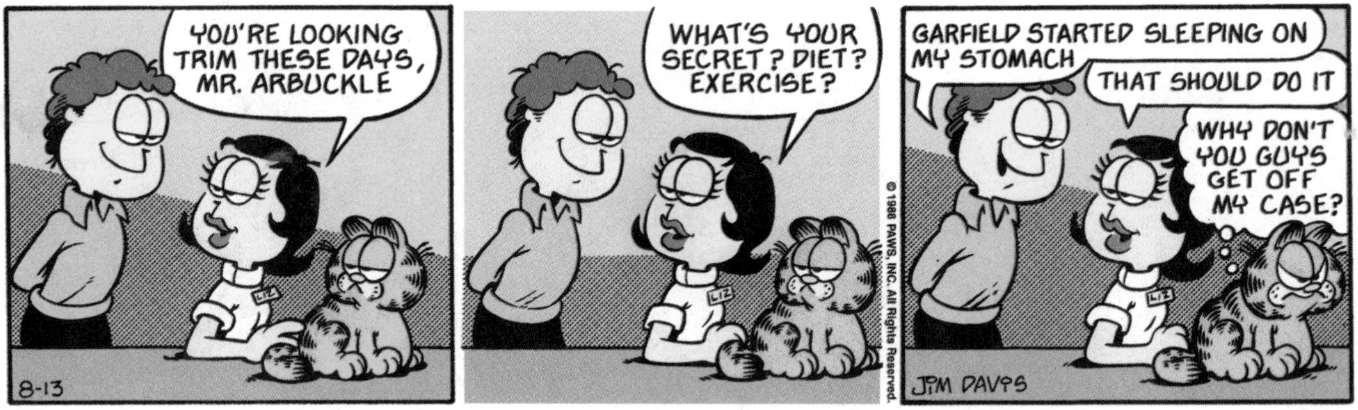
YOU'RE LOOKING TRIM THESE DAYS, MR. ARBUCKLE
8-13
WHAT'S YOUR SECRET? DIET? EXERCISE?
GARFIELD STARTED SLEEPING ON MY STOMACH
THAT SHOULD DO IT
WHY DON'T YOU GUYS GET OFF MY CASE?
© 1988 PAWS, INC. All Rights Reserved.
JIM DAVIS

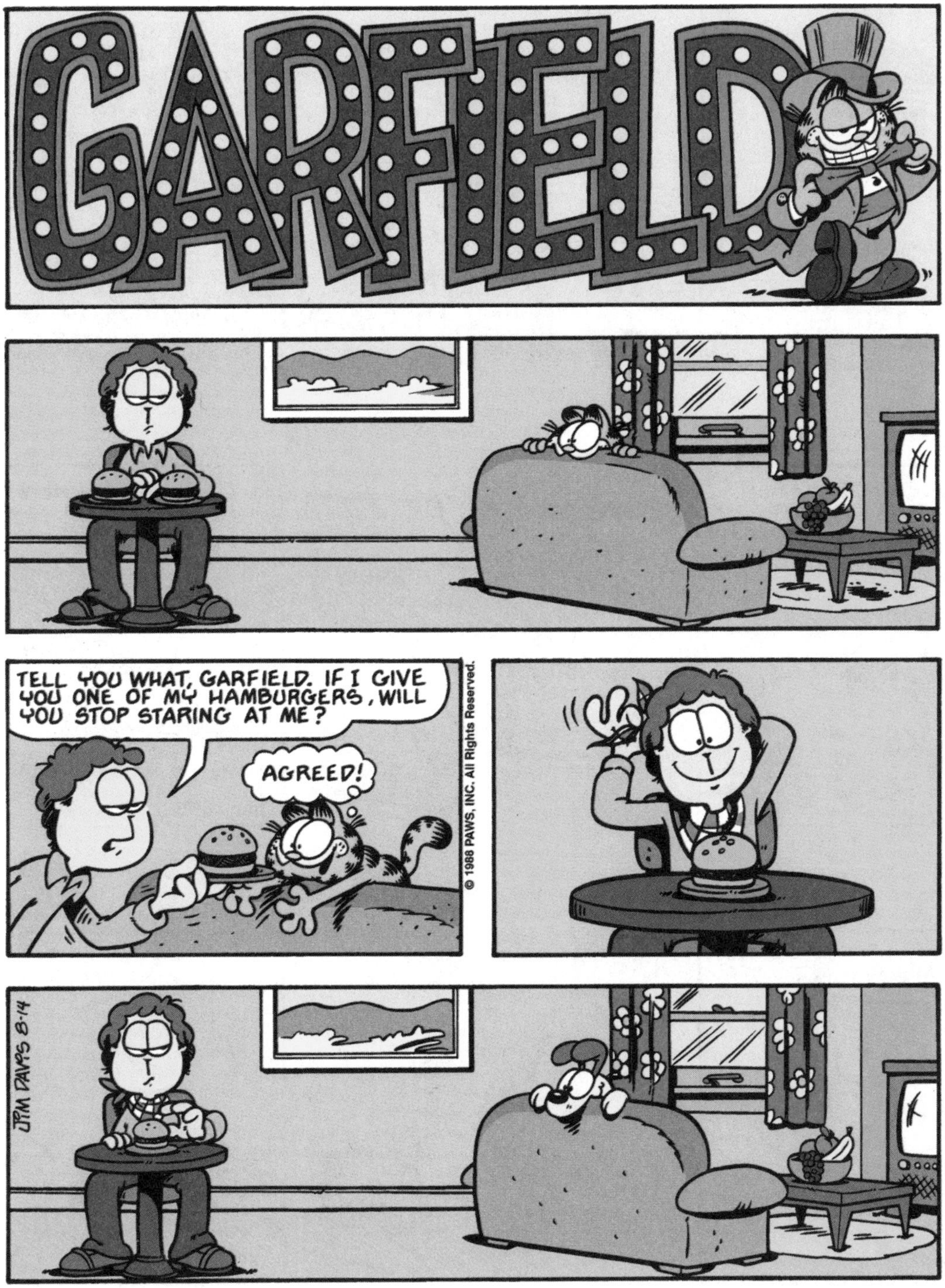
GARFIELD
TELL YOU WHAT, GARFIELD. IF I GIVE YOU ONE OF MY HAMBURGERS, WILL YOU STOP STARING AT ME?
AGREED!
© 1988 PAWS, INC. All Rights Reserved.
JIM DAVIS 8-14

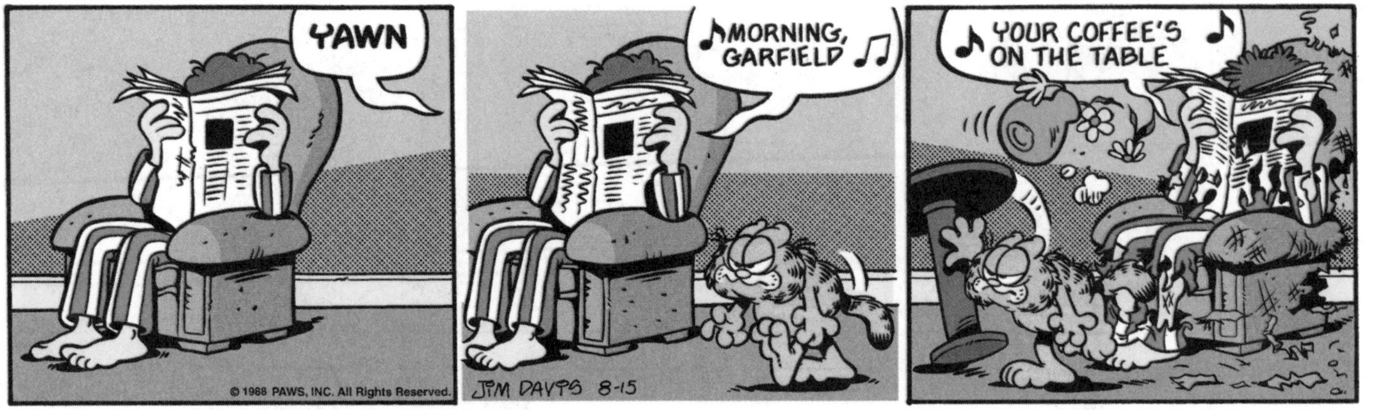
YAWN
© 1988 PAWS, INC. All Rights Reserved.
MORNING, GARFIELD
JIM DAVIS 8-15
YOUR COFFEE'S ON THE TABLE

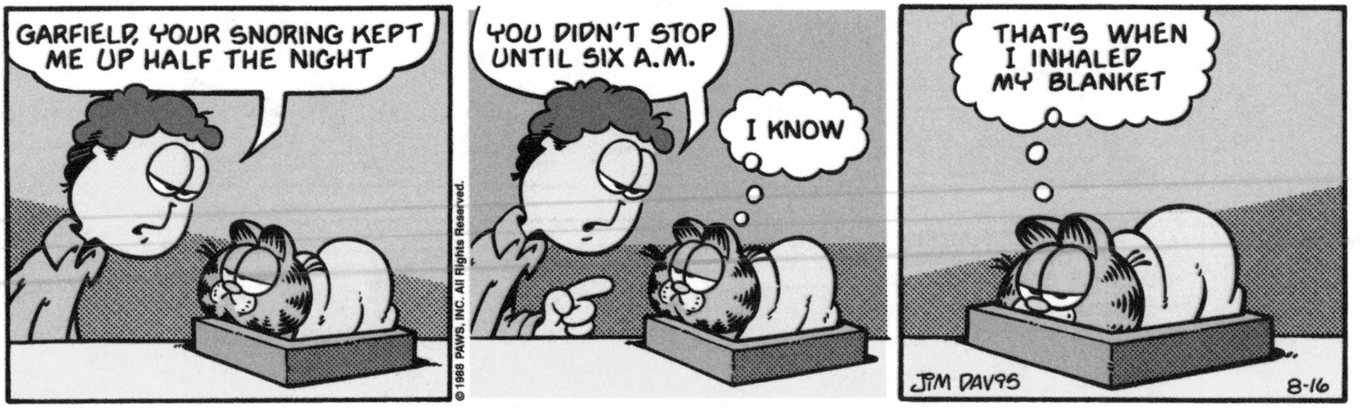
GARFIELD, YOUR SNORING KEPT ME UP HALF THE NIGHT
© 1988 PAWS, INC. All Rights Reserved.
YOU DIDN'T STOP UNTIL SIX A.M.
I KNOW
THAT'S WHEN I INHALED MY BLANKET
JIM DAVIS
8-16

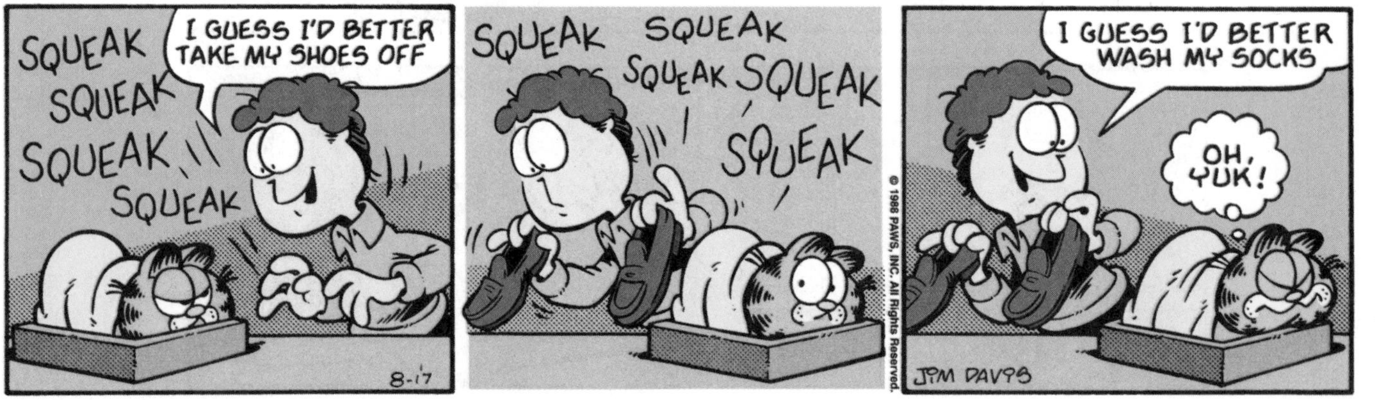
SQUEAK
SQUEAK
SQUEAK
SQUEAK
I GUESS I'D BETTER TAKE MY SHOES OFF
8-17
SQUEAK
SQUEAK
SQUEAK
SQUEAK
SQUEAK
© 1988 PAWS, INC. All Rights Reserved.
I GUESS I'D BETTER WASH MY SOCKS
OH, YUK!
JIM DAVIS

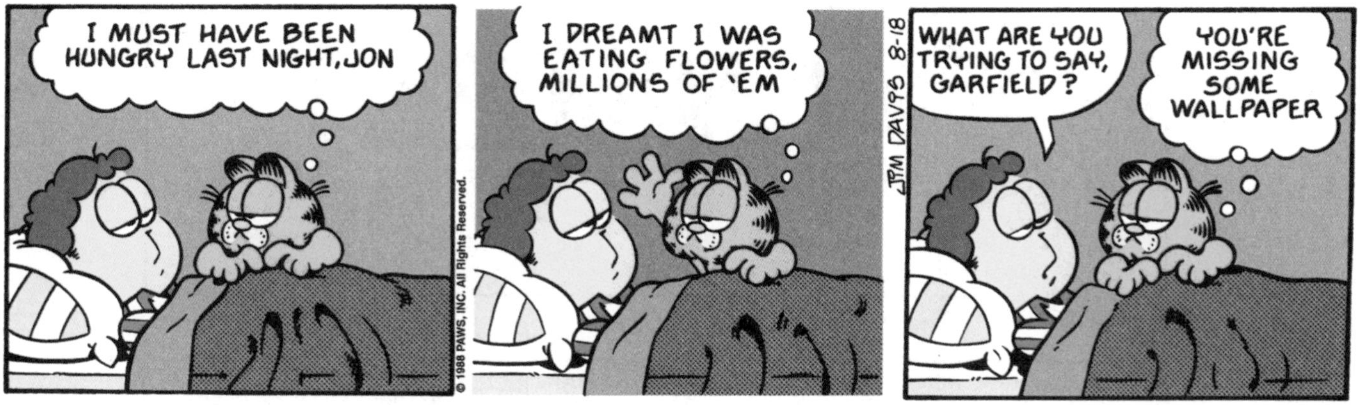
I MUST HAVE BEEN HUNGRY LAST NIGHT, JON
© 1988 PAWS, INC. All Rights Reserved.
I DREAMT I WAS EATING FLOWERS, MILLIONS OF 'EM
JIM DAVIS 8-18
WHAT ARE YOU TRYING TO SAY, GARFIELD?
YOU'RE MISSING SOME WALLPAPER

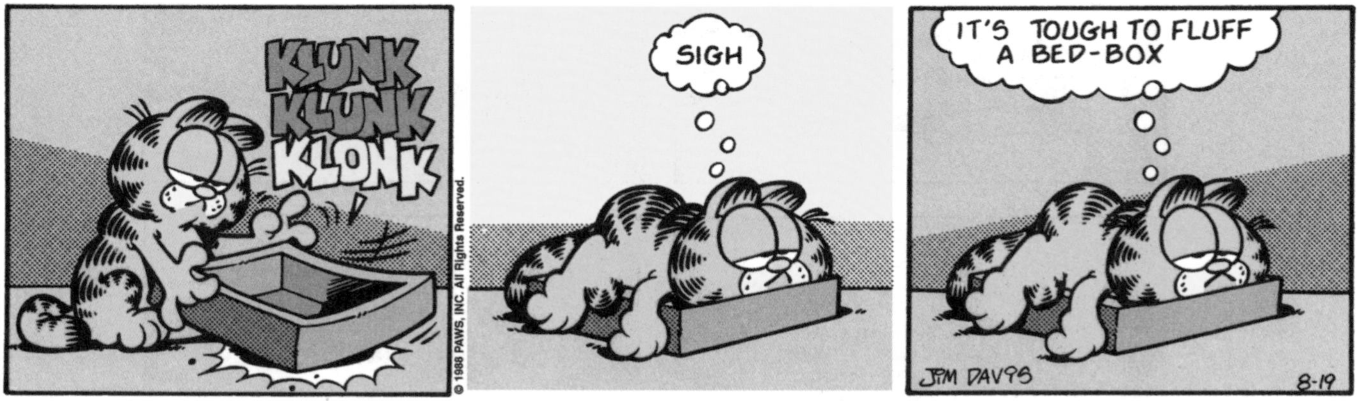
KLUNK KLUNK KLONK
© 1988 PAWS, INC. All Rights Reserved.
SIGH
IT'S TOUGH TO FLUFF A BED-BOX
JIM DAVIS
8-19

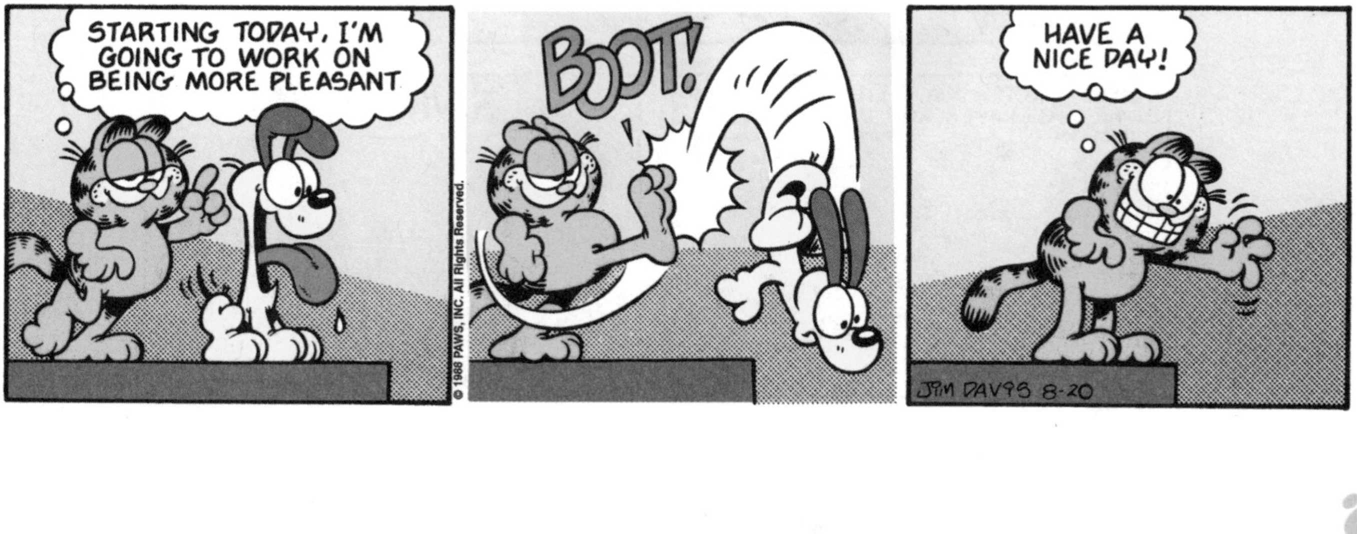
STARTING TODAY, I'M GOING TO WORK ON BEING MORE PLEASANT
© 1988 PAWS, INC. All Rights Reserved.
BOOT!
HAVE A NICE DAY!
JIM DAVIS 8-20

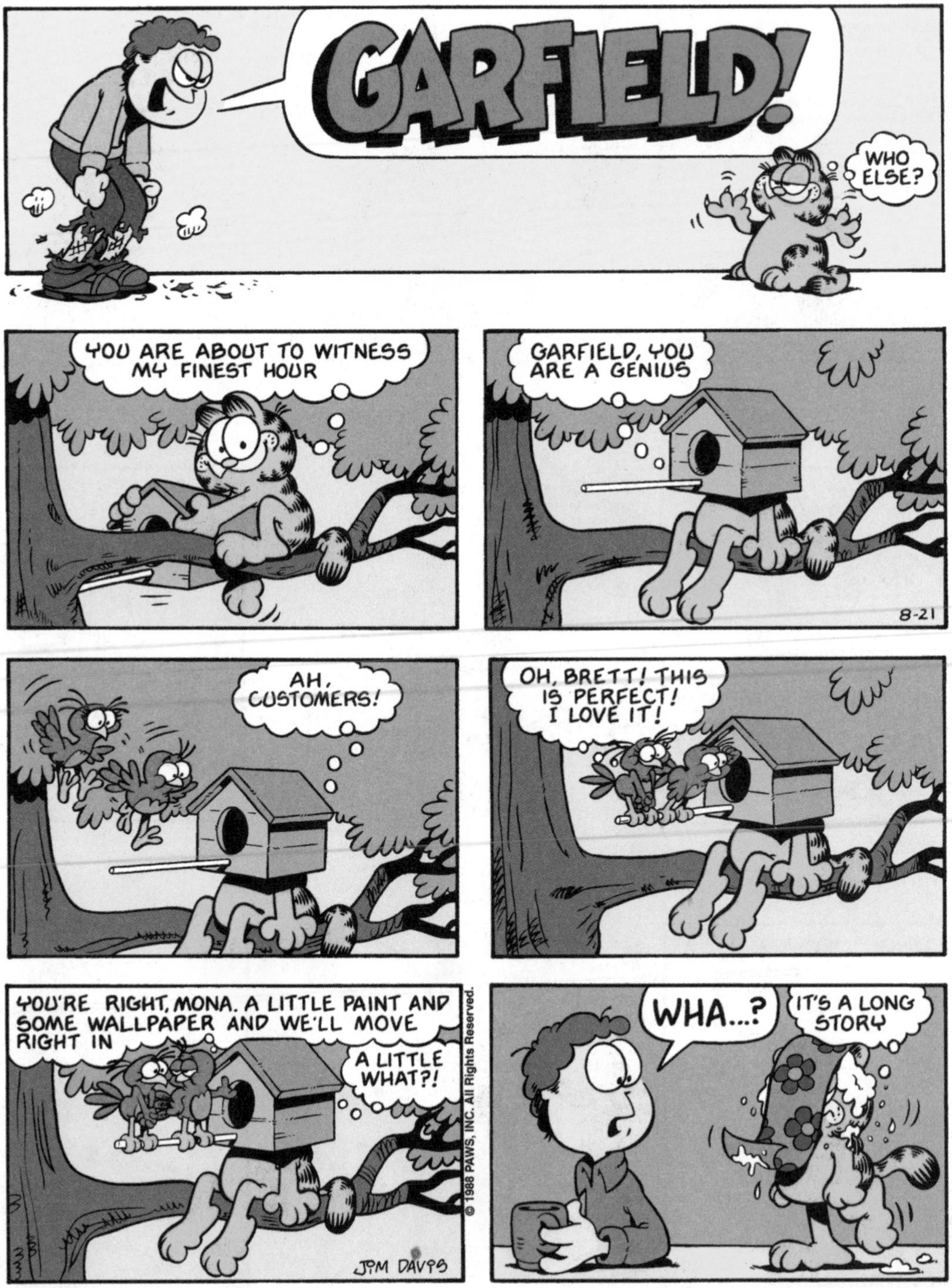
GARFIELD!
WHO ELSE?
YOU ARE ABOUT TO WITNESS MY FINEST HOUR
GARFIELD, YOU ARE A GENIUS
8-21
AH, CUSTOMERS!
OH, BRETT! THIS IS PERFECT! I LOVE IT!
YOU'RE RIGHT, MONA. A LITTLE PAINT AND SOME WALLPAPER AND WE'LL MOVE RIGHT IN
A LITTLE WHAT?!
JIM DAVIS
© 1988 PAWS, INC. All Rights Reserved.
WHA...?
IT'S A LONG STORY

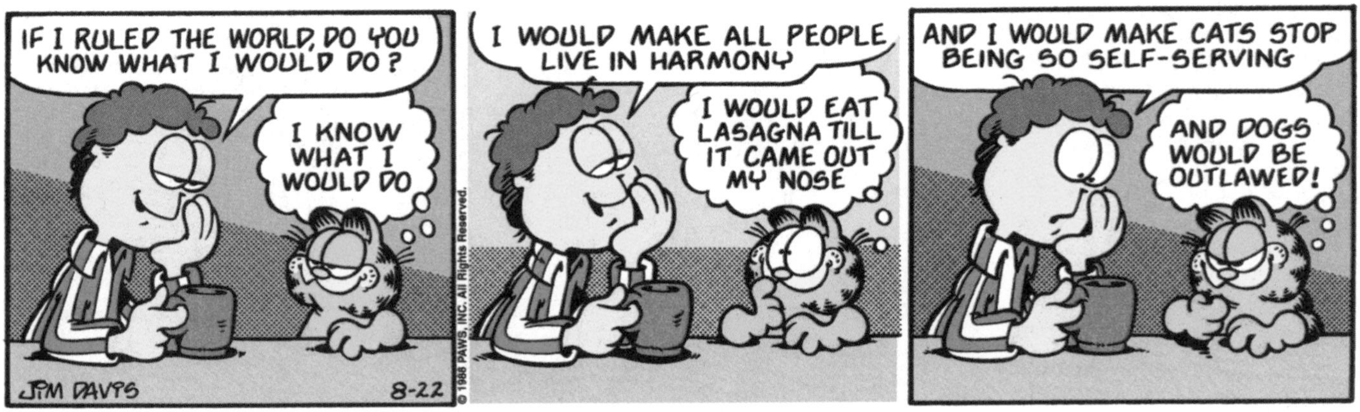
IF I RULED THE WORLD, DO YOU KNOW WHAT I WOULD DO?
I KNOW WHAT I WOULD DO
JIM DAVIS 8-22
© 1988 PAWS, INC. All Rights Reserved.
I WOULD MAKE ALL PEOPLE LIVE IN HARMONY
I WOULD EAT LASAGNA TILL IT CAME OUT MY NOSE
AND I WOULD MAKE CATS STOP BEING SO SELF-SERVING
AND DOGS WOULD BE OUTLAWED!

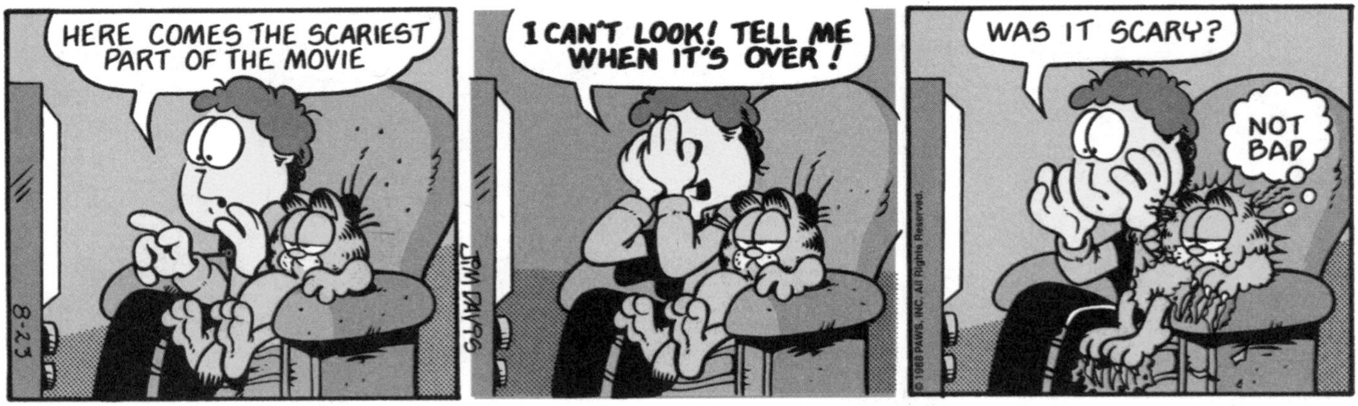
HERE COMES THE SCARIEST PART OF THE MOVIE
8-23
JIM DAVIS
I CAN'T LOOK! TELL ME WHEN IT'S OVER!
© 1988 PAWS, INC. All Rights Reserved.
WAS IT SCARY?
NOT BAD

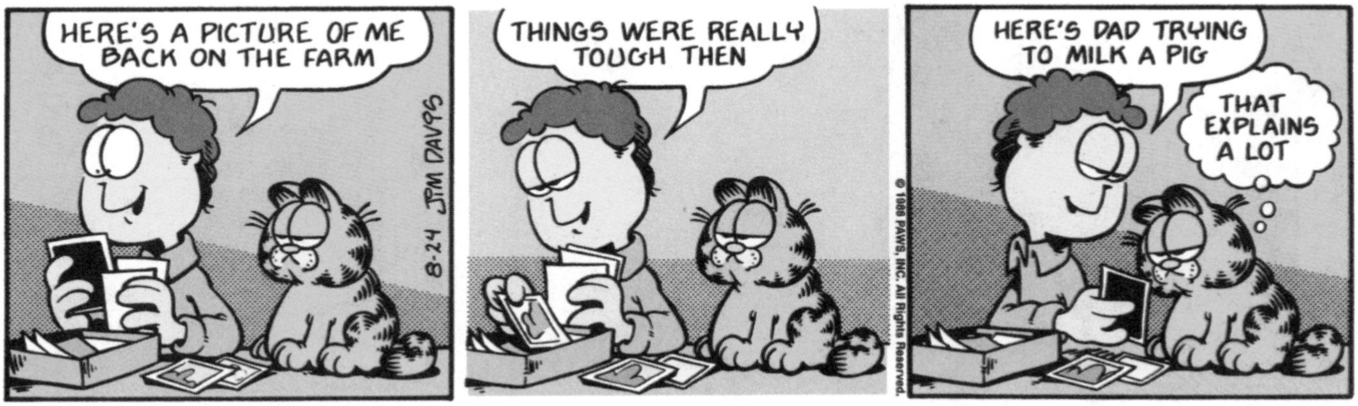
HERE'S A PICTURE OF ME BACK ON THE FARM
8-24 JIM DAVIS
THINGS WERE REALLY TOUGH THEN
© 1988 PAWS, INC. All Rights Reserved.
HERE'S DAD TRYING TO MILK A PIG
THAT EXPLAINS A LOT

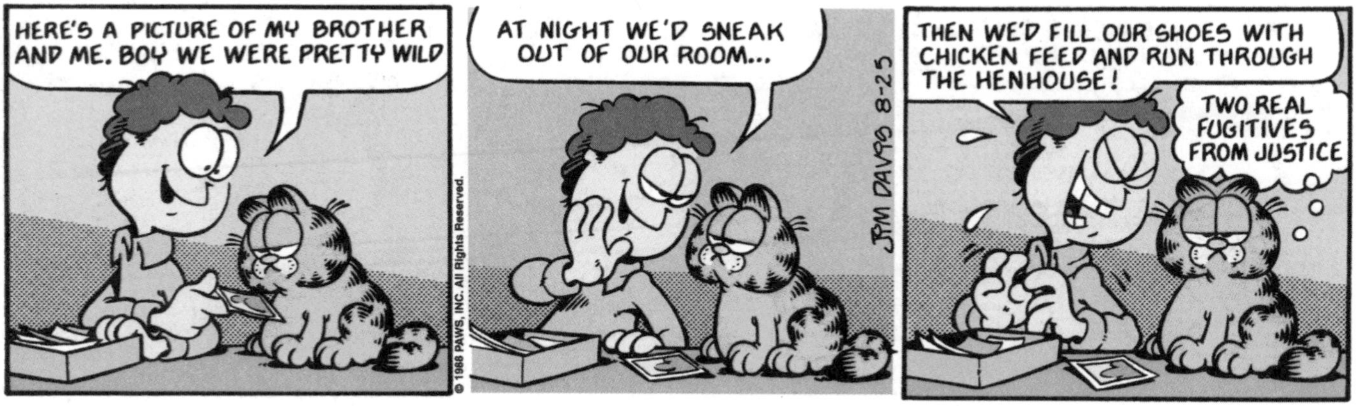
HERE'S A PICTURE OF MY BROTHER AND ME. BOY WE WERE PRETTY WILD
© 1988 PAWS, INC. All Rights Reserved.
AT NIGHT WE'D SNEAK OUT OF OUR ROOM...
JIM DAVIS 8-25
THEN WE'D FILL OUR SHOES WITH CHICKEN FEED AND RUN THROUGH THE HENHOUSE!
TWO REAL FUGITIVES FROM JUSTICE

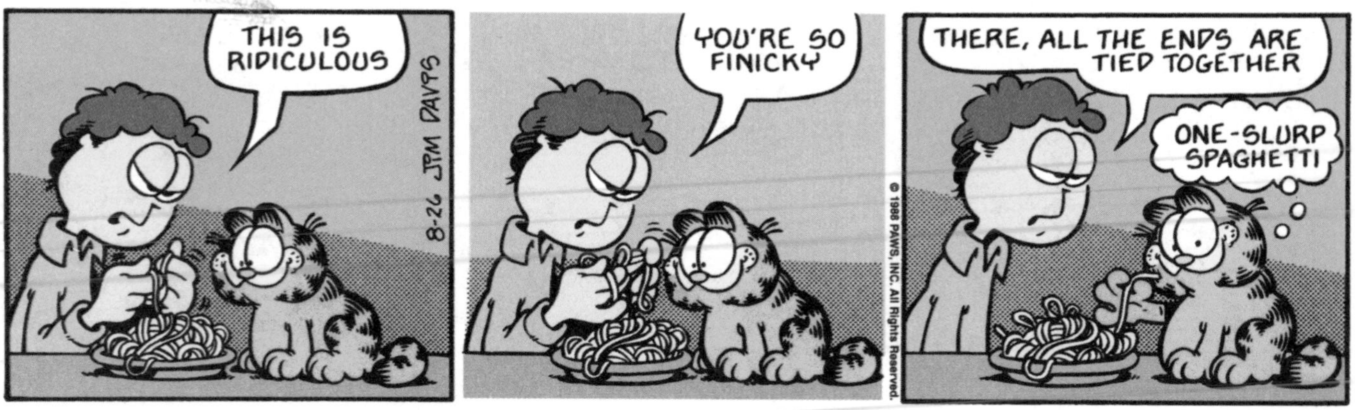
THIS IS RIDICULOUS
JIM DAVIS 8-26
YOU'RE SO FINICKY
© 1988 PAWS, INC. All Rights Reserved.
THERE, ALL THE ENDS ARE TIED TOGETHER
ONE-SLURP SPAGHETTI

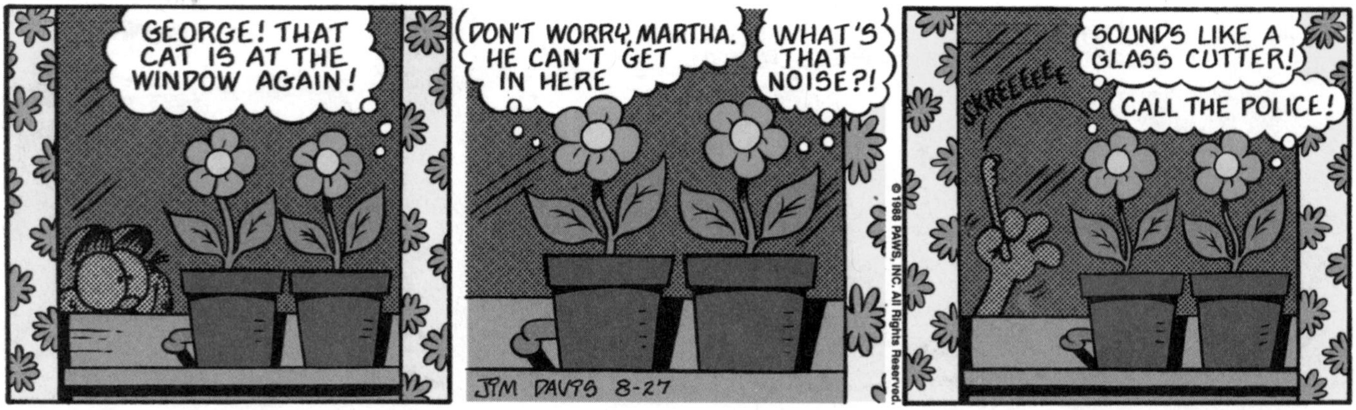
GEORGE! THAT CAT IS AT THE WINDOW AGAIN!
DON'T WORRY, MARTHA. HE CAN'T GET IN HERE
WHAT'S THAT NOISE?!
JIM DAVIS 8-27
© 1988 PAWS, INC. All Rights Reserved.
SKREEEEEE
SOUNDS LIKE A GLASS CUTTER!
CALL THE POLICE!

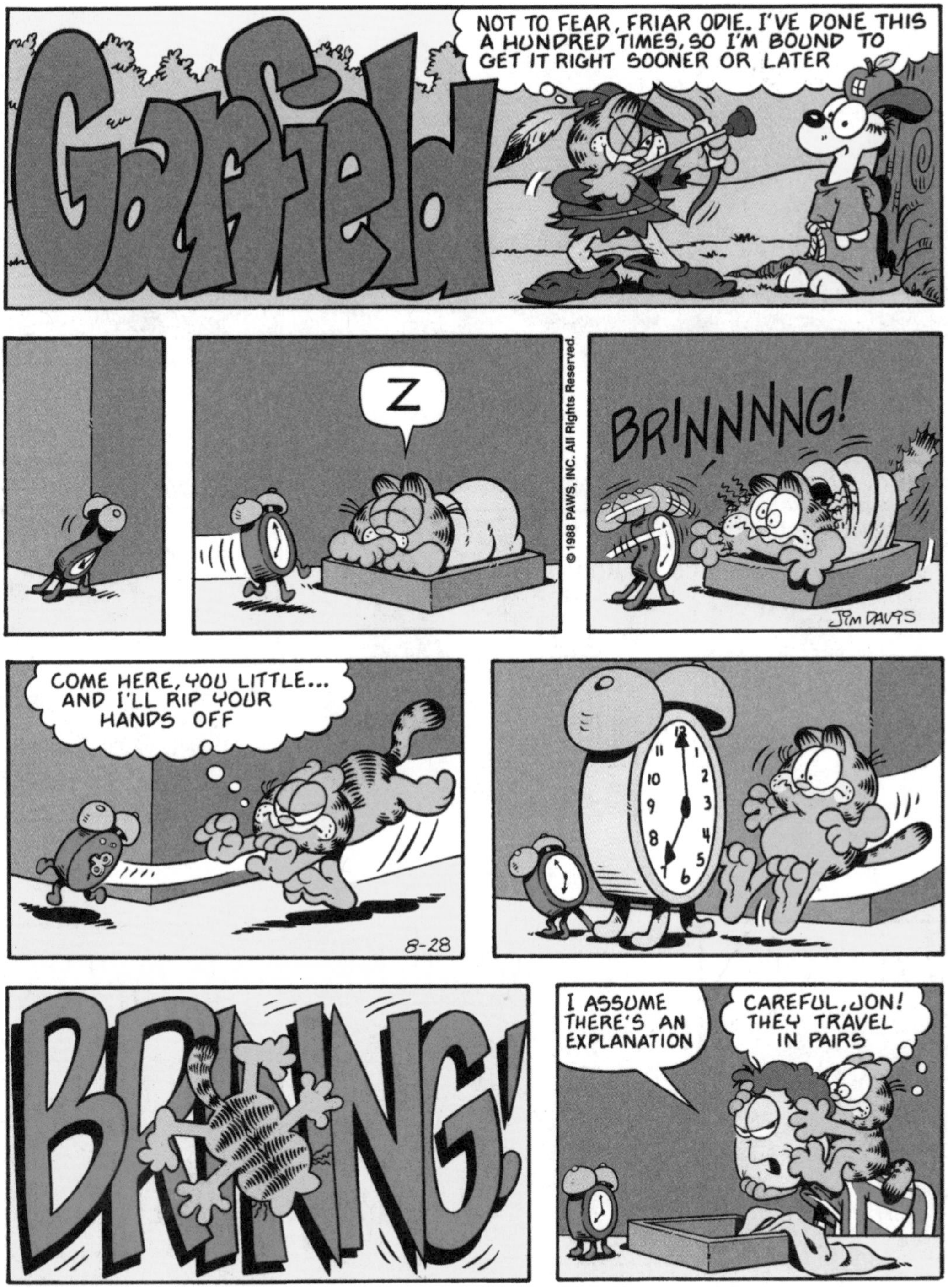
Garfield
NOT TO FEAR, FRIAR ODIE. I'VE DONE THIS A HUNDRED TIMES, SO I'M BOUND TO GET IT RIGHT SOONER OR LATER
Z
© 1988 PAWS, INC. All Rights Reserved.
BRINNNNG!
JIM DAVIS
COME HERE, YOU LITTLE... AND I'LL RIP YOUR HANDS OFF
8-28
BRIIING!
I ASSUME THERE'S AN EXPLANATION
CAREFUL, JON! THEY TRAVEL IN PAIRS

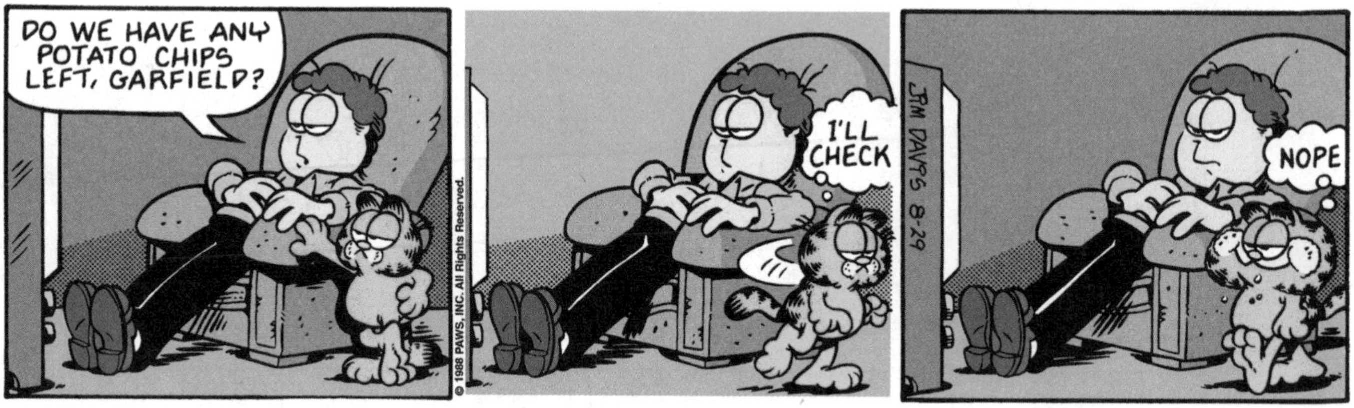
DO WE HAVE ANY POTATO CHIPS LEFT, GARFIELD?
© 1988 PAWS, INC. All Rights Reserved.
I'LL CHECK
JIM DAVIS 8-29
NOPE

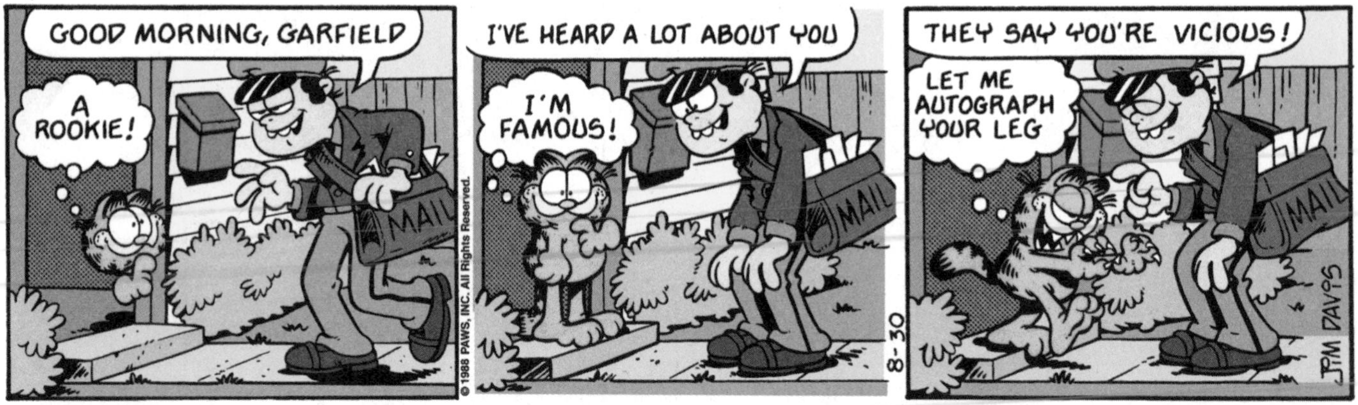
GOOD MORNING, GARFIELD
A ROOKIE!
MAIL
© 1988 PAWS, INC. All Rights Reserved.
I'VE HEARD A LOT ABOUT YOU
I'M FAMOUS!
MAIL
8-30
THEY SAY YOU'RE VICIOUS!
LET ME AUTOGRAPH YOUR LEG
MAIL
JIM DAVIS

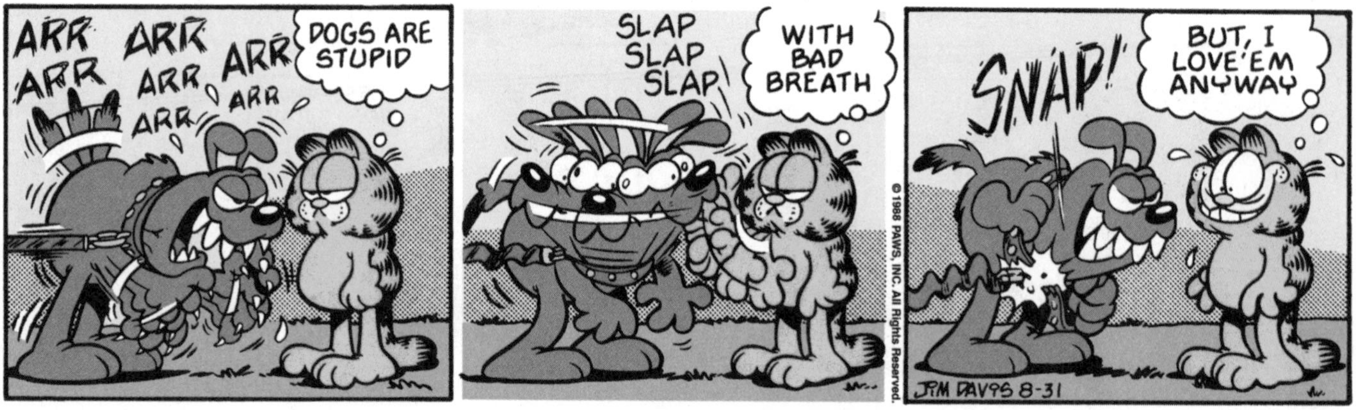
ARR ARR ARR ARR ARR ARR ARR ARR
DOGS ARE STUPID
SLAP SLAP SLAP
WITH BAD BREATH
© 1988 PAWS, INC. All Rights Reserved.
SNAP!
BUT, I LOVE'EM ANYWAY
JIM DAVIS 8-31

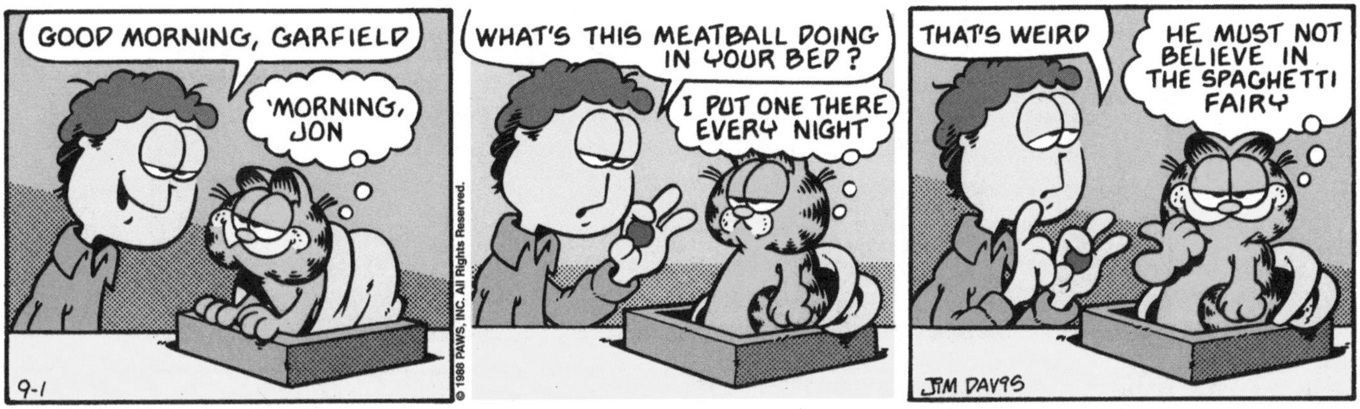
GOOD MORNING, GARFIELD
'MORNING, JON
9-1
© 1988 PAWS, INC. All Rights Reserved.
WHAT'S THIS MEATBALL DOING IN YOUR BED?
I PUT ONE THERE EVERY NIGHT
THAT'S WEIRD
HE MUST NOT BELIEVE IN THE SPAGHETTI FAIRY
JIM DAVIS

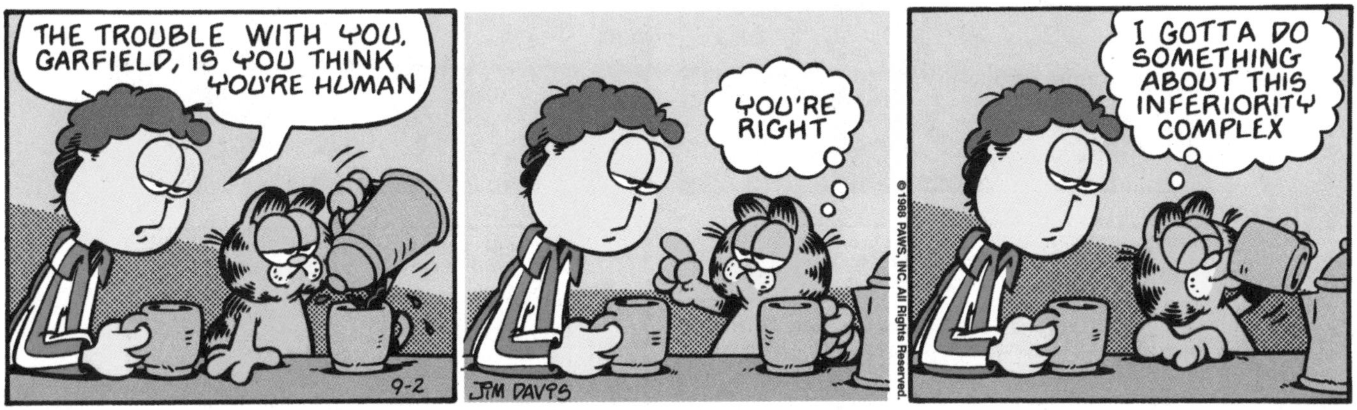
THE TROUBLE WITH YOU, GARFIELD, IS YOU THINK YOU'RE HUMAN
9-2
JIM DAVIS
YOU'RE RIGHT
© 1988 PAWS, INC. All Rights Reserved.
I GOTTA DO SOMETHING ABOUT THIS INFERIORITY COMPLEX

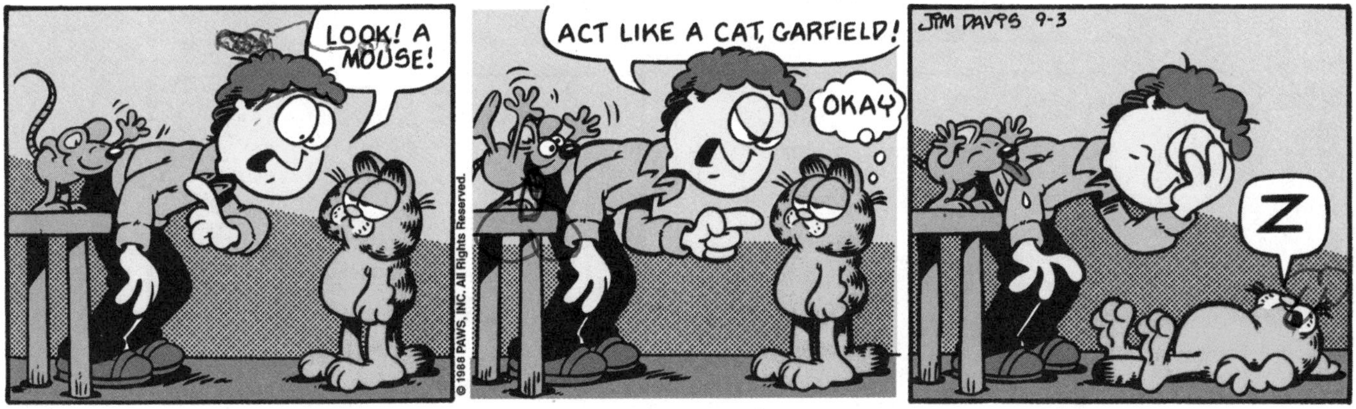
LOOK! A MOUSE!
© 1988 PAWS, INC. All Rights Reserved.
ACT LIKE A CAT, GARFIELD!
OKAY
JIM DAVIS 9-3
Z

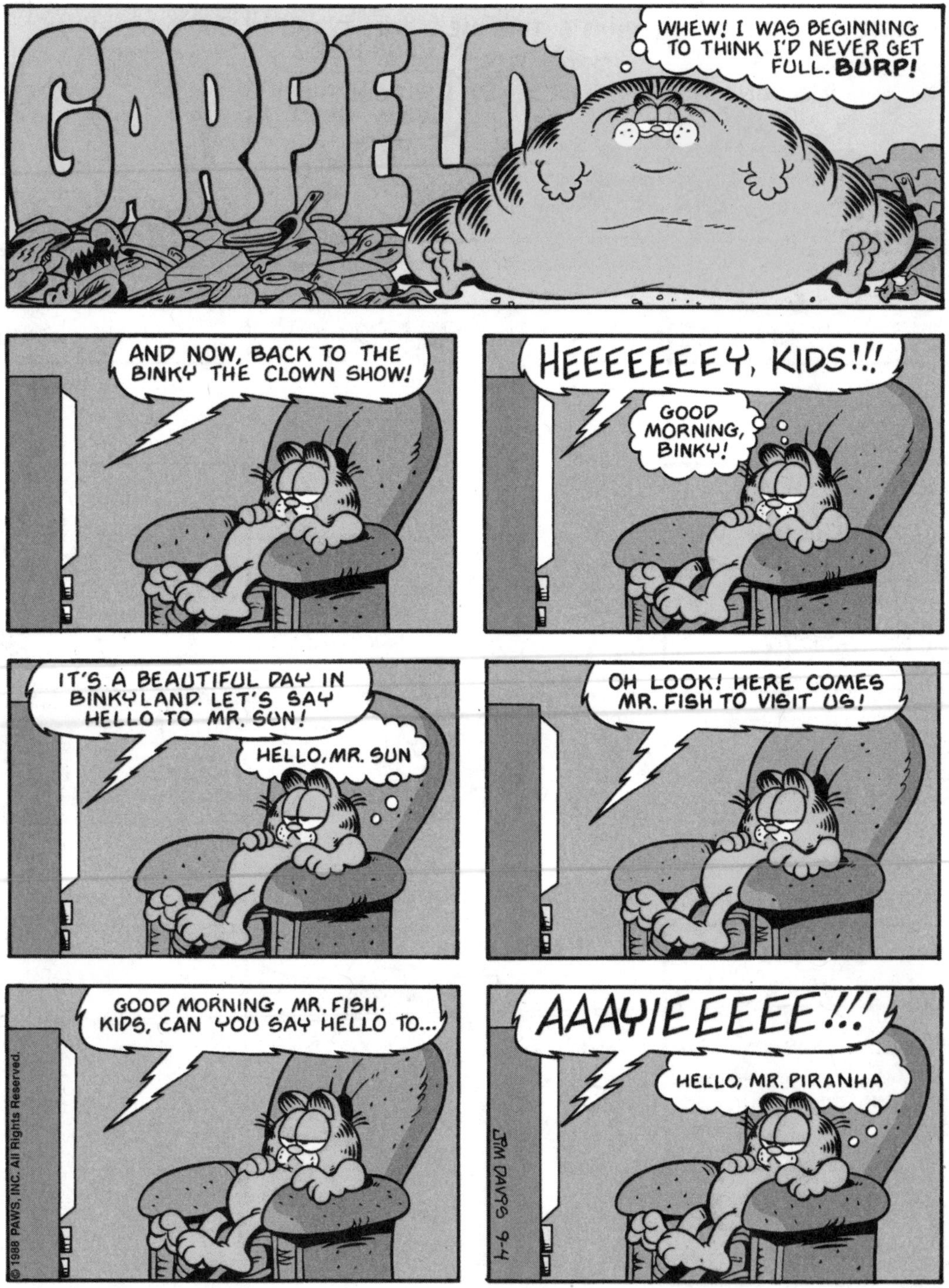
GARFIELD
WHEW! I WAS BEGINNING TO THINK I'D NEVER GET FULL. **BURP!**
AND NOW, BACK TO THE BINKY THE CLOWN SHOW!
HEEEEEEEY, KIDS!!!
GOOD MORNING, BINKY!
IT'S A BEAUTIFUL DAY IN BINKYLAND. LET'S SAY HELLO TO MR. SUN!
HELLO, MR. SUN
OH LOOK! HERE COMES MR. FISH TO VISIT US!
GOOD MORNING, MR. FISH. KIDS, CAN YOU SAY HELLO TO...
© 1988 PAWS, INC. All Rights Reserved.
AAAYIEEEEE!!!
HELLO, MR. PIRANHA
JIM DAVIS 9-4

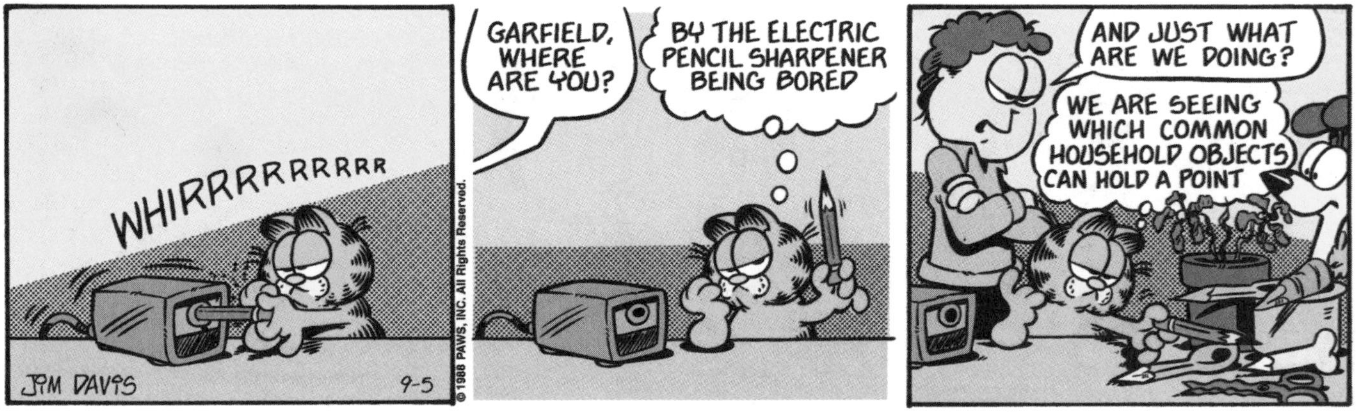
WHIRRRRRRRRRR
JIM DAVIS
9-5
© 1988 PAWS, INC. All Rights Reserved.
GARFIELD, WHERE ARE YOU?
BY THE ELECTRIC PENCIL SHARPENER BEING BORED
AND JUST WHAT ARE WE DOING?
WE ARE SEEING WHICH COMMON HOUSEHOLD OBJECTS CAN HOLD A POINT

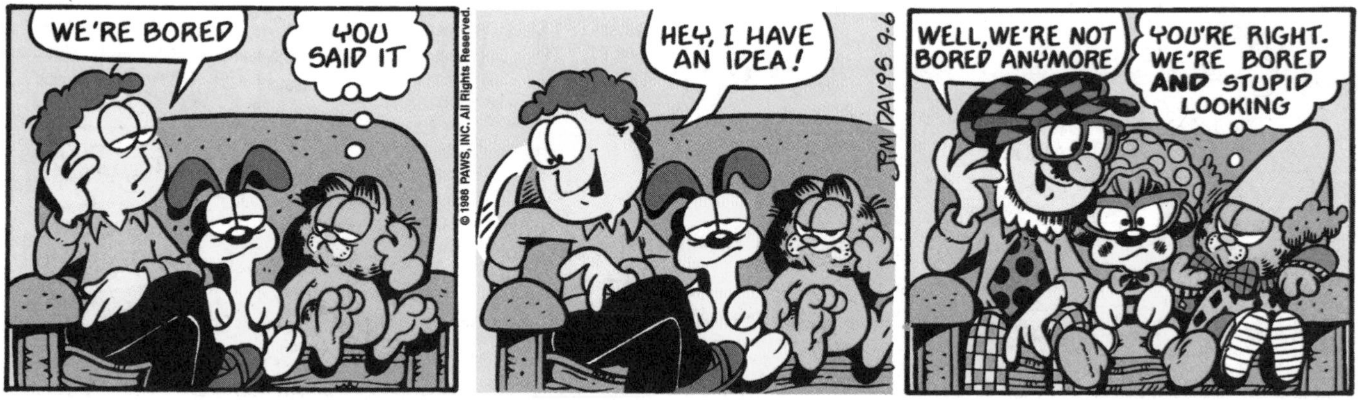
WE'RE BORED
YOU SAID IT
© 1988 PAWS, INC. All Rights Reserved.
HEY, I HAVE AN IDEA!
JIM DAVIS 9-6
WELL, WE'RE NOT BORED ANYMORE
YOU'RE RIGHT. WE'RE BORED AND STUPID LOOKING

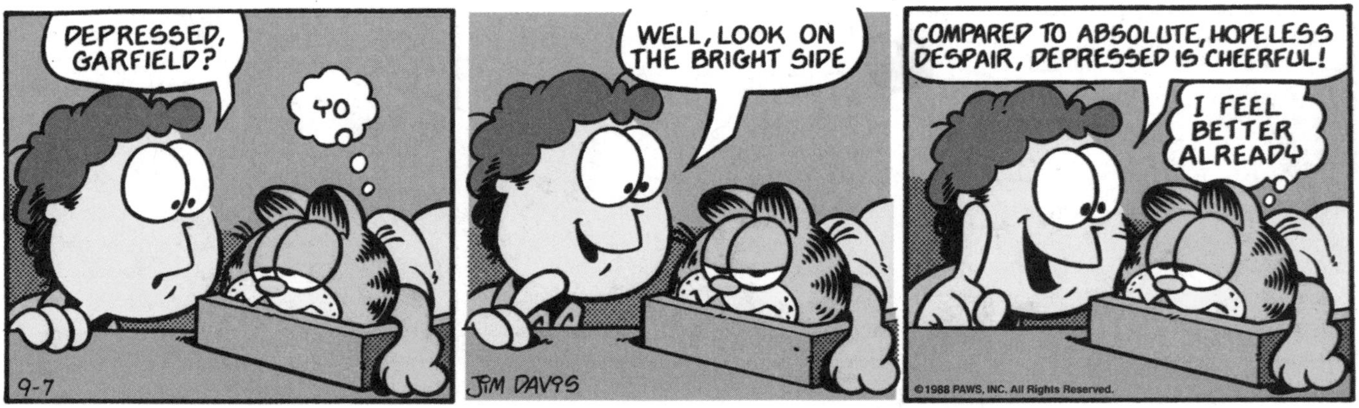
DEPRESSED, GARFIELD?
YO
9-7
WELL, LOOK ON THE BRIGHT SIDE
JIM DAVIS
COMPARED TO ABSOLUTE, HOPELESS DESPAIR, DEPRESSED IS CHEERFUL!
I FEEL BETTER ALREADY
©1988 PAWS, INC. All Rights Reserved.

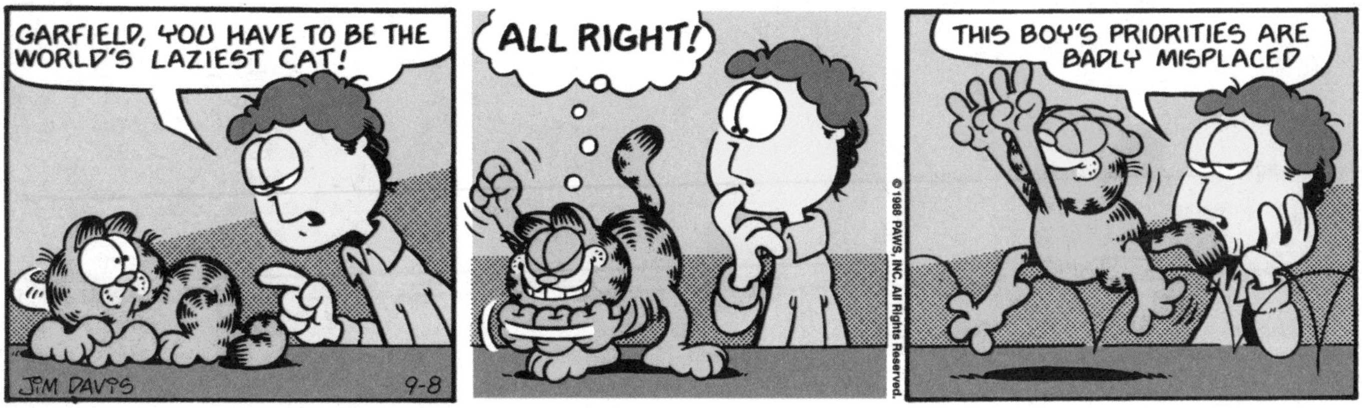
GARFIELD, YOU HAVE TO BE THE WORLD'S LAZIEST CAT!
JIM DAVIS
9-8
ALL RIGHT!
© 1988 PAWS, INC. All Rights Reserved.
THIS BOY'S PRIORITIES ARE BADLY MISPLACED

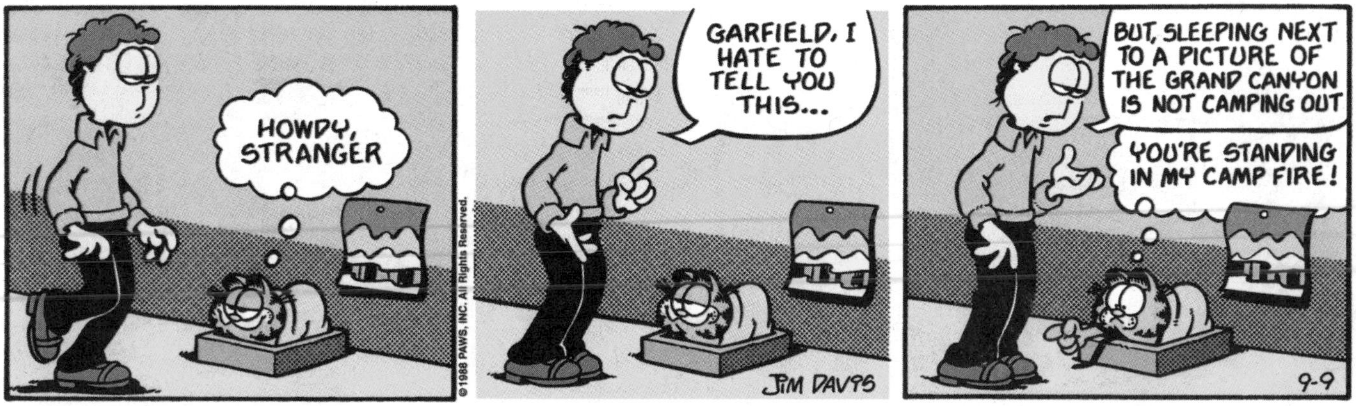
HOWDY, STRANGER
©1988 PAWS, INC. All Rights Reserved.
GARFIELD, I HATE TO TELL YOU THIS...
JIM DAVIS
BUT, SLEEPING NEXT TO A PICTURE OF THE GRAND CANYON IS NOT CAMPING OUT
YOU'RE STANDING IN MY CAMP FIRE!
9-9

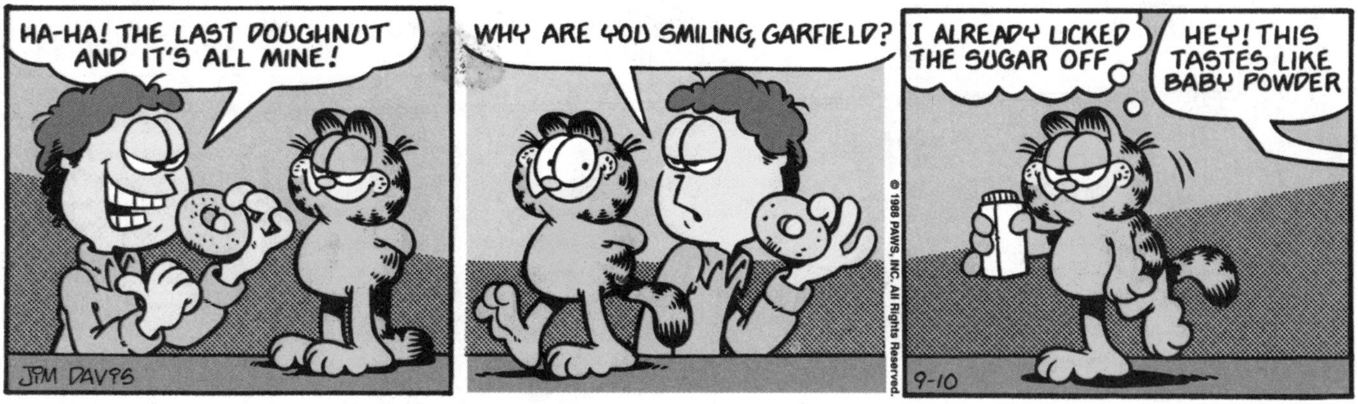
HA-HA! THE LAST DOUGHNUT AND IT'S ALL MINE!
JIM DAVIS
WHY ARE YOU SMILING, GARFIELD?
© 1988 PAWS, INC. All Rights Reserved.
I ALREADY LICKED THE SUGAR OFF
HEY! THIS TASTES LIKE BABY POWDER
9-10

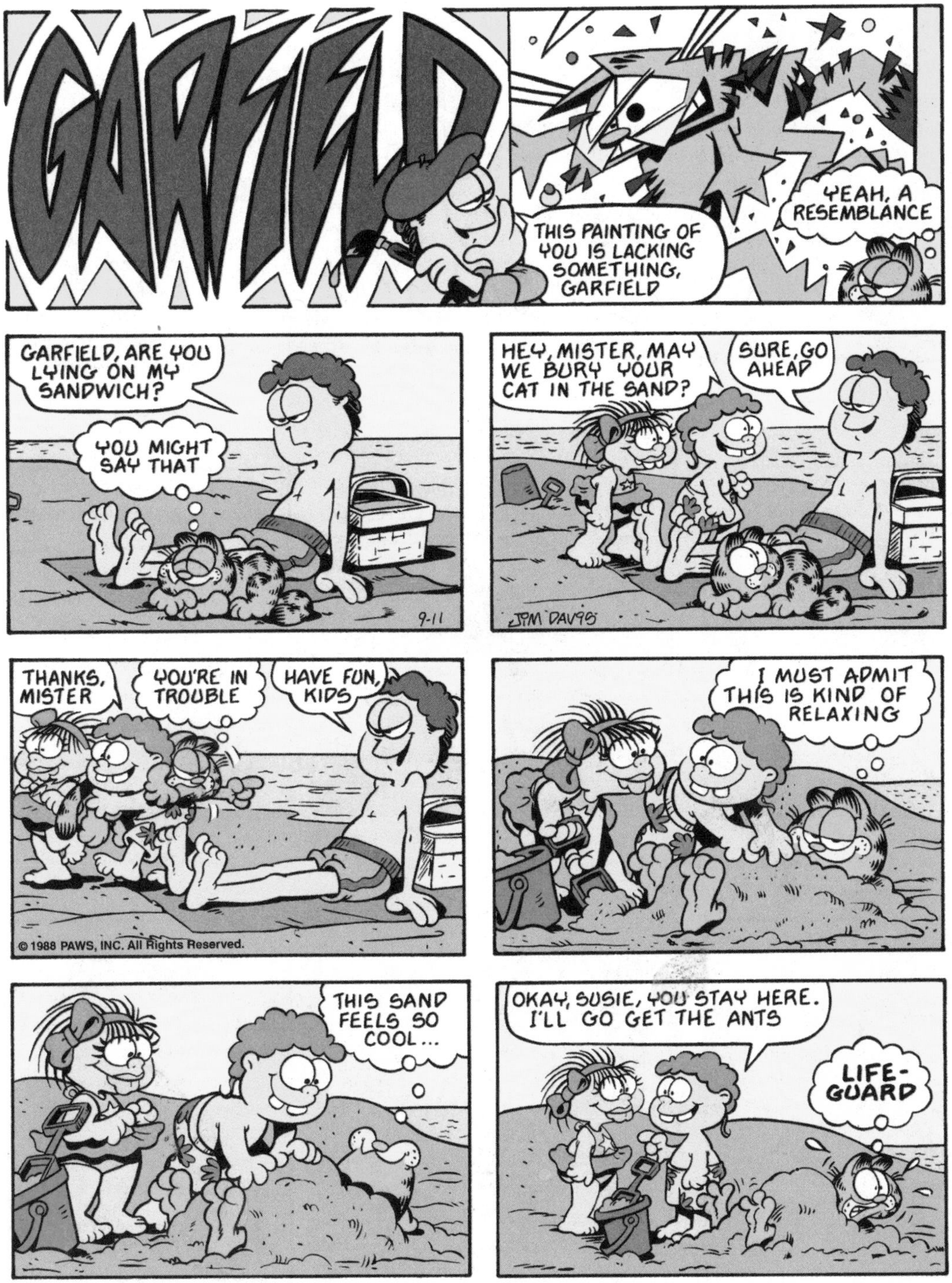
GARFIELD
THIS PAINTING OF YOU IS LACKING SOMETHING, GARFIELD
YEAH, A RESEMBLANCE
GARFIELD, ARE YOU LYING ON MY SANDWICH?
YOU MIGHT SAY THAT
9-11
HEY, MISTER, MAY WE BURY YOUR CAT IN THE SAND?
SURE, GO AHEAD
JIM DAVIS
THANKS, MISTER
YOU'RE IN TROUBLE
HAVE FUN, KIDS
© 1988 PAWS, INC. All Rights Reserved.
I MUST ADMIT THIS IS KIND OF RELAXING
THIS SAND FEELS SO COOL...
OKAY, SUSIE, YOU STAY HERE. I'LL GO GET THE ANTS
LIFE-GUARD

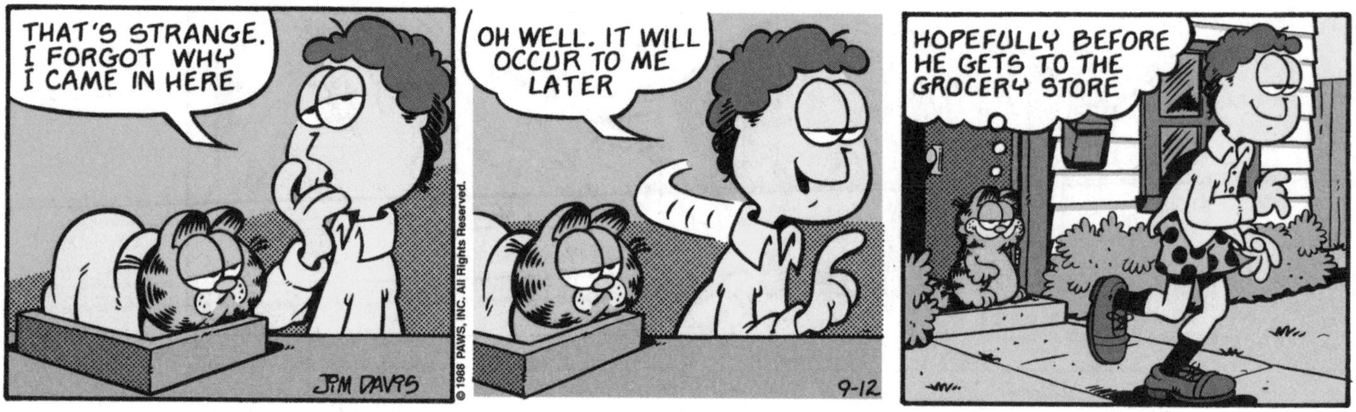
THAT'S STRANGE. I FORGOT WHY I CAME IN HERE
© 1988 PAWS, INC. All Rights Reserved.
OH WELL. IT WILL OCCUR TO ME LATER
HOPEFULLY BEFORE HE GETS TO THE GROCERY STORE

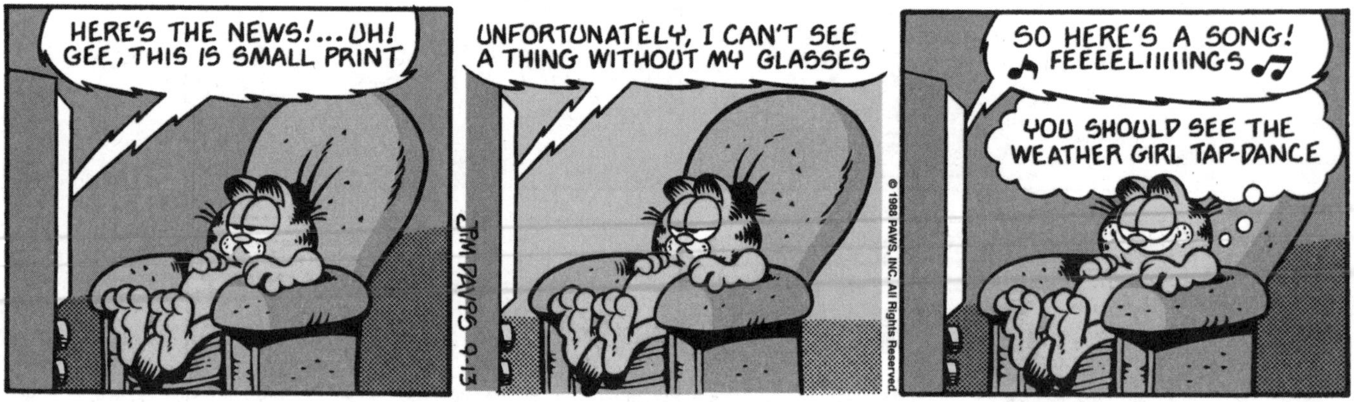
HERE'S THE NEWS!... UH! GEE, THIS IS SMALL PRINT
UNFORTUNATELY, I CAN'T SEE A THING WITHOUT MY GLASSES
© 1988 PAWS, INC. All Rights Reserved.
SO HERE'S A SONG! FEEEELIIIIIINGS
YOU SHOULD SEE THE WEATHER GIRL TAP-DANCE

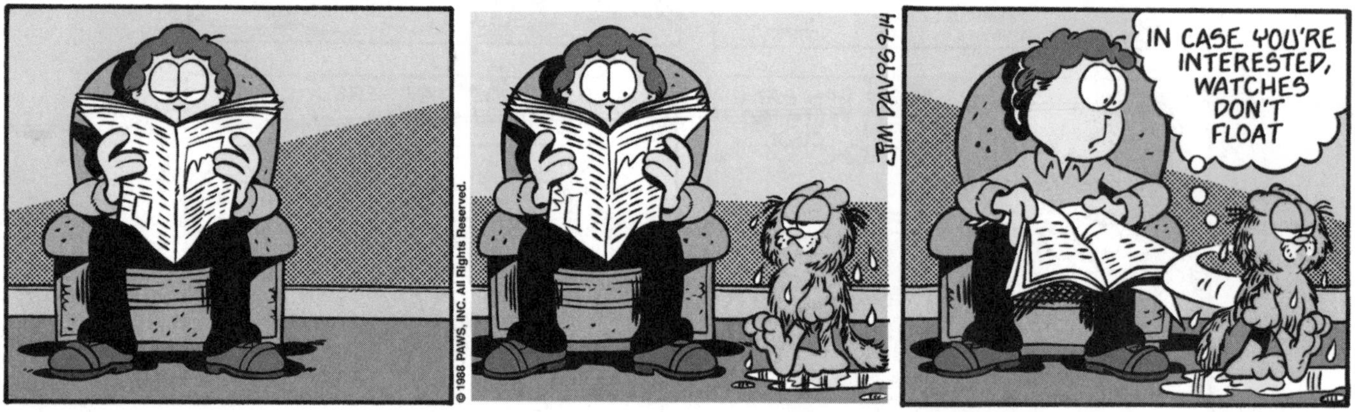
© 1988 PAWS, INC. All Rights Reserved.
IN CASE YOU'RE INTERESTED, WATCHES DON'T FLOAT

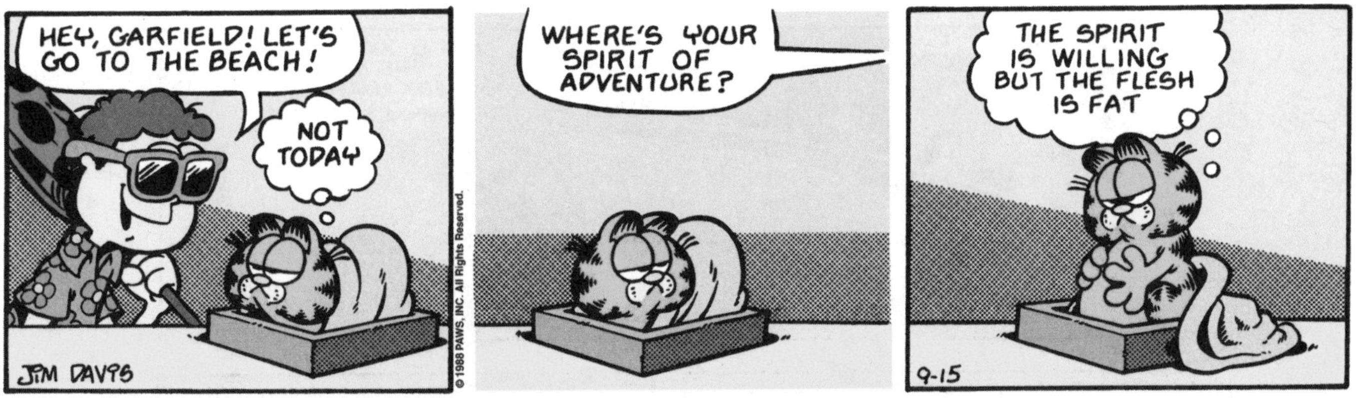
HEY, GARFIELD! LET'S GO TO THE BEACH!
NOT TODAY
JIM DAVIS
© 1988 PAWS, INC. All Rights Reserved.
WHERE'S YOUR SPIRIT OF ADVENTURE?
THE SPIRIT IS WILLING BUT THE FLESH IS FAT
9-15

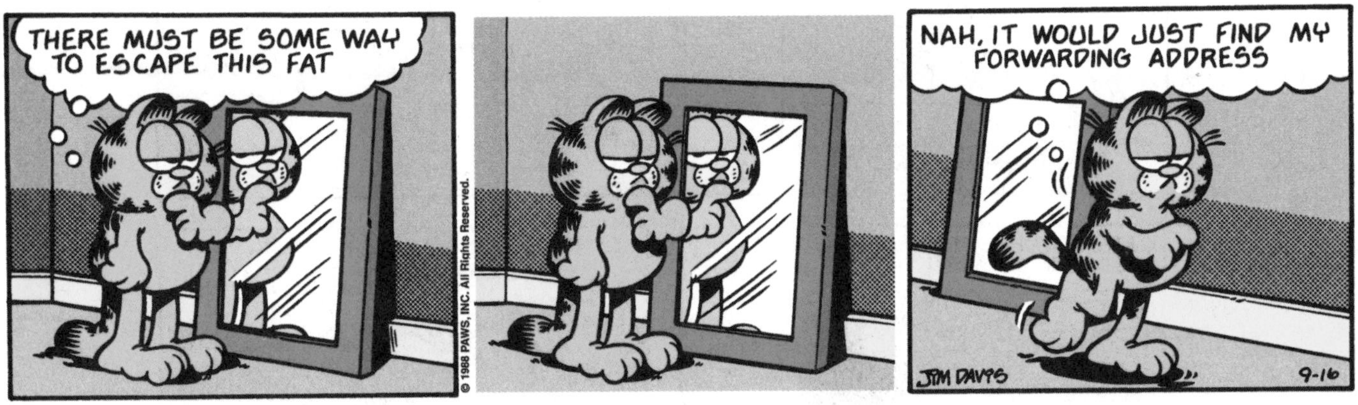
THERE MUST BE SOME WAY TO ESCAPE THIS FAT
© 1988 PAWS, INC. All Rights Reserved.
NAH, IT WOULD JUST FIND MY FORWARDING ADDRESS
JIM DAVIS
9-16

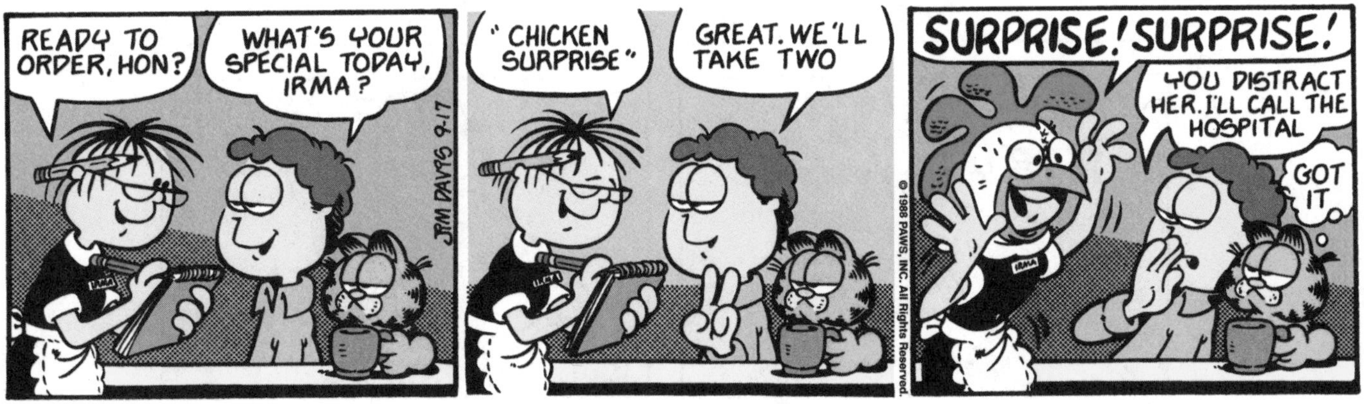
READY TO ORDER, HON?
WHAT'S YOUR SPECIAL TODAY, IRMA?
JIM DAVIS 9-17
"CHICKEN SURPRISE"
GREAT. WE'LL TAKE TWO
© 1988 PAWS, INC. All Rights Reserved.
SURPRISE! SURPRISE!
YOU DISTRACT HER. I'LL CALL THE HOSPITAL
GOT IT

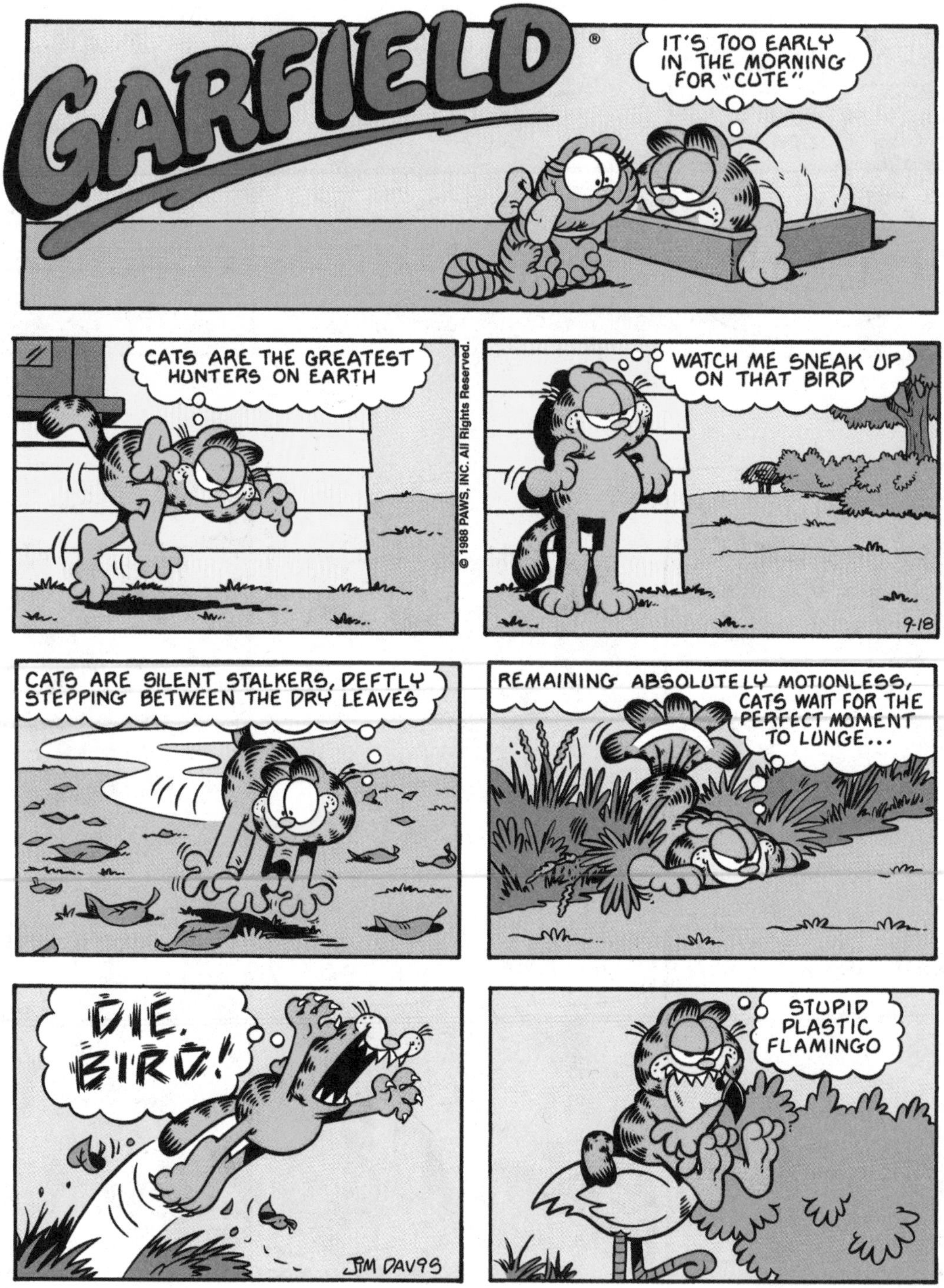
GARFIELD®
IT'S TOO EARLY IN THE MORNING FOR "CUTE"
CATS ARE THE GREATEST HUNTERS ON EARTH
WATCH ME SNEAK UP ON THAT BIRD
9-18
CATS ARE SILENT STALKERS, DEFTLY STEPPING BETWEEN THE DRY LEAVES
REMAINING ABSOLUTELY MOTIONLESS, CATS WAIT FOR THE PERFECT MOMENT TO LUNGE...
DIE, BIRD!
JIM DAVIS
STUPID PLASTIC FLAMINGO

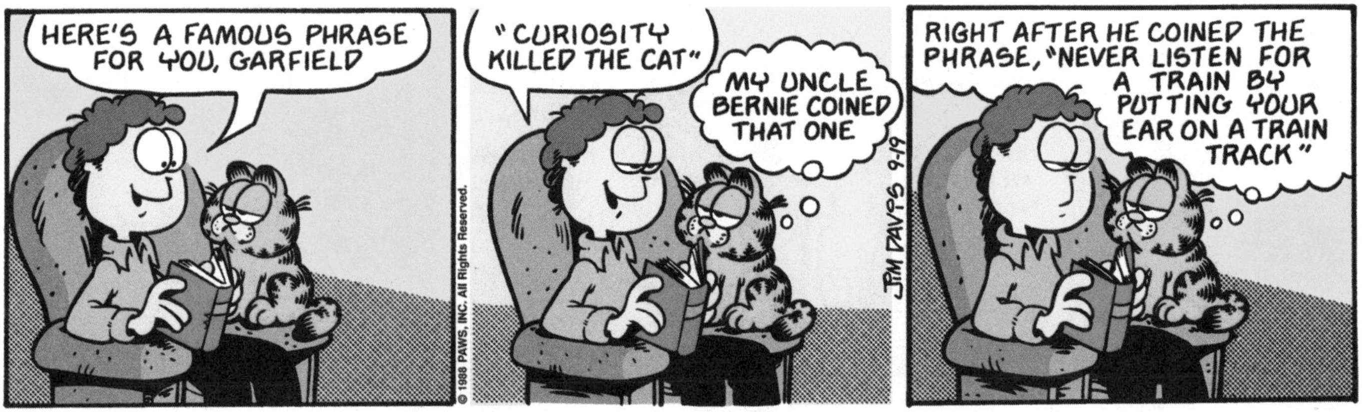
HERE'S A FAMOUS PHRASE FOR YOU, GARFIELD
© 1988 PAWS, INC. All Rights Reserved.
"CURIOSITY KILLED THE CAT"
MY UNCLE BERNIE COINED THAT ONE
JIM DAVIS 9-19
RIGHT AFTER HE COINED THE PHRASE, "NEVER LISTEN FOR A TRAIN BY PUTTING YOUR EAR ON A TRAIN TRACK"

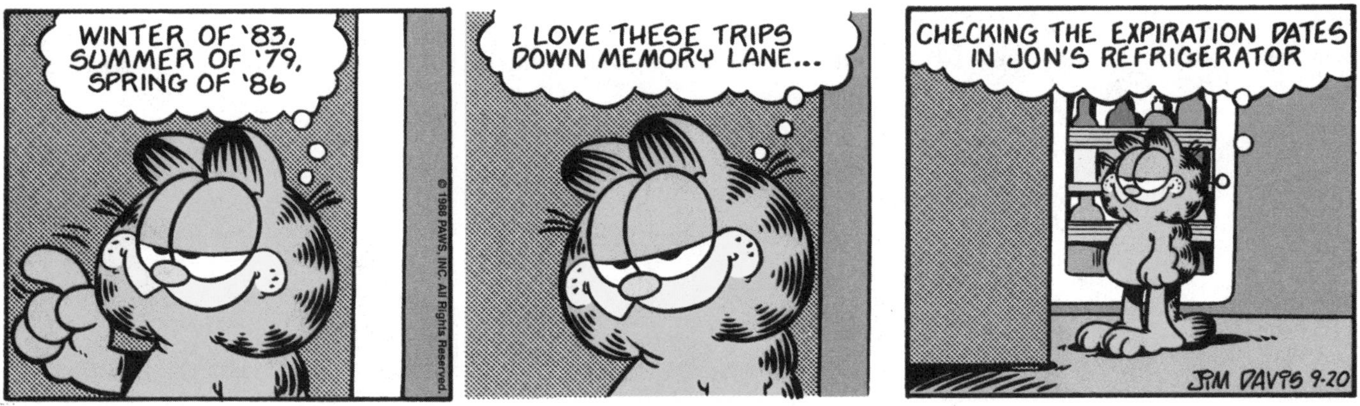
WINTER OF '83, SUMMER OF '79, SPRING OF '86
© 1988 PAWS, INC. All Rights Reserved.
I LOVE THESE TRIPS DOWN MEMORY LANE...
CHECKING THE EXPIRATION DATES IN JON'S REFRIGERATOR
JIM DAVIS 9-20

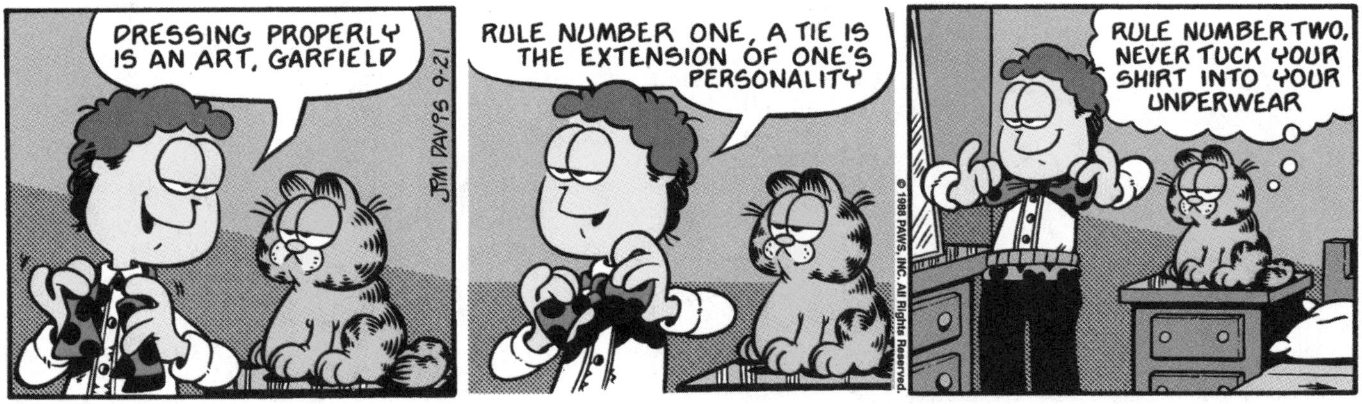
DRESSING PROPERLY IS AN ART, GARFIELD
JIM DAVIS 9-21
RULE NUMBER ONE, A TIE IS THE EXTENSION OF ONE'S PERSONALITY
© 1988 PAWS, INC. All Rights Reserved.
RULE NUMBER TWO, NEVER TUCK YOUR SHIRT INTO YOUR UNDERWEAR

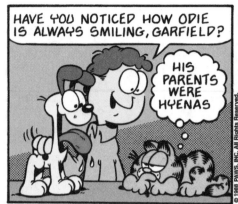

HAVE YOU NOTICED HOW ODIE IS ALWAYS SMILING, GARFIELD?
HIS PARENTS WERE HYENAS
© 1988 PAWS, INC. All Rights Reserved.
WHY DON'T YOU EVER SMILE?
I HAVE MY REASONS
IF HE THOUGHT HE WERE PLEASING ME, HE'D STOP TRYING
JIM DAVIS 9-22

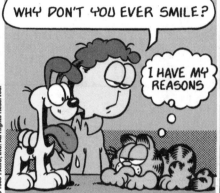

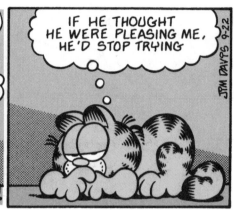

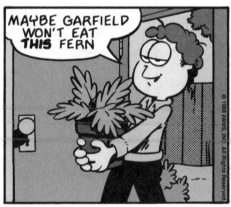

MAYBE GARFIELD WON'T EAT **THIS** FERN
© 1988 PAWS, INC. All Rights Reserved.
DO YOU KNOW WHAT THIS IS?
I SURE DO
JIM DAVIS 9-23
IT'S THE TRIUMPH OF HOPE OVER EXPERIENCE

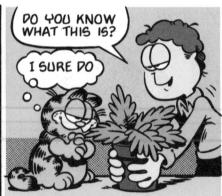

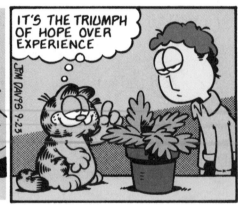

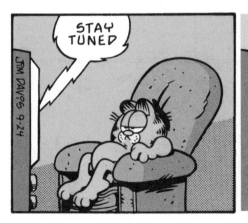

STAY TUNED
JIM DAVIS 9-24
COMING UP NEXT IS SOME MINDLESS DRIVEL GUARANTEED TO INSULT YOUR INTELLECT
© 1988 PAWS, INC. All Rights Reserved.
JON! YOUR SHOW'S ON!

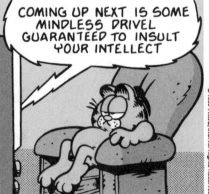

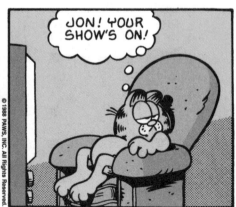

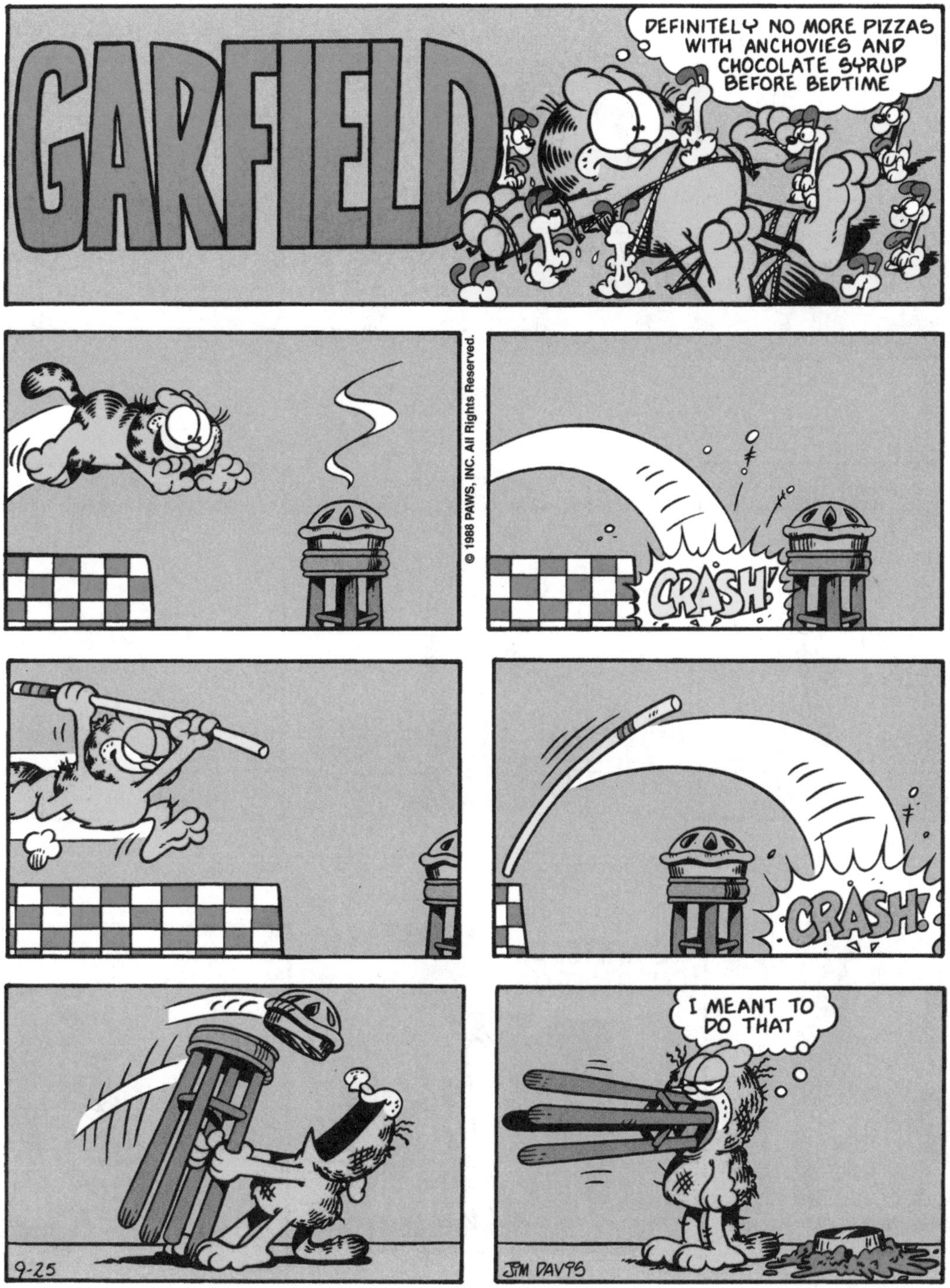
GARFIELD
DEFINITELY NO MORE PIZZAS WITH ANCHOVIES AND CHOCOLATE SYRUP BEFORE BEDTIME
© 1988 PAWS, INC. All Rights Reserved.
CRASH!
CRASH!
I MEANT TO DO THAT
9-25
JIM DAVIS

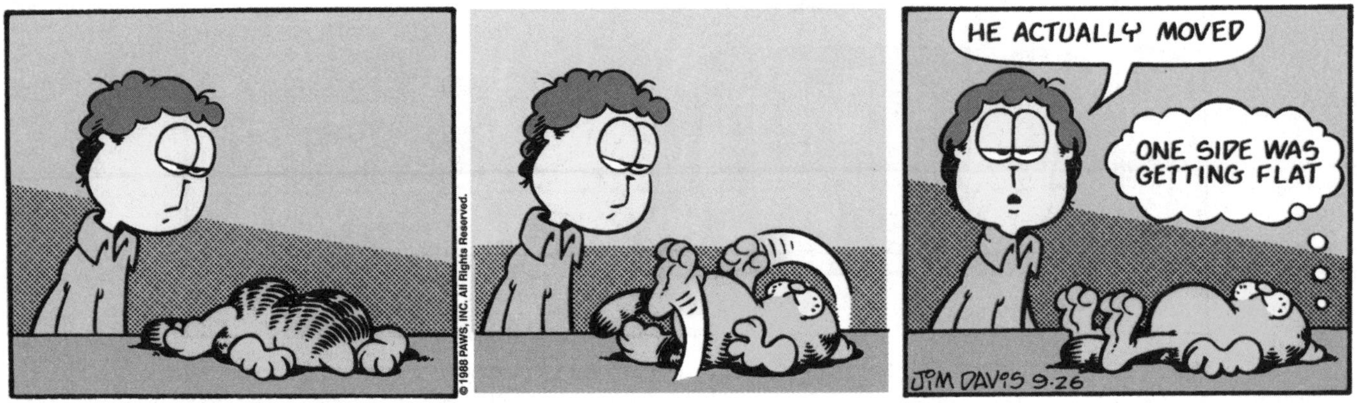
© 1988 PAWS, INC. All Rights Reserved.
HE ACTUALLY MOVED
ONE SIDE WAS GETTING FLAT
JIM DAVIS 9-26

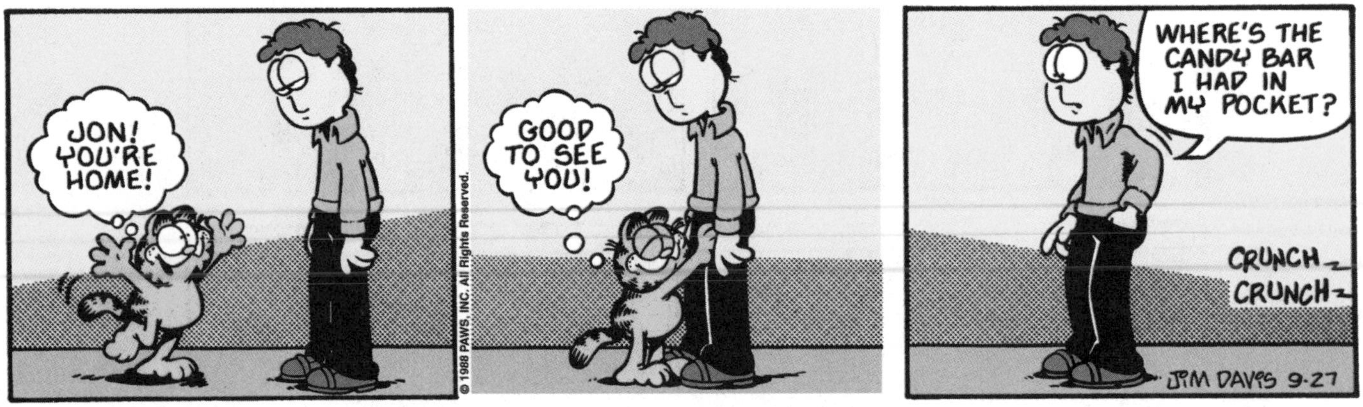
© 1988 PAWS, INC. All Rights Reserved.
JON! YOU'RE HOME!
GOOD TO SEE YOU!
WHERE'S THE CANDY BAR I HAD IN MY POCKET?
CRUNCH
CRUNCH
JIM DAVIS 9-27

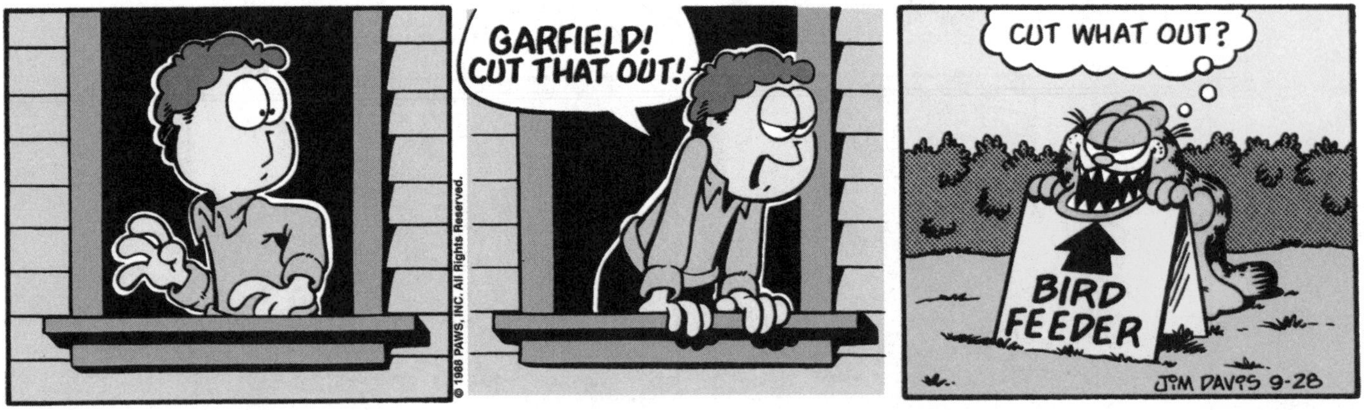
© 1988 PAWS, INC. All Rights Reserved.
GARFIELD! CUT THAT OUT!
CUT WHAT OUT?
BIRD FEEDER
JIM DAVIS 9-28

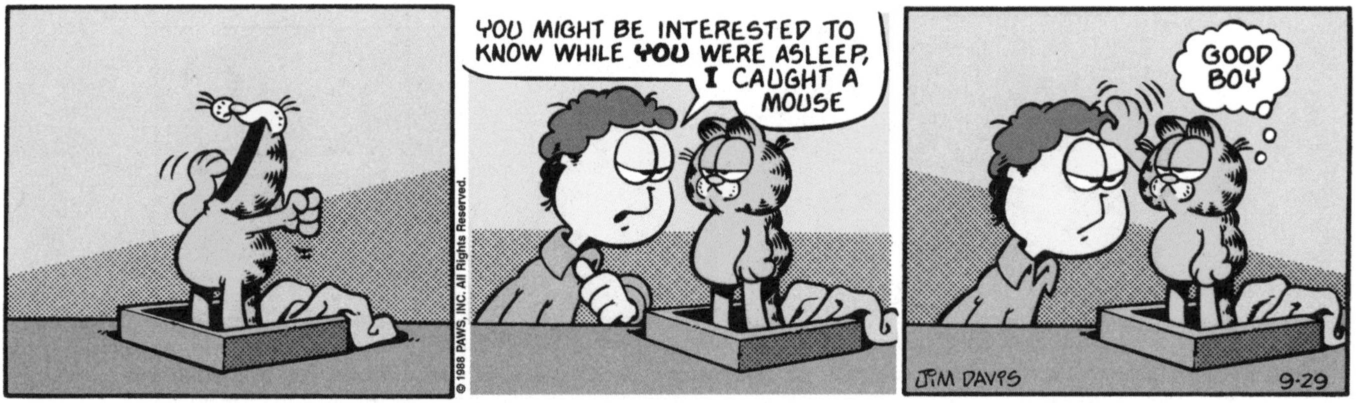
© 1988 PAWS, INC. All Rights Reserved.
YOU MIGHT BE INTERESTED TO KNOW WHILE YOU WERE ASLEEP, I CAUGHT A MOUSE
GOOD BOY
JIM DAVIS 9-29

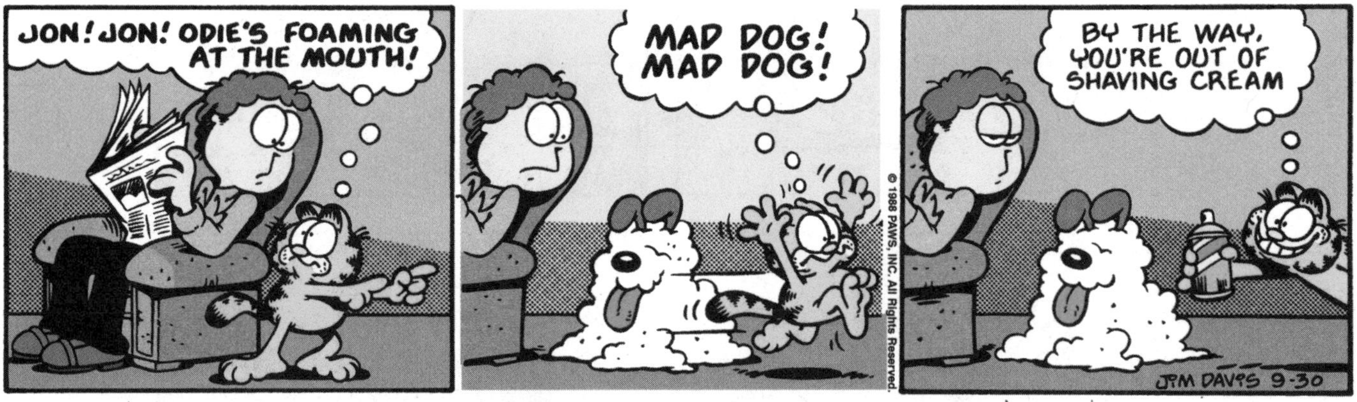
JON! JON! ODIE'S FOAMING AT THE MOUTH!
MAD DOG! MAD DOG!
© 1988 PAWS, INC. All Rights Reserved.
BY THE WAY, YOU'RE OUT OF SHAVING CREAM
JIM DAVIS 9-30

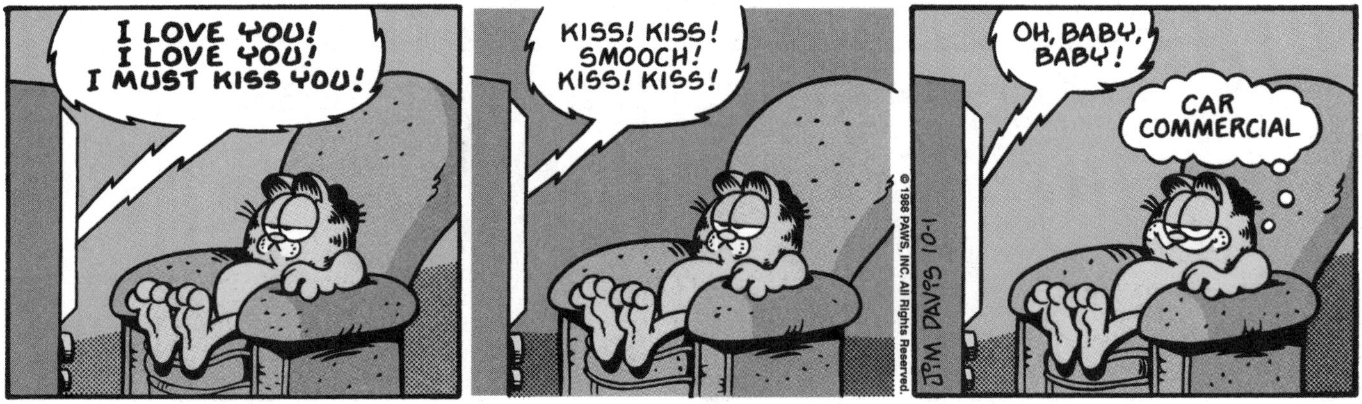
I LOVE YOU! I LOVE YOU! I MUST KISS YOU!
KISS! KISS! SMOOCH! KISS! KISS!
© 1988 PAWS, INC. All Rights Reserved.
JIM DAVIS 10-1
OH, BABY, BABY!
CAR COMMERCIAL

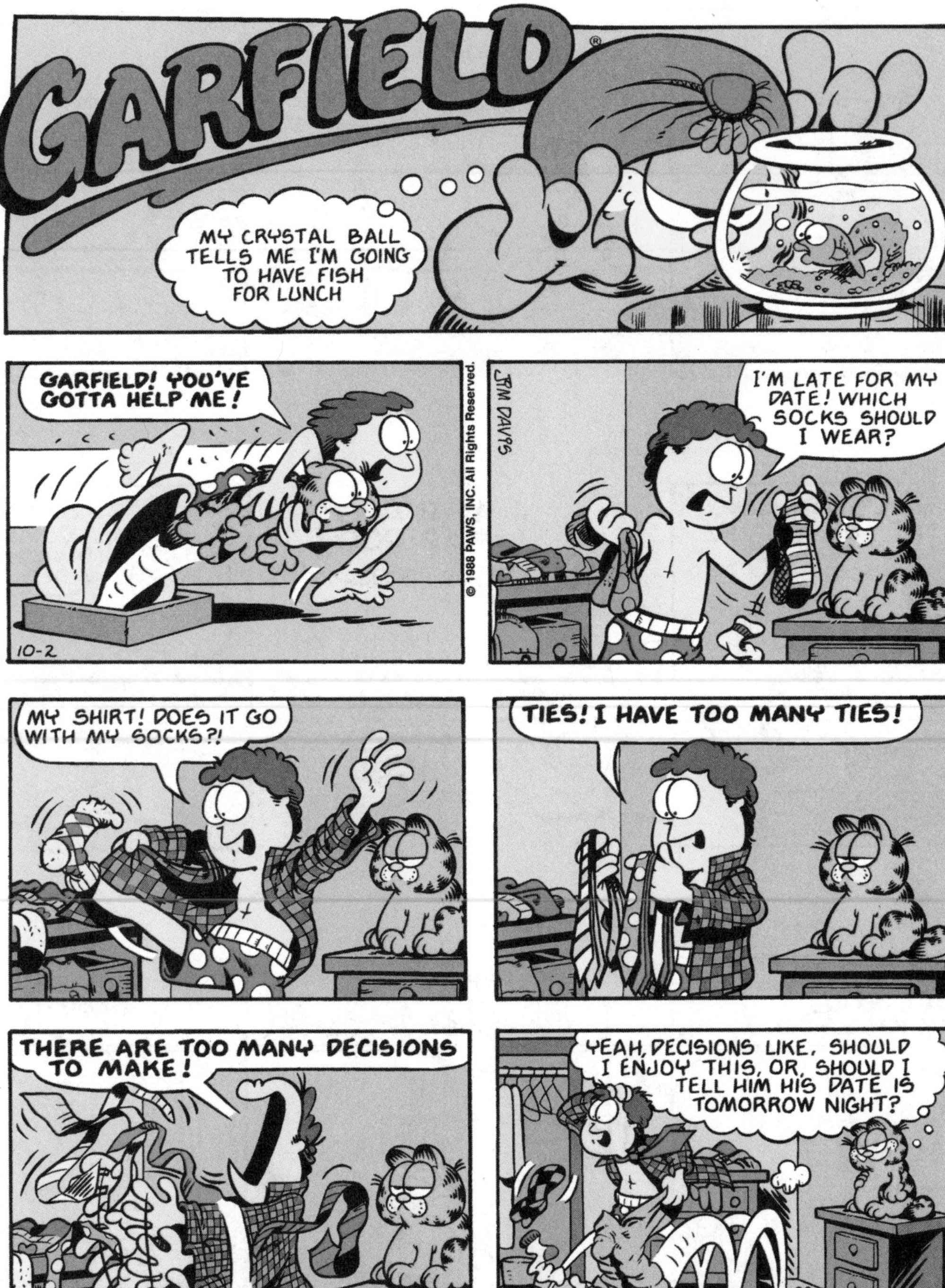
GARFIELD®
MY CRYSTAL BALL TELLS ME I'M GOING TO HAVE FISH FOR LUNCH
GARFIELD! YOU'VE GOTTA HELP ME!
10-2
© 1988 PAWS, INC. All Rights Reserved.
JIM DAVIS
I'M LATE FOR MY DATE! WHICH SOCKS SHOULD I WEAR?
MY SHIRT! DOES IT GO WITH MY SOCKS?!
TIES! I HAVE TOO MANY TIES!
THERE ARE TOO MANY DECISIONS TO MAKE!
YEAH, DECISIONS LIKE, SHOULD I ENJOY THIS, OR, SHOULD I TELL HIM HIS DATE IS TOMORROW NIGHT?

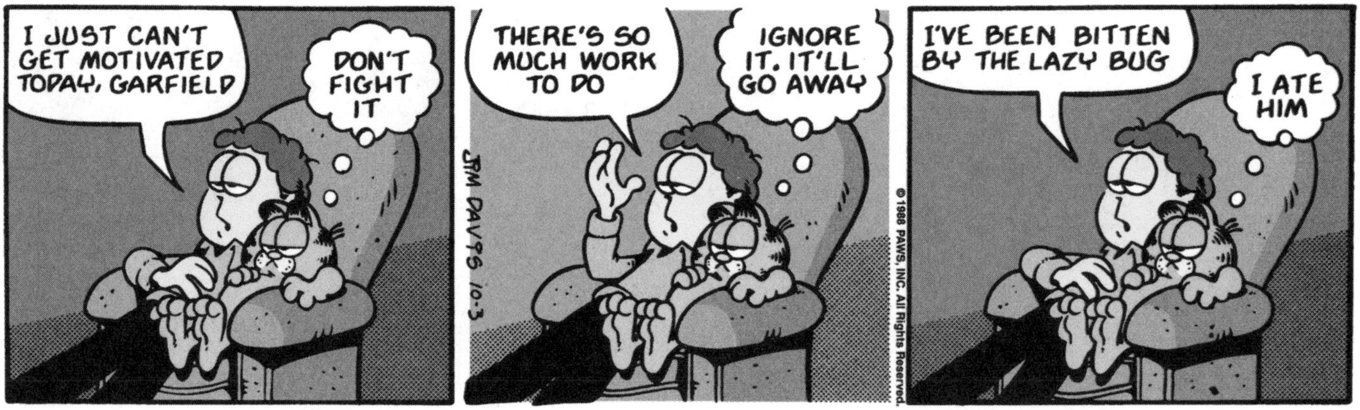
I JUST CAN'T GET MOTIVATED TODAY, GARFIELD
DON'T FIGHT IT
THERE'S SO MUCH WORK TO DO
IGNORE IT. IT'LL GO AWAY
JIM DAVIS 10-3
© 1988 PAWS, INC. All Rights Reserved.
I'VE BEEN BITTEN BY THE LAZY BUG
I ATE HIM

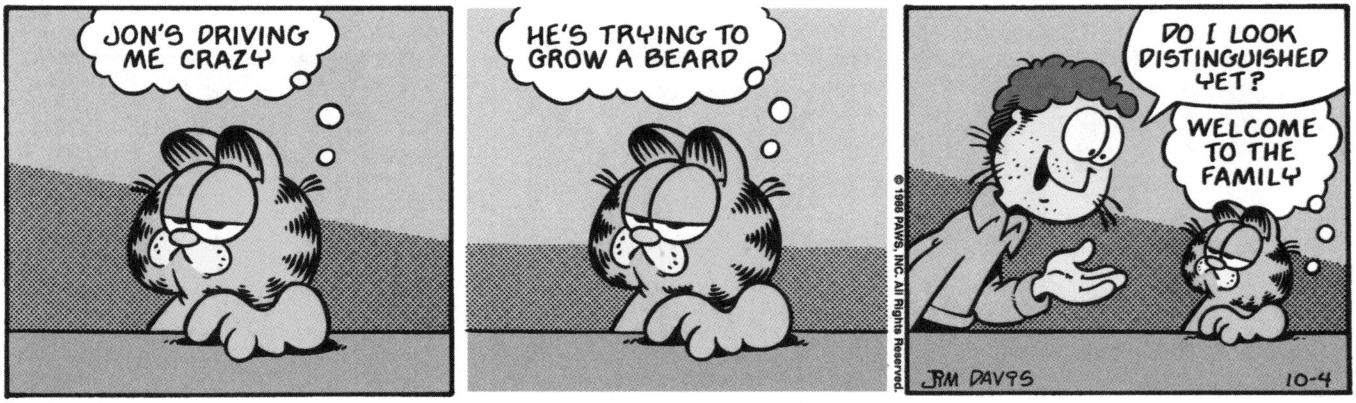
JON'S DRIVING ME CRAZY
HE'S TRYING TO GROW A BEARD
© 1988 PAWS, INC. All Rights Reserved.
DO I LOOK DISTINGUISHED YET?
WELCOME TO THE FAMILY
JIM DAVIS
10-4

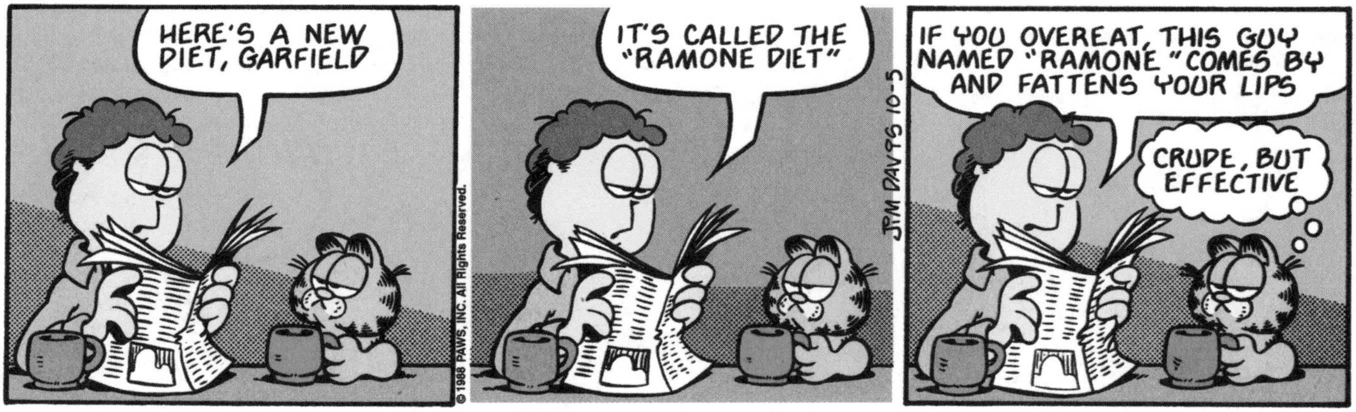
HERE'S A NEW DIET, GARFIELD
© 1988 PAWS, INC. All Rights Reserved.
IT'S CALLED THE "RAMONE DIET"
JIM DAVIS 10-5
IF YOU OVEREAT, THIS GUY NAMED "RAMONE" COMES BY AND FATTENS YOUR LIPS
CRUDE, BUT EFFECTIVE

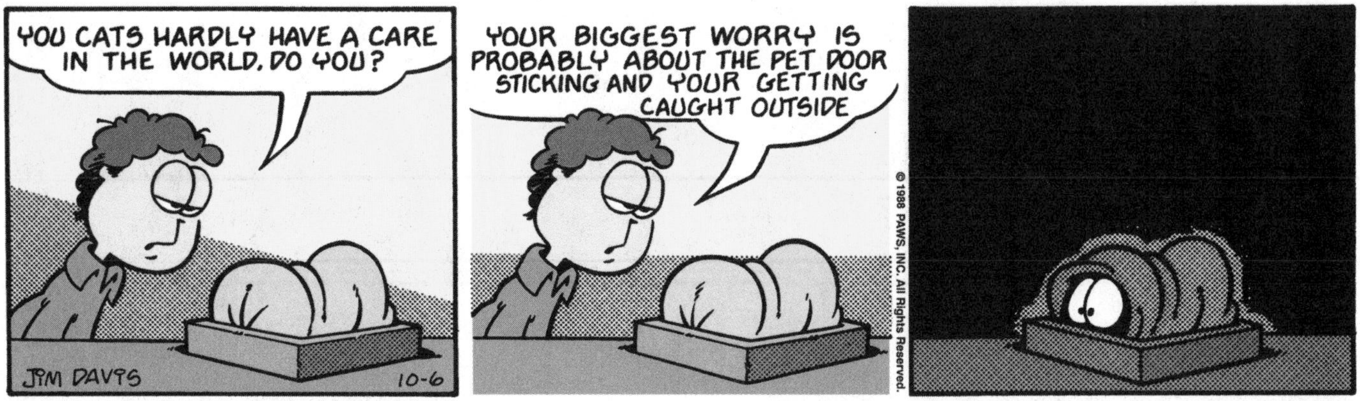
YOU CATS HARDLY HAVE A CARE IN THE WORLD, DO YOU?
YOUR BIGGEST WORRY IS PROBABLY ABOUT THE PET DOOR STICKING AND YOUR GETTING CAUGHT OUTSIDE
JIM DAVIS 10-6
© 1988 PAWS, INC. All Rights Reserved.

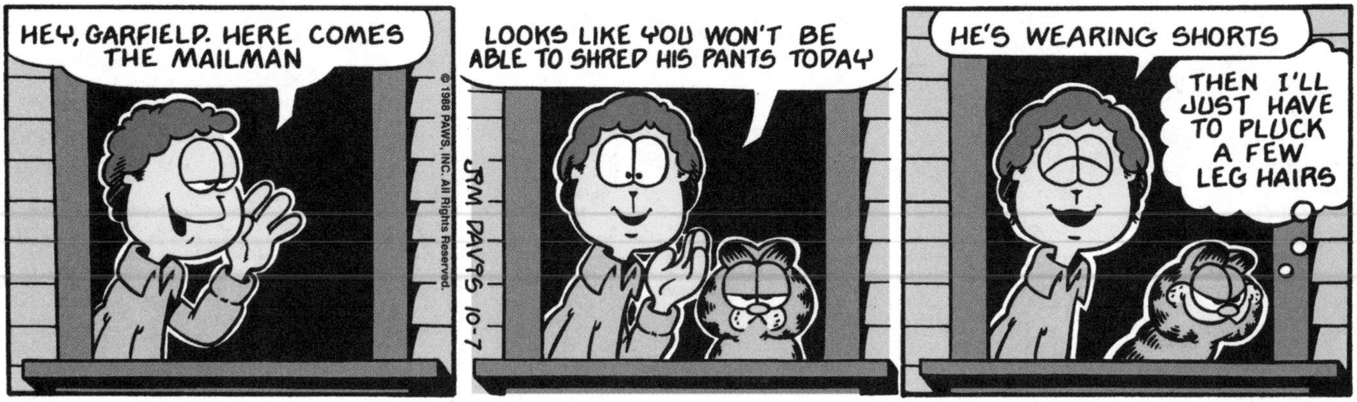
HEY, GARFIELD. HERE COMES THE MAILMAN
LOOKS LIKE YOU WON'T BE ABLE TO SHRED HIS PANTS TODAY
HE'S WEARING SHORTS
THEN I'LL JUST HAVE TO PLUCK A FEW LEG HAIRS
JIM DAVIS 10-7
© 1988 PAWS, INC. All Rights Reserved.

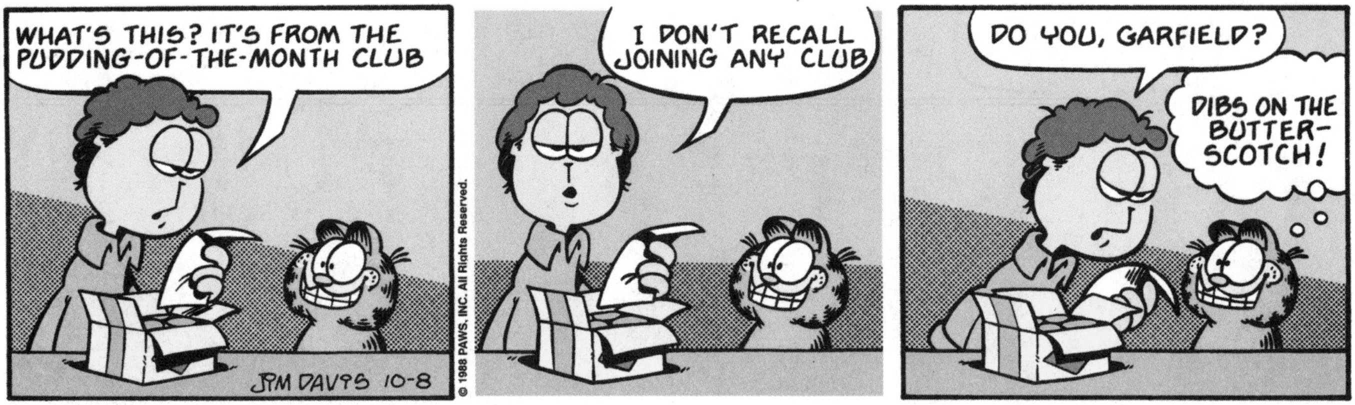
WHAT'S THIS? IT'S FROM THE PUDDING-OF-THE-MONTH CLUB
I DON'T RECALL JOINING ANY CLUB
DO YOU, GARFIELD?
DIBS ON THE BUTTER-SCOTCH!
JIM DAVIS 10-8
© 1988 PAWS, INC. All Rights Reserved.

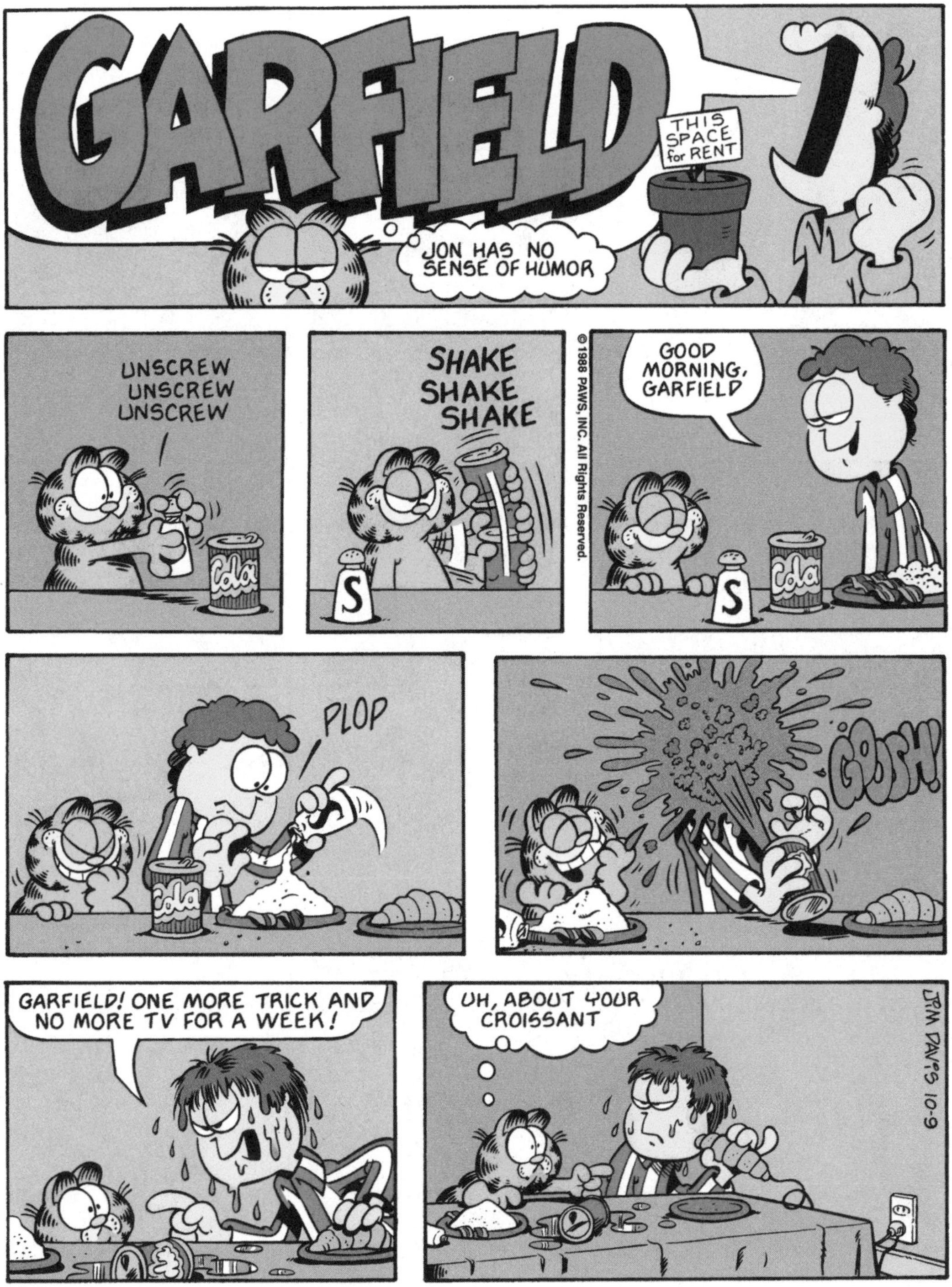
GARFIELD
THIS SPACE for RENT
JON HAS NO SENSE OF HUMOR
UNSCREW UNSCREW UNSCREW
SHAKE SHAKE SHAKE
© 1988 PAWS, INC. All Rights Reserved.
GOOD MORNING, GARFIELD
PLOP
GUSH!
GARFIELD! ONE MORE TRICK AND NO MORE TV FOR A WEEK!
UH, ABOUT YOUR CROISSANT
JIM DAVIS 10-9

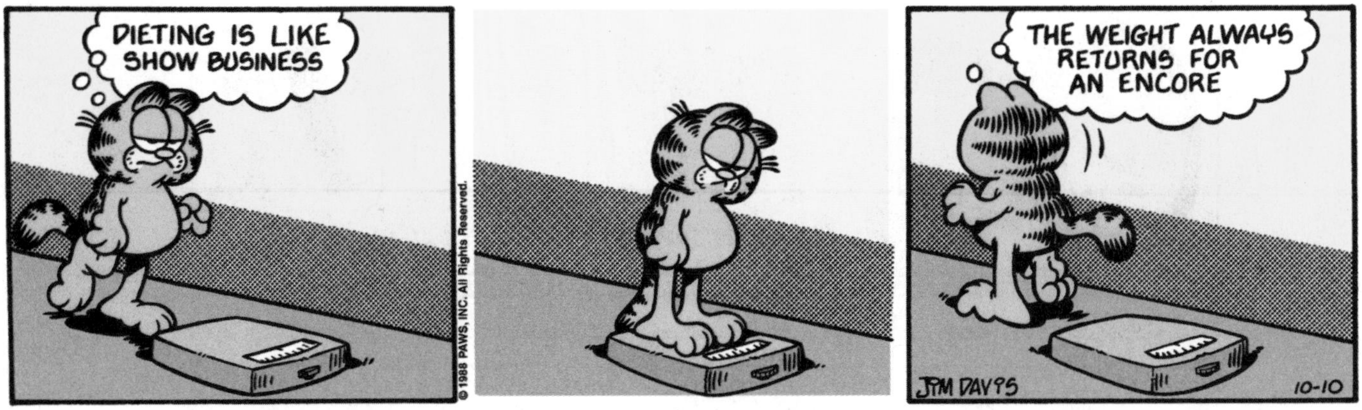
DIETING IS LIKE SHOW BUSINESS
© 1988 PAWS, INC. All Rights Reserved.
THE WEIGHT ALWAYS RETURNS FOR AN ENCORE
JIM DAVIS
10-10

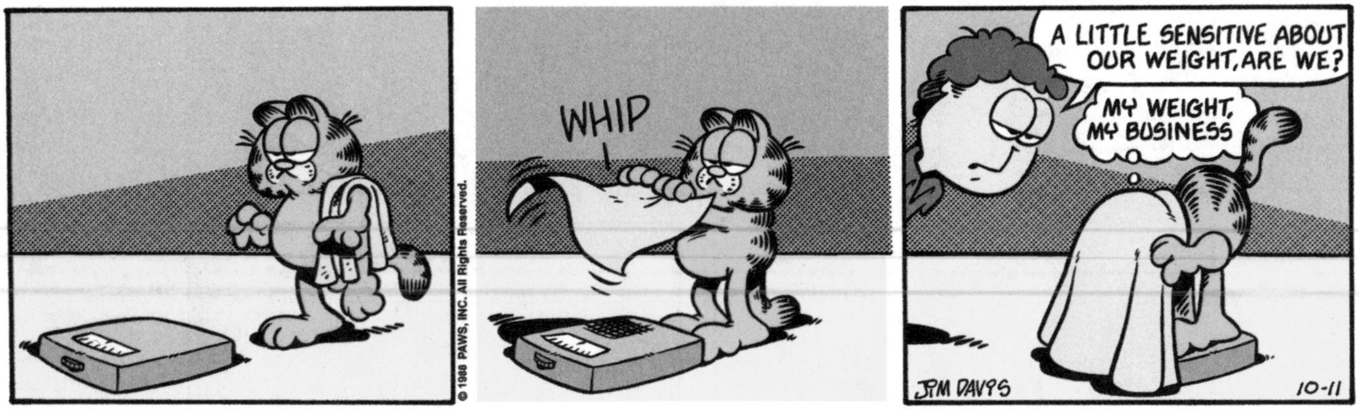
© 1988 PAWS, INC. All Rights Reserved.
WHIP
A LITTLE SENSITIVE ABOUT OUR WEIGHT, ARE WE?
MY WEIGHT, MY BUSINESS
JIM DAVIS
10-11

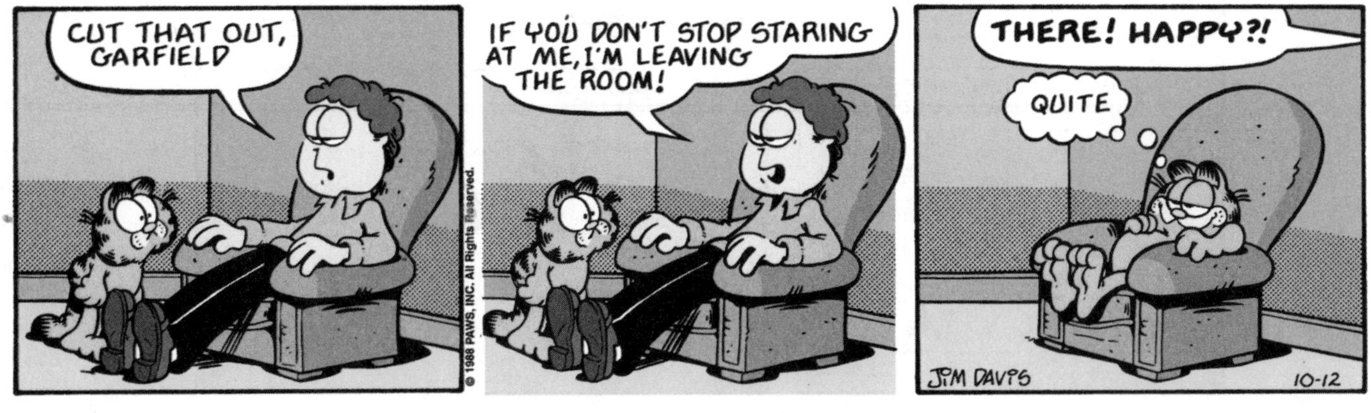
CUT THAT OUT, GARFIELD
© 1988 PAWS, INC. All Rights Reserved.
IF YOU DON'T STOP STARING AT ME, I'M LEAVING THE ROOM!
THERE! HAPPY?!
QUITE
JIM DAVIS
10-12

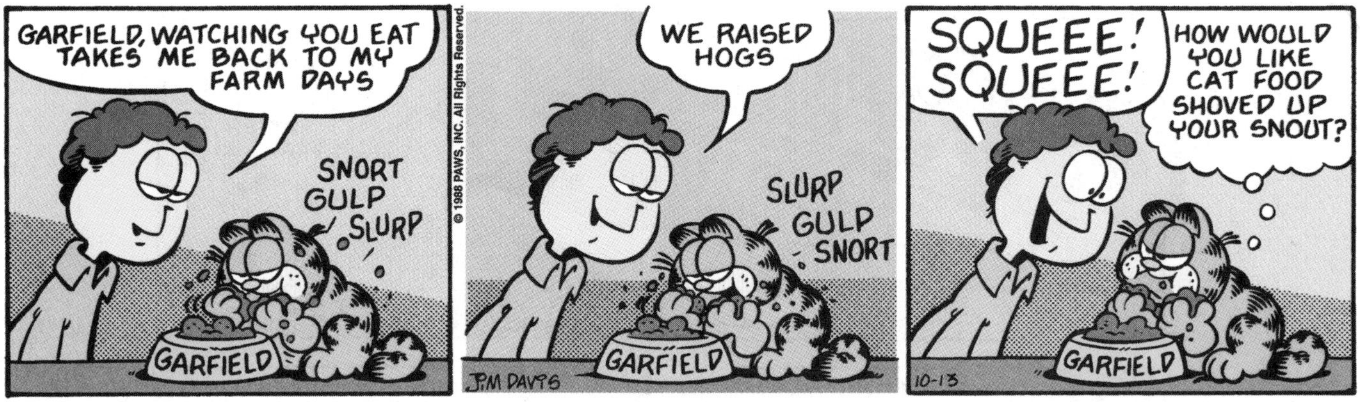
GARFIELD, WATCHING YOU EAT TAKES ME BACK TO MY FARM DAYS
SNORT GULP SLURP
GARFIELD
© 1988 PAWS, INC. All Rights Reserved.
WE RAISED HOGS
SLURP GULP SNORT
GARFIELD
JIM DAVIS
SQUEEE! SQUEEE!
HOW WOULD YOU LIKE CAT FOOD SHOVED UP YOUR SNOUT?
GARFIELD
10-13

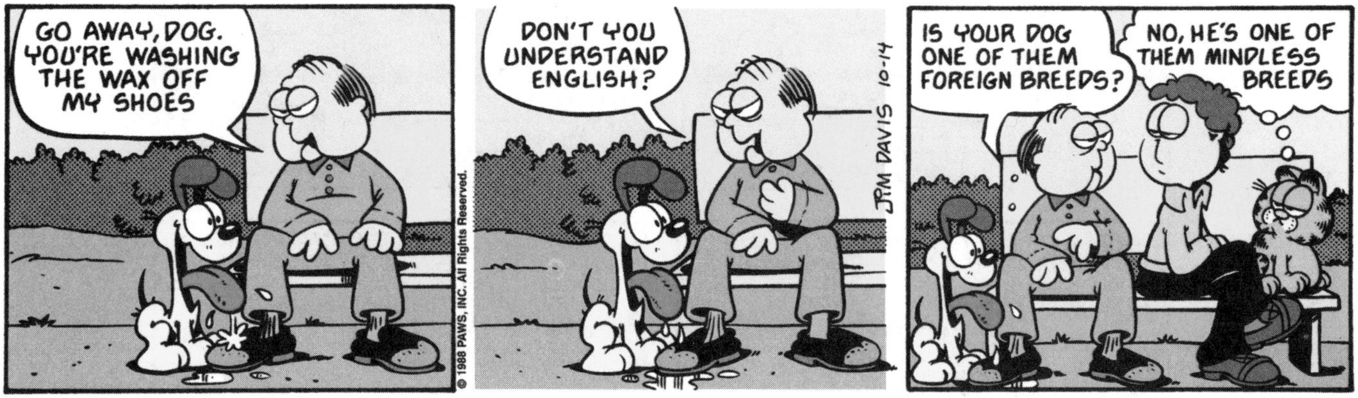
GO AWAY, DOG. YOU'RE WASHING THE WAX OFF MY SHOES
© 1988 PAWS, INC. All Rights Reserved.
DON'T YOU UNDERSTAND ENGLISH?
JIM DAVIS 10-14
IS YOUR DOG ONE OF THEM FOREIGN BREEDS?
NO, HE'S ONE OF THEM MINDLESS BREEDS

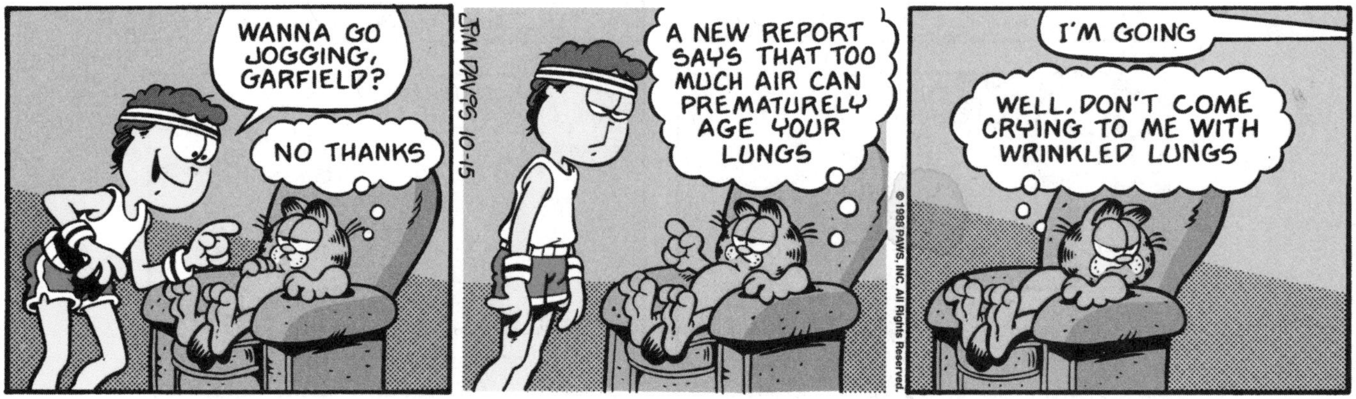
WANNA GO JOGGING, GARFIELD?
NO THANKS
JIM DAVIS 10-15
A NEW REPORT SAYS THAT TOO MUCH AIR CAN PREMATURELY AGE YOUR LUNGS
© 1988 PAWS, INC. All Rights Reserved.
I'M GOING
WELL, DON'T COME CRYING TO ME WITH WRINKLED LUNGS

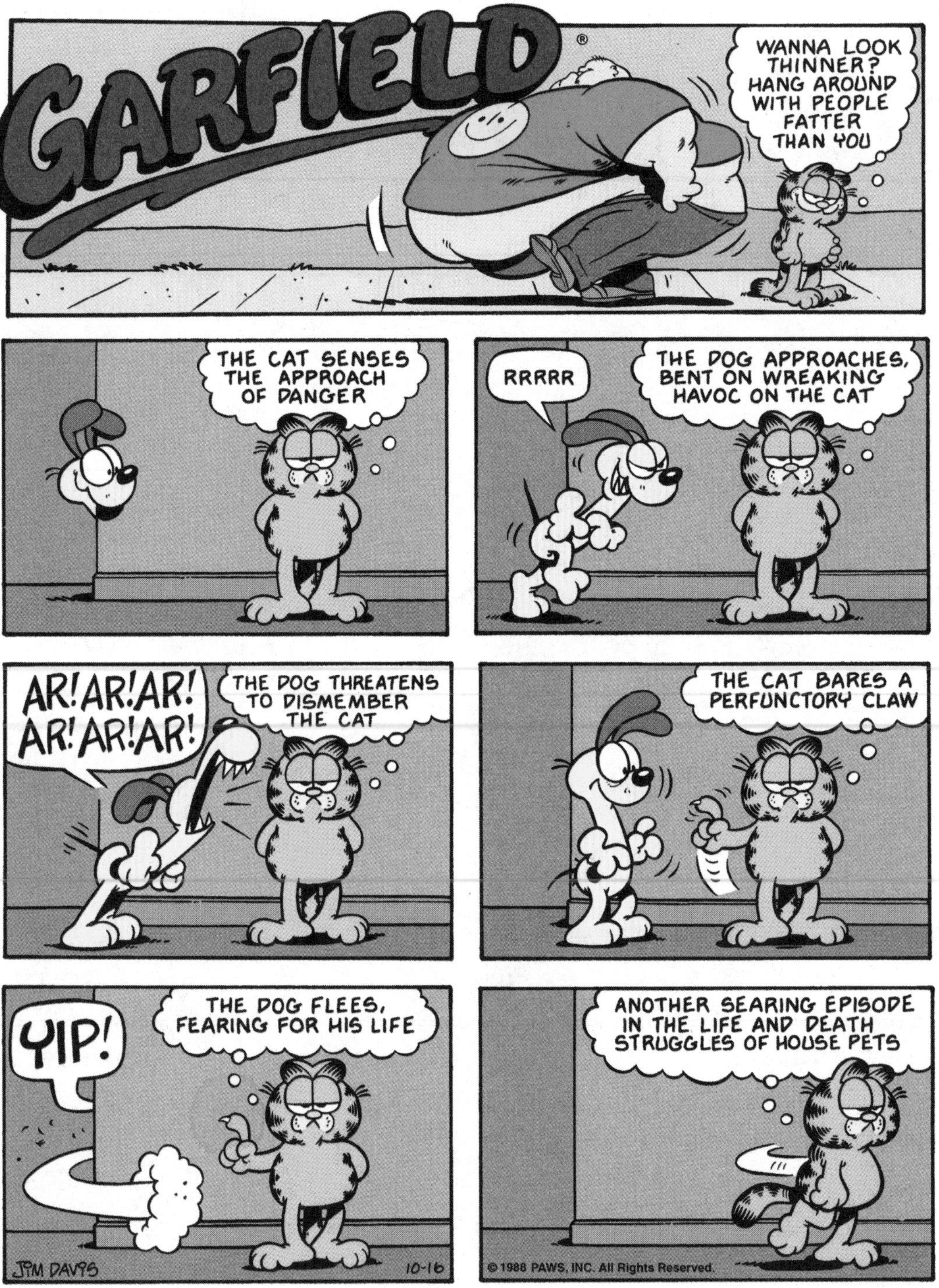
GARFIELD®
WANNA LOOK THINNER? HANG AROUND WITH PEOPLE FATTER THAN YOU
THE CAT SENSES THE APPROACH OF DANGER
RRRRR
THE DOG APPROACHES, BENT ON WREAKING HAVOC ON THE CAT
AR! AR! AR! AR! AR! AR!
THE DOG THREATENS TO DISMEMBER THE CAT
THE CAT BARES A PERFUNCTORY CLAW
YIP!
THE DOG FLEES, FEARING FOR HIS LIFE
ANOTHER SEARING EPISODE IN THE LIFE AND DEATH STRUGGLES OF HOUSE PETS
JIM DAVIS
10-16

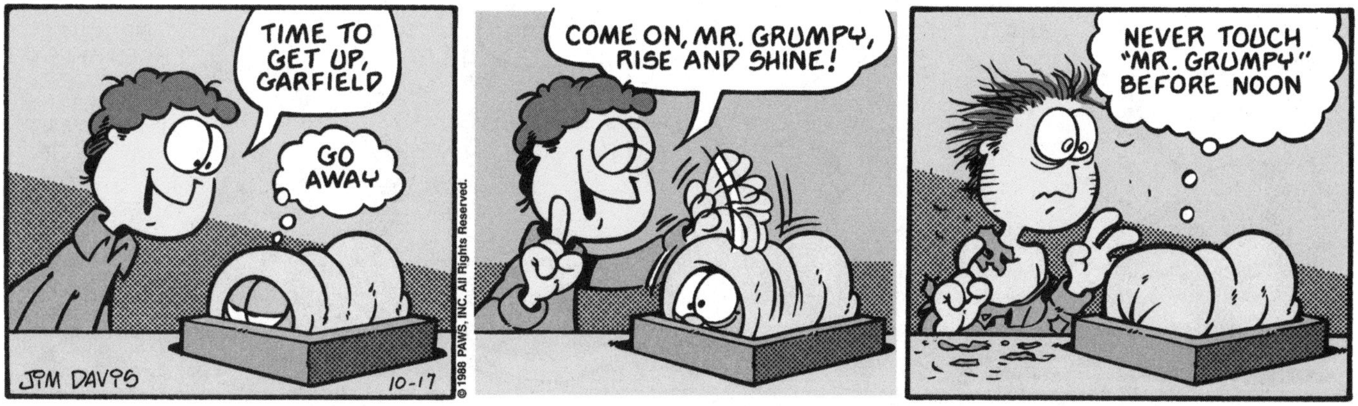
TIME TO GET UP, GARFIELD
GO AWAY
JIM DAVIS 10-17
© 1988 PAWS, INC. All Rights Reserved.
COME ON, MR. GRUMPY, RISE AND SHINE!
NEVER TOUCH "MR. GRUMPY" BEFORE NOON

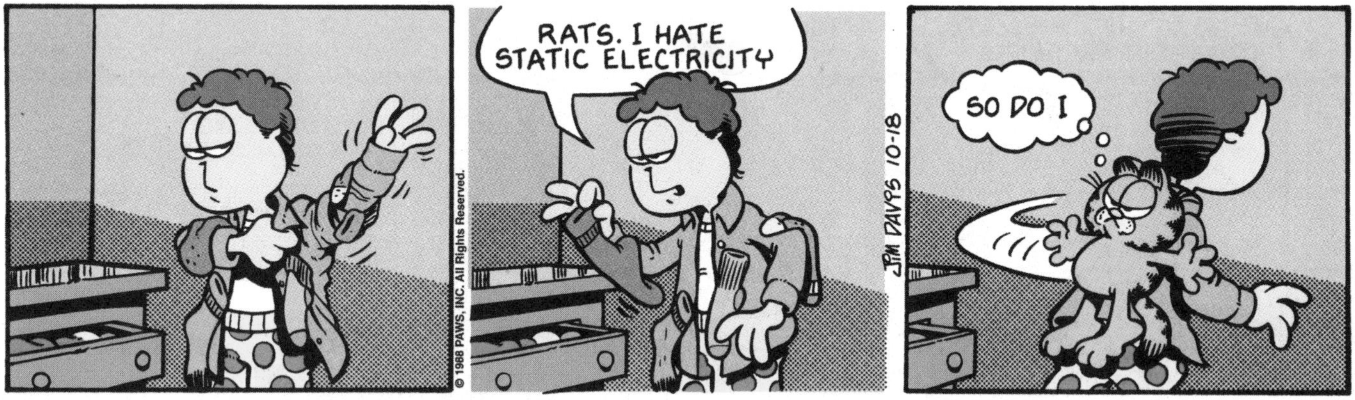
© 1988 PAWS, INC. All Rights Reserved.
RATS. I HATE STATIC ELECTRICITY
JIM DAVIS 10-18
SO DO I

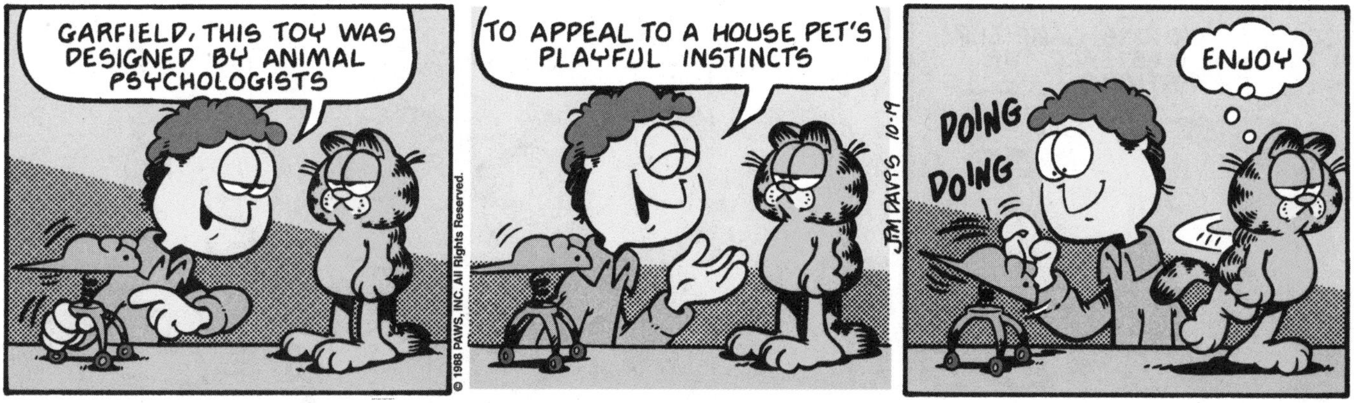
GARFIELD, THIS TOY WAS DESIGNED BY ANIMAL PSYCHOLOGISTS
© 1988 PAWS, INC. All Rights Reserved.
TO APPEAL TO A HOUSE PET'S PLAYFUL INSTINCTS
JIM DAVIS 10-19
DOING
DOING
ENJOY

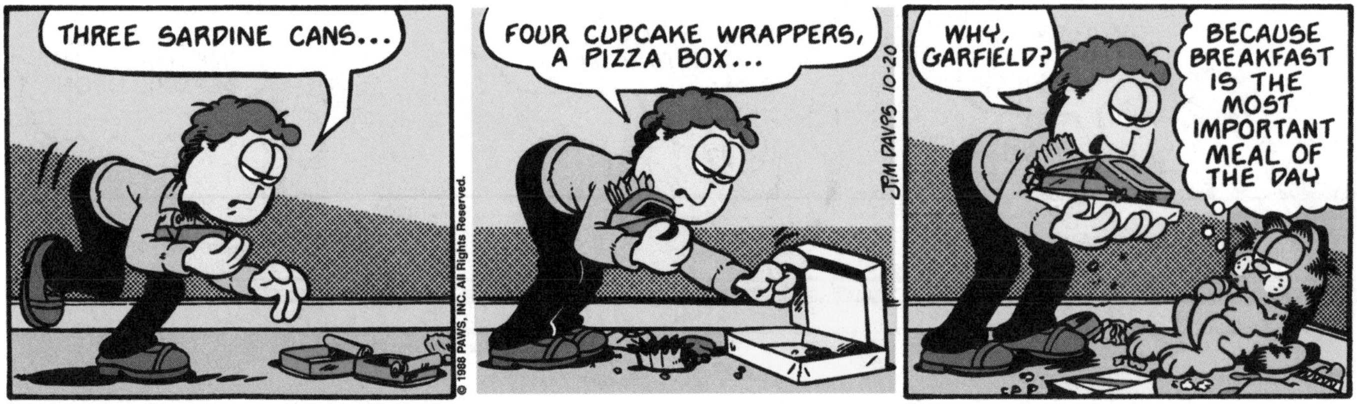
THREE SARDINE CANS...
© 1988 PAWS, INC. All Rights Reserved.
FOUR CUPCAKE WRAPPERS, A PIZZA BOX...
JIM DAVIS 10-20
WHY, GARFIELD?
BECAUSE BREAKFAST IS THE MOST IMPORTANT MEAL OF THE DAY

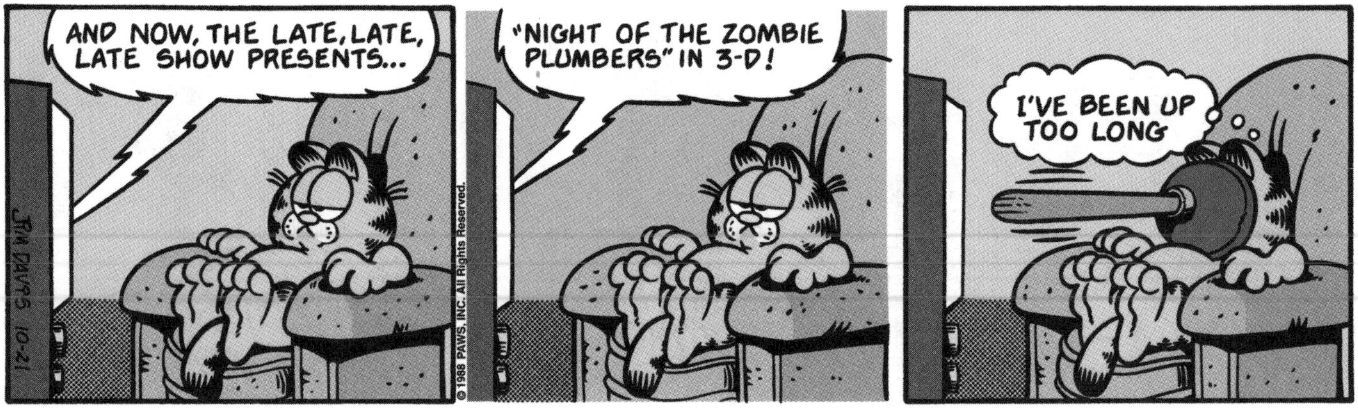
AND NOW, THE LATE, LATE, LATE SHOW PRESENTS...
JIM DAVIS 10-21
© 1988 PAWS, INC. All Rights Reserved.
"NIGHT OF THE ZOMBIE PLUMBERS" IN 3-D!
I'VE BEEN UP TOO LONG

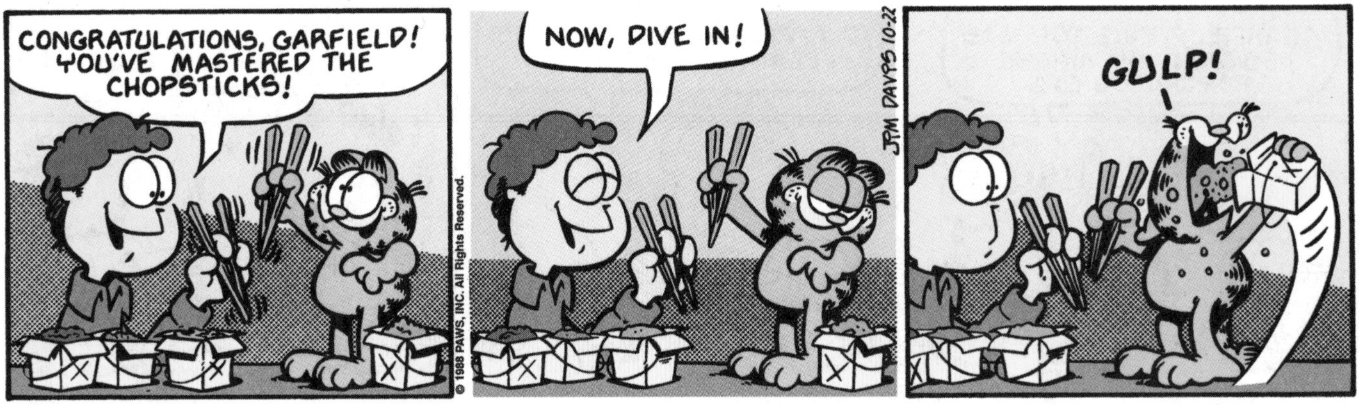
CONGRATULATIONS, GARFIELD! YOU'VE MASTERED THE CHOPSTICKS!
© 1988 PAWS, INC. All Rights Reserved.
NOW, DIVE IN!
JIM DAVIS 10-22
GULP!

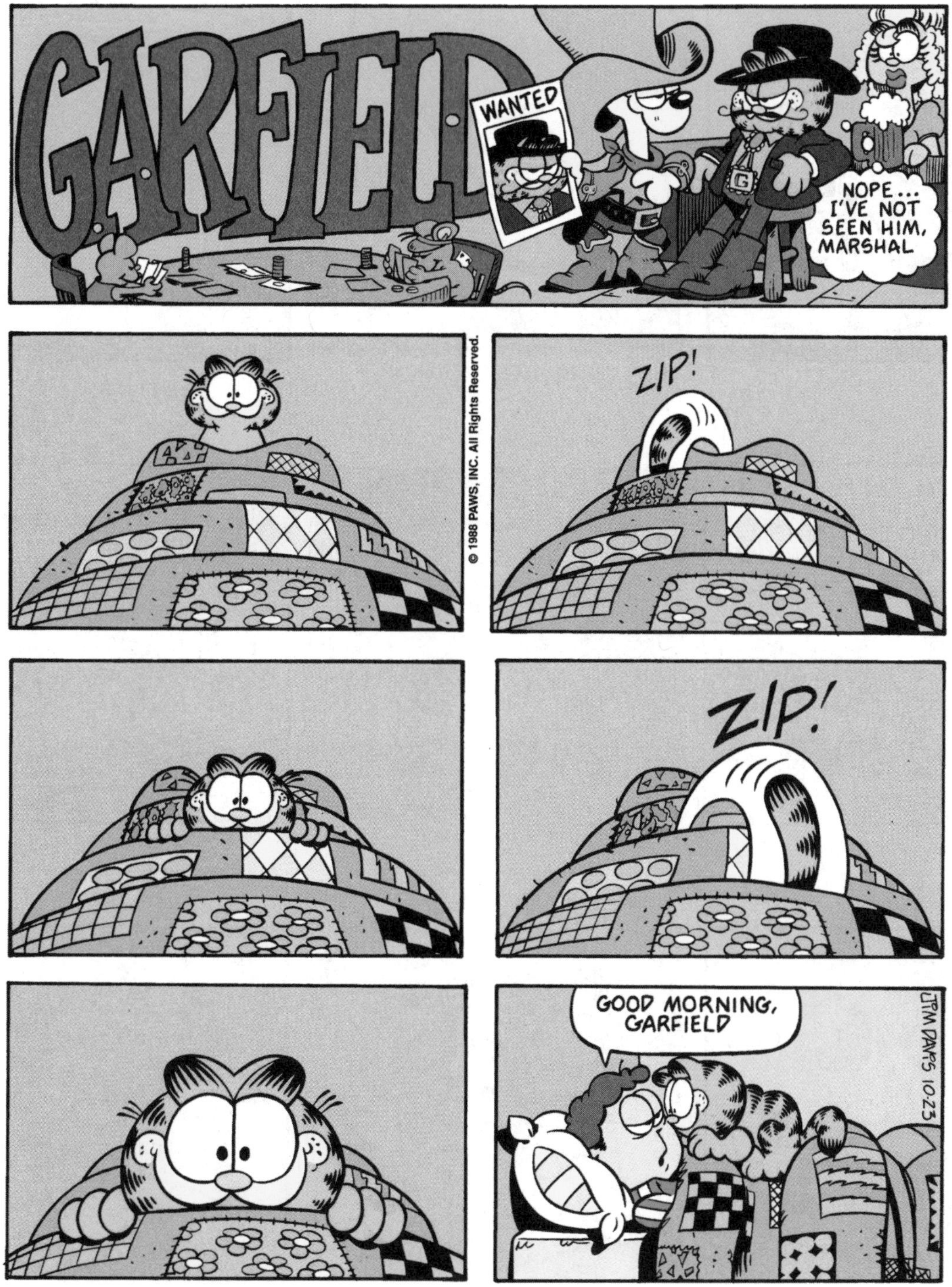
GARFIELD
WANTED
NOPE... I'VE NOT SEEN HIM, MARSHAL
© 1988 PAWS, INC. All Rights Reserved.
ZIP!
ZIP!
GOOD MORNING, GARFIELD
JPM DAVIS 10-23

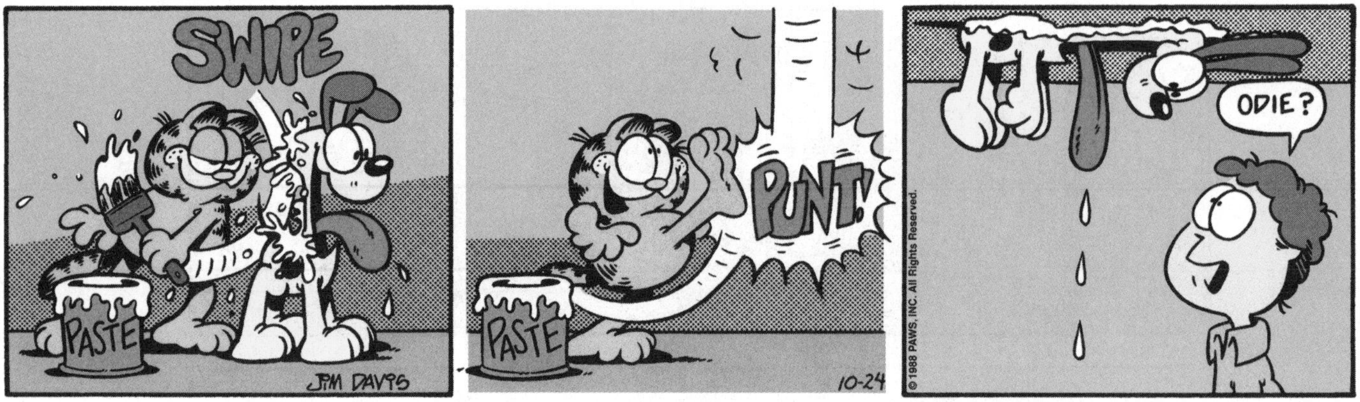
SWIPE
PASTE
JIM DAVIS
PUNT!
PASTE
10-24
© 1988 PAWS, INC. All Rights Reserved.
ODIE?

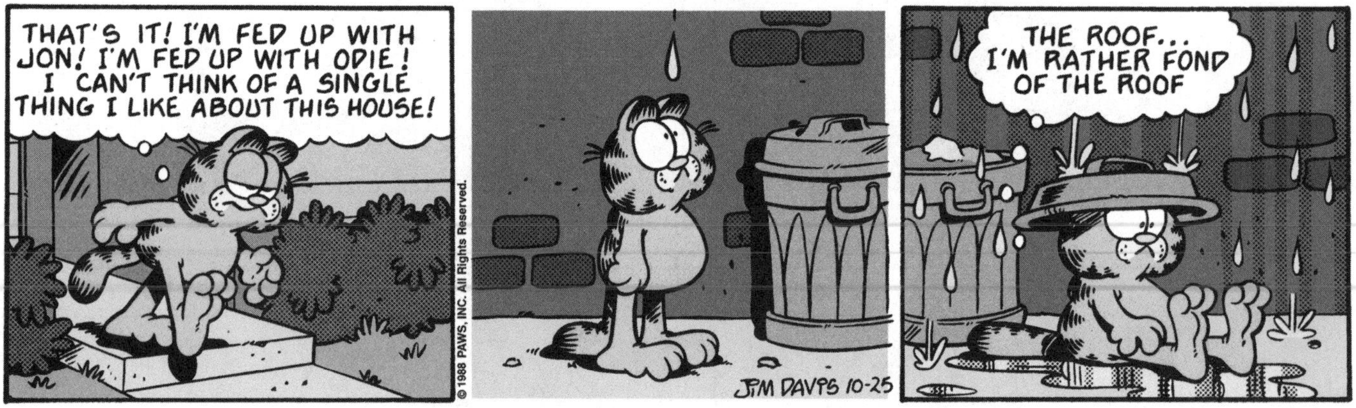
THAT'S IT! I'M FED UP WITH JON! I'M FED UP WITH ODIE! I CAN'T THINK OF A SINGLE THING I LIKE ABOUT THIS HOUSE!
© 1988 PAWS, INC. All Rights Reserved.
JIM DAVIS 10-25
THE ROOF... I'M RATHER FOND OF THE ROOF

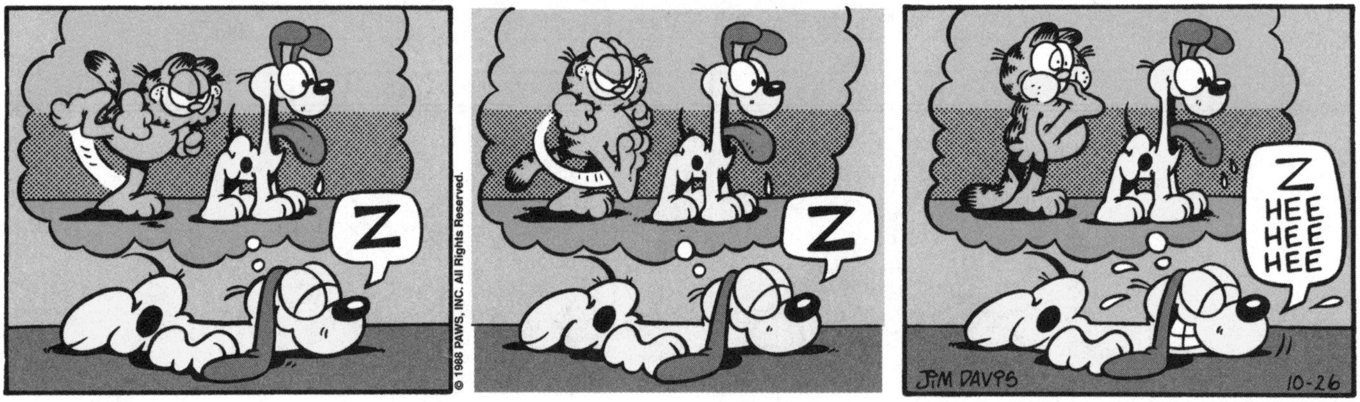
Z
© 1988 PAWS, INC. All Rights Reserved.
Z
Z HEE HEE HEE
JIM DAVIS
10-26

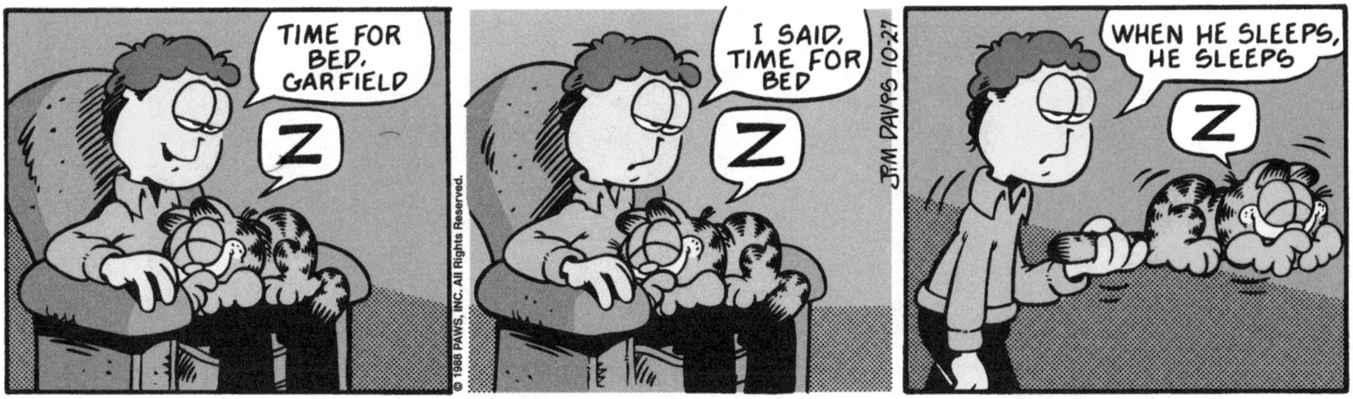
TIME FOR BED, GARFIELD
Z
© 1988 PAWS, INC. All Rights Reserved.
I SAID, TIME FOR BED
Z
JIM DAVIS 10-27
WHEN HE SLEEPS, HE SLEEPS
Z

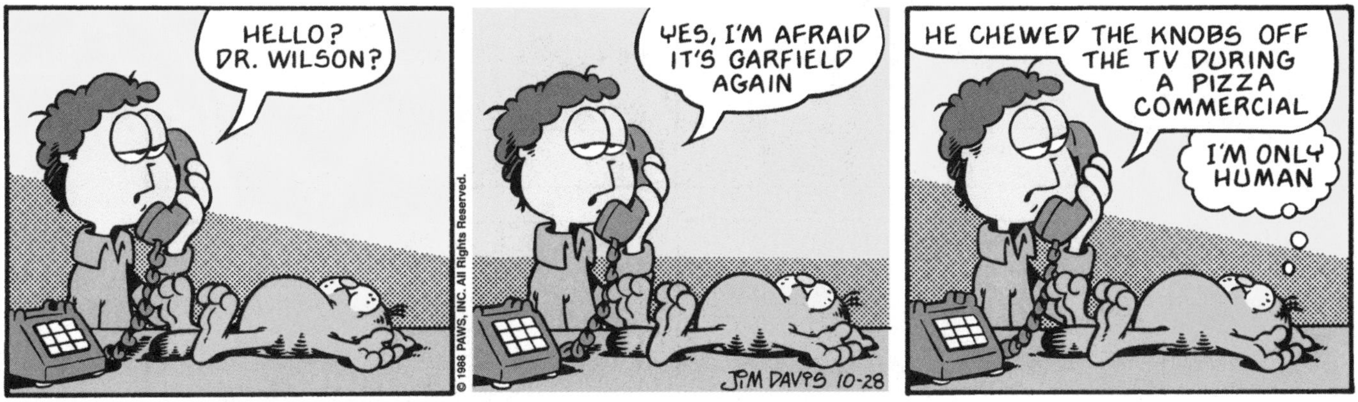
HELLO? DR. WILSON?
© 1988 PAWS, INC. All Rights Reserved.
YES, I'M AFRAID IT'S GARFIELD AGAIN
JIM DAVIS 10-28
HE CHEWED THE KNOBS OFF THE TV DURING A PIZZA COMMERCIAL
I'M ONLY HUMAN

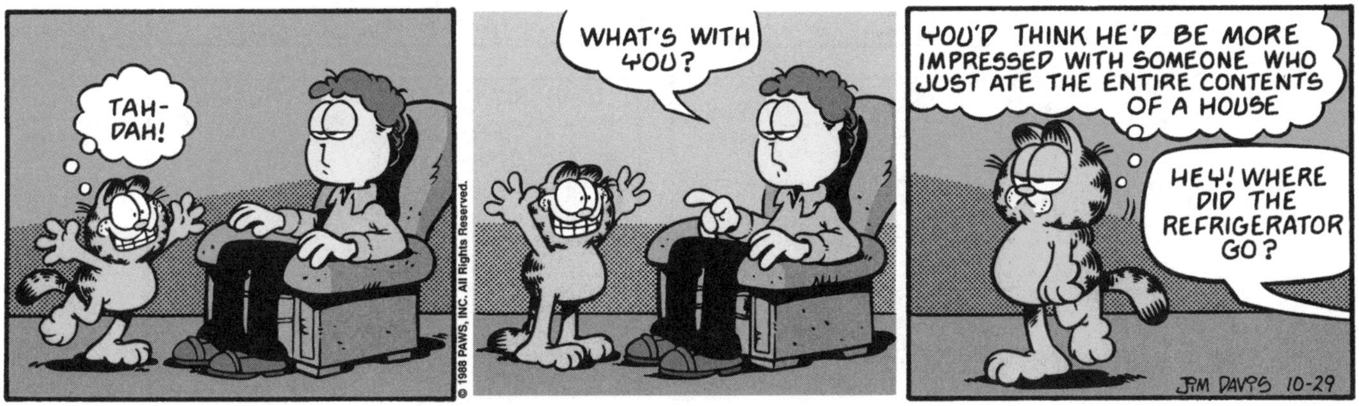
TAH-DAH!
© 1988 PAWS, INC. All Rights Reserved.
WHAT'S WITH YOU?
YOU'D THINK HE'D BE MORE IMPRESSED WITH SOMEONE WHO JUST ATE THE ENTIRE CONTENTS OF A HOUSE
HEY! WHERE DID THE REFRIGERATOR GO?
JIM DAVIS 10-29

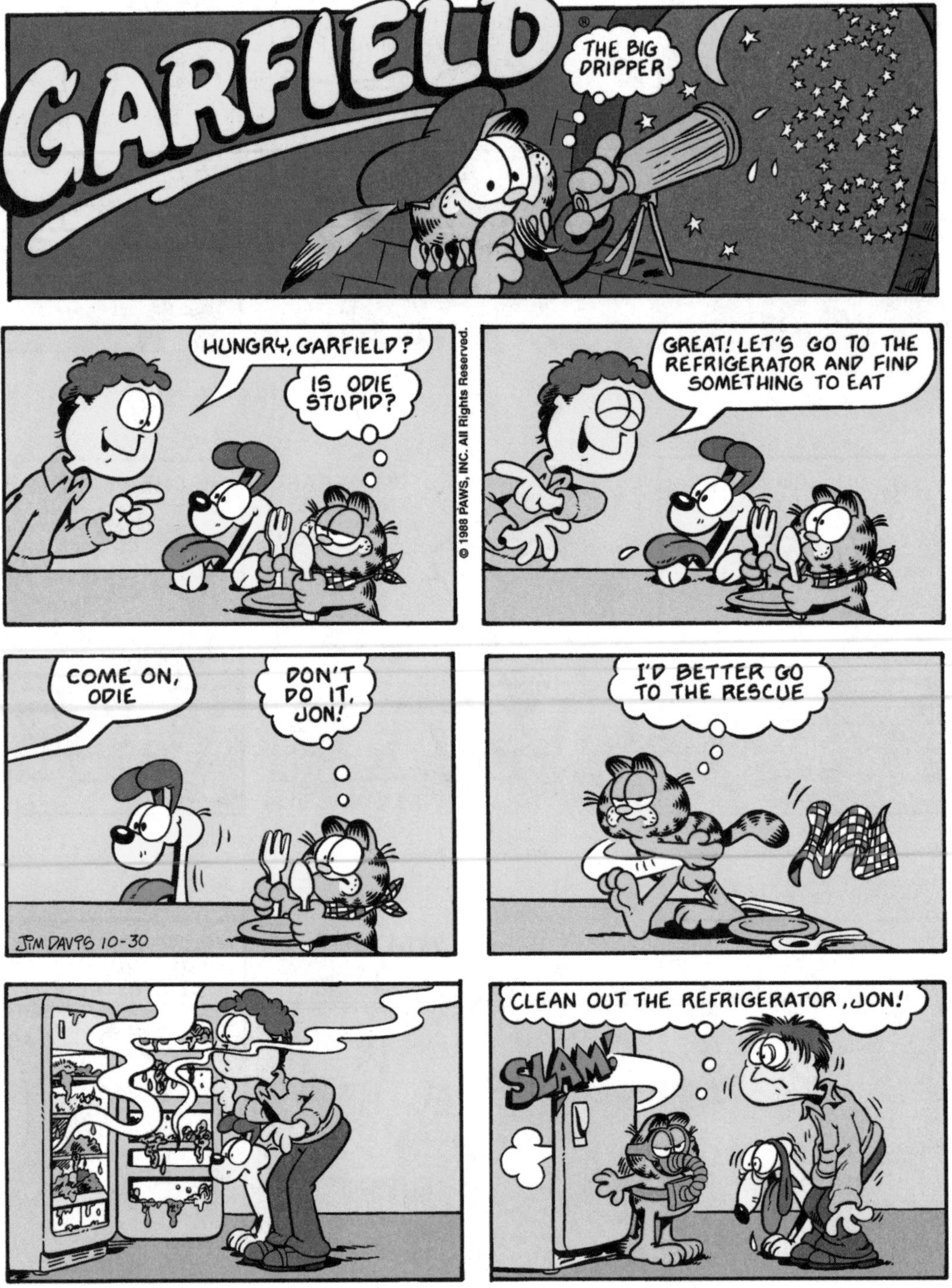
GARFIELD®
THE BIG DRIPPER
HUNGRY, GARFIELD?
IS ODIE STUPID?
GREAT! LET'S GO TO THE REFRIGERATOR AND FIND SOMETHING TO EAT
COME ON, ODIE
DON'T DO IT, JON!
I'D BETTER GO TO THE RESCUE
SLAM!
CLEAN OUT THE REFRIGERATOR, JON!
JIM DAVIS 10-30

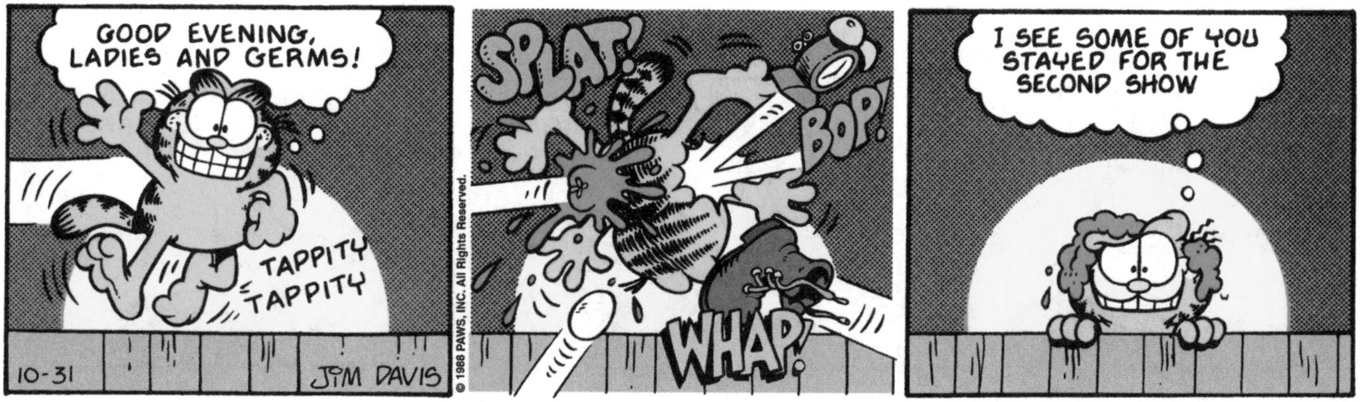
GOOD EVENING, LADIES AND GERMS!
TAPPITY TAPPITY
10-31
JIM DAVIS
© 1988 PAWS, INC. All Rights Reserved.
SPLAT!
BOP!
WHAP!
I SEE SOME OF YOU STAYED FOR THE SECOND SHOW

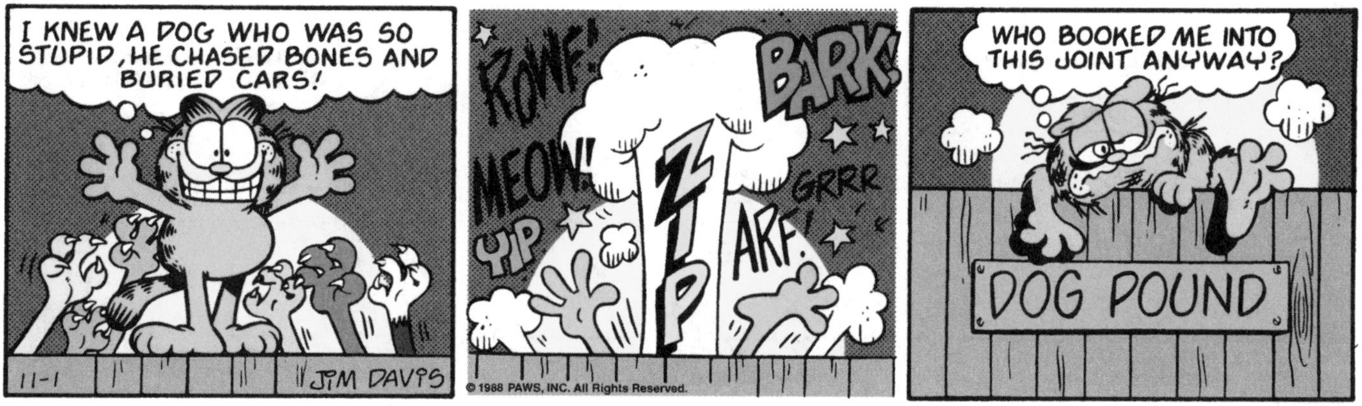
I KNEW A DOG WHO WAS SO STUPID, HE CHASED BONES AND BURIED CARS!
11-1
JIM DAVIS
ROWF!
BARK!
MEOW!
YIP
ZIP
GRRR
ARF!
© 1988 PAWS, INC. All Rights Reserved.
WHO BOOKED ME INTO THIS JOINT ANYWAY?
DOG POUND

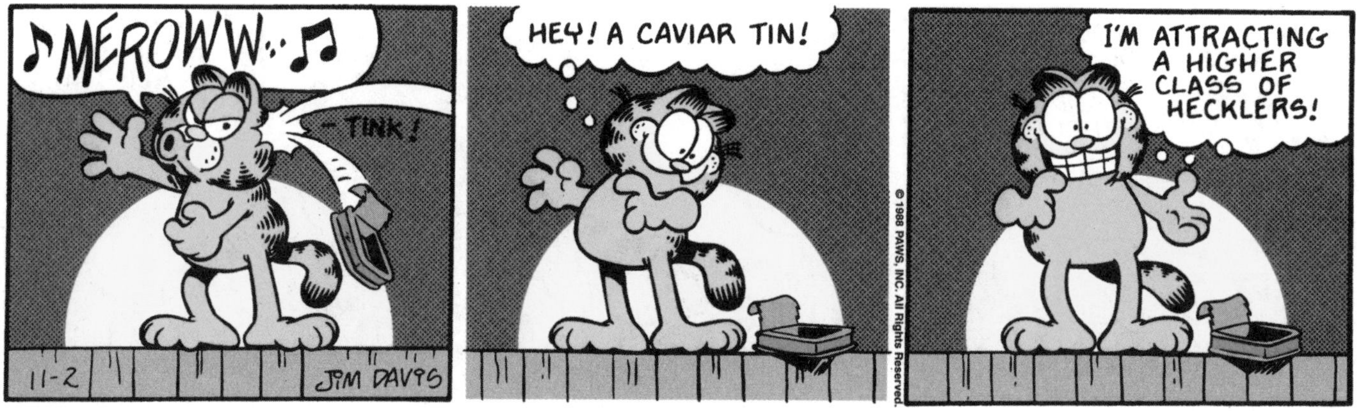
♪MEROWW.:.♫
TINK!
11-2
JIM DAVIS
HEY! A CAVIAR TIN!
© 1988 PAWS, INC. All Rights Reserved.
I'M ATTRACTING A HIGHER CLASS OF HECKLERS!

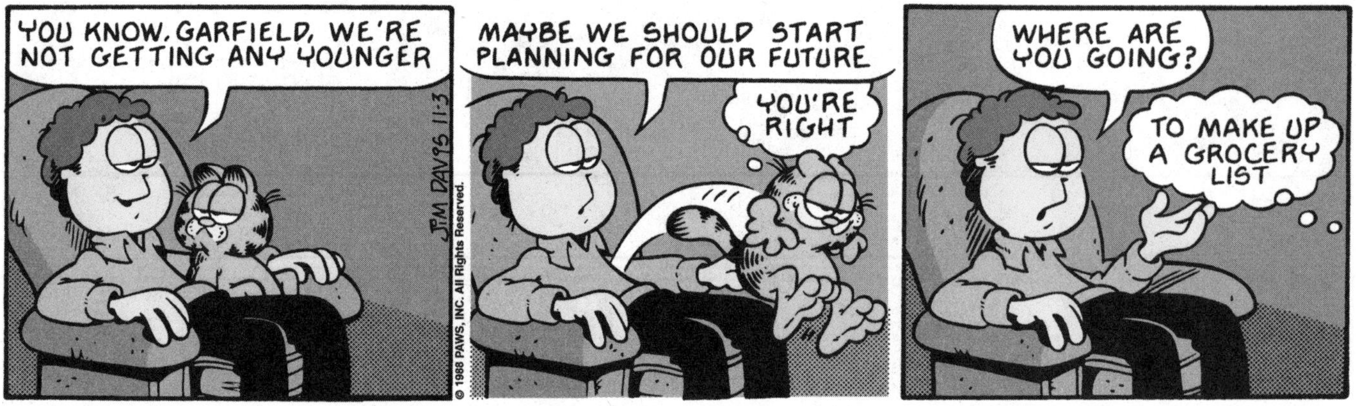
YOU KNOW, GARFIELD, WE'RE NOT GETTING ANY YOUNGER
JIM DAVIS 11-3
© 1988 PAWS, INC. All Rights Reserved.
MAYBE WE SHOULD START PLANNING FOR OUR FUTURE
YOU'RE RIGHT
WHERE ARE YOU GOING?
TO MAKE UP A GROCERY LIST

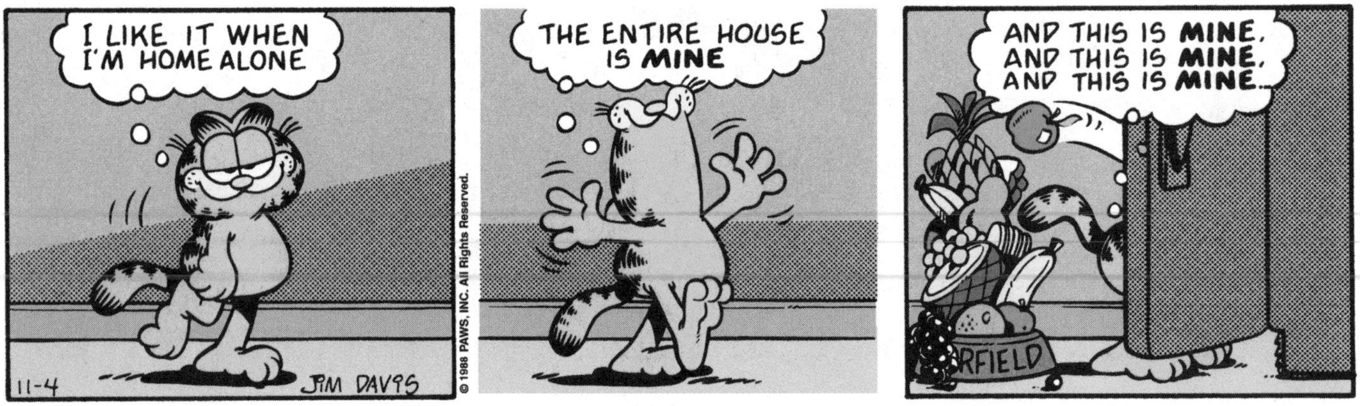
I LIKE IT WHEN I'M HOME ALONE
11-4
JIM DAVIS
© 1988 PAWS, INC. All Rights Reserved.
THE ENTIRE HOUSE IS **MINE**
AND THIS IS **MINE**, AND THIS IS **MINE**, AND THIS IS **MINE**...
RFIELD

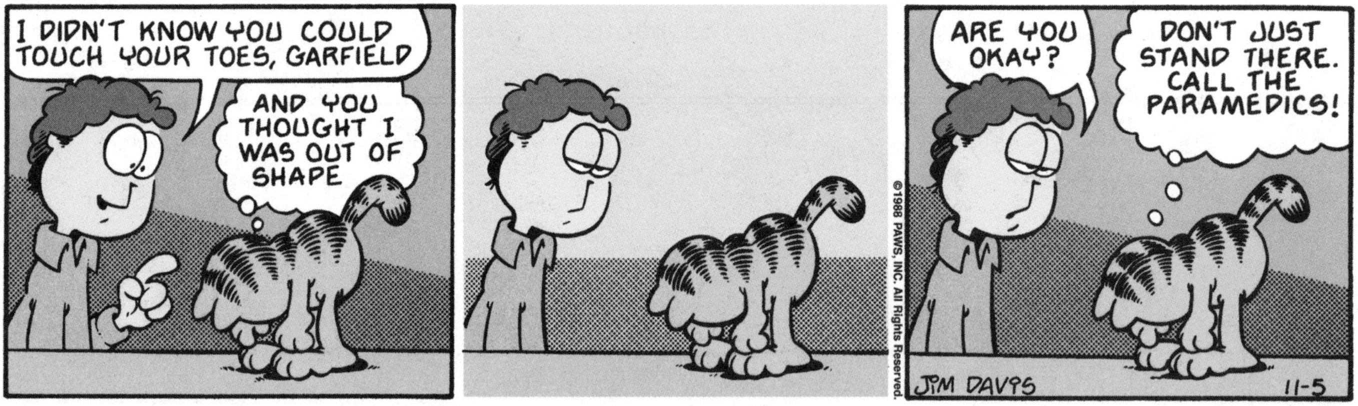
I DIDN'T KNOW YOU COULD TOUCH YOUR TOES, GARFIELD
AND YOU THOUGHT I WAS OUT OF SHAPE
© 1988 PAWS, INC. All Rights Reserved.
ARE YOU OKAY?
DON'T JUST STAND THERE. CALL THE PARAMEDICS!
JIM DAVIS
11-5

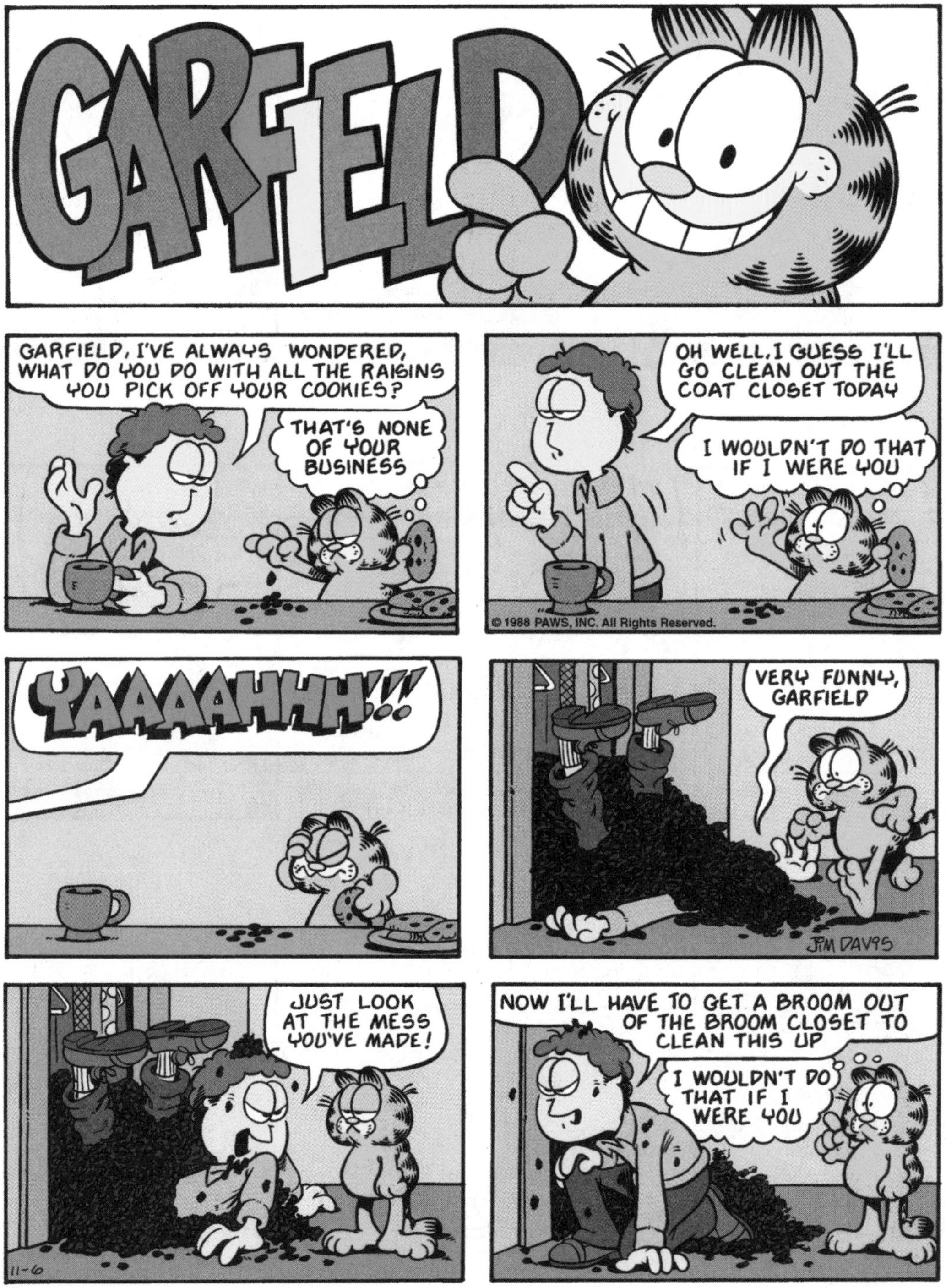
GARFIELD
GARFIELD, I'VE ALWAYS WONDERED, WHAT DO YOU DO WITH ALL THE RAISINS YOU PICK OFF YOUR COOKIES?
THAT'S NONE OF YOUR BUSINESS
OH WELL. I GUESS I'LL GO CLEAN OUT THE COAT CLOSET TODAY
I WOULDN'T DO THAT IF I WERE YOU
© 1988 PAWS, INC. All Rights Reserved.
YAAAAHHH!!!
VERY FUNNY, GARFIELD
JIM DAVIS
JUST LOOK AT THE MESS YOU'VE MADE!
11-6
NOW I'LL HAVE TO GET A BROOM OUT OF THE BROOM CLOSET TO CLEAN THIS UP
I WOULDN'T DO THAT IF I WERE YOU

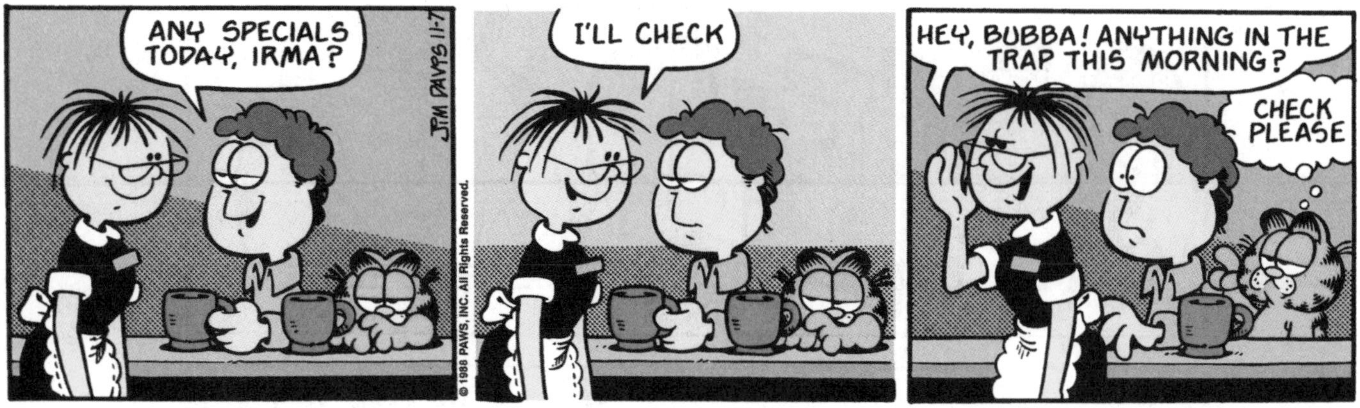
ANY SPECIALS TODAY, IRMA?
JIM DAVIS 11-7
© 1988 PAWS, INC. All Rights Reserved.
I'LL CHECK
HEY, BUBBA! ANYTHING IN THE TRAP THIS MORNING?
CHECK PLEASE

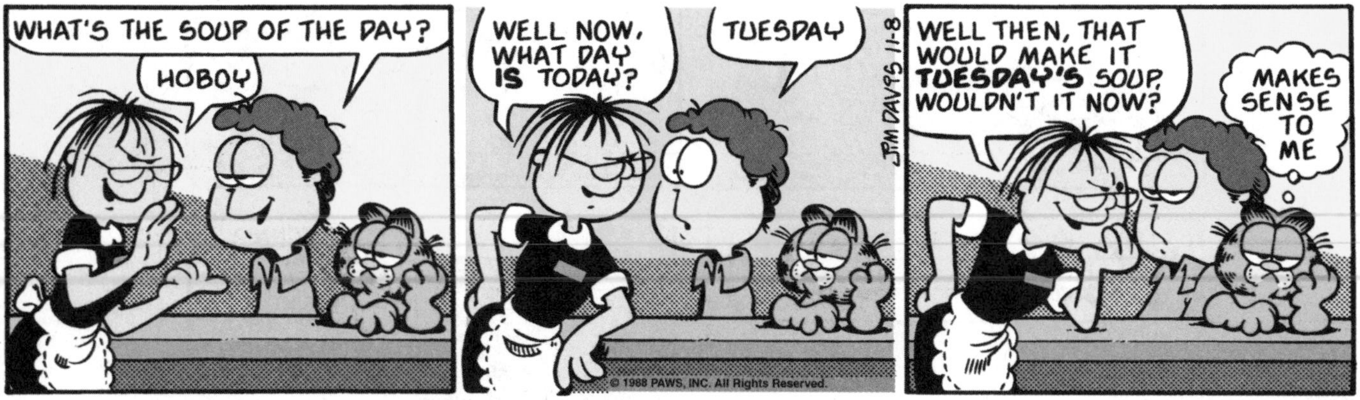
WHAT'S THE SOUP OF THE DAY?
HOBOY
WELL NOW, WHAT DAY **IS** TODAY?
TUESDAY
© 1988 PAWS, INC. All Rights Reserved.
JIM DAVIS 11-8
WELL THEN, THAT WOULD MAKE IT **TUESDAY'S** SOUP, WOULDN'T IT NOW?
MAKES SENSE TO ME

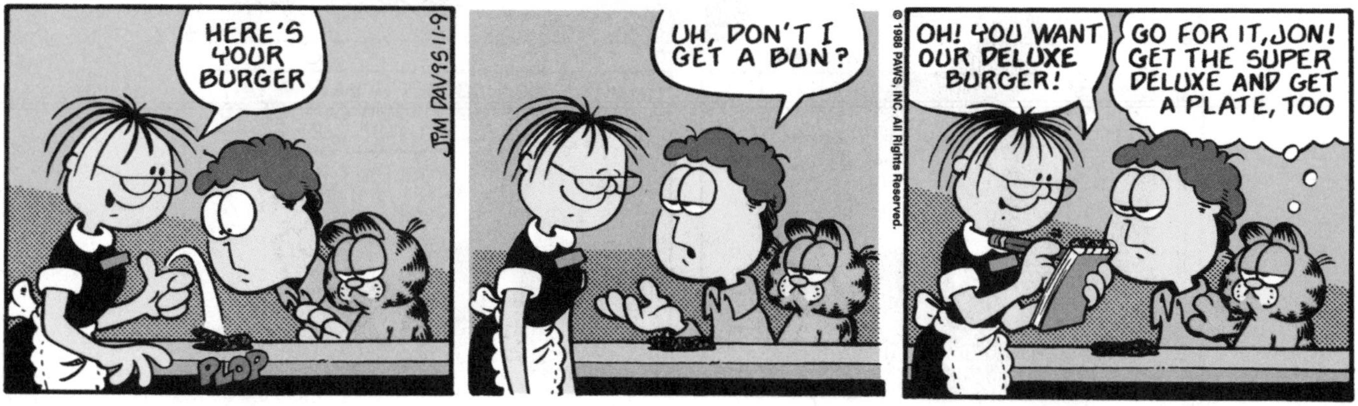
HERE'S YOUR BURGER
PLOP
JIM DAVIS 11-9
UH, DON'T I GET A BUN?
© 1988 PAWS, INC. All Rights Reserved.
OH! YOU WANT OUR **DELUXE** BURGER!
GO FOR IT, JON! GET THE SUPER DELUXE AND GET A PLATE, TOO

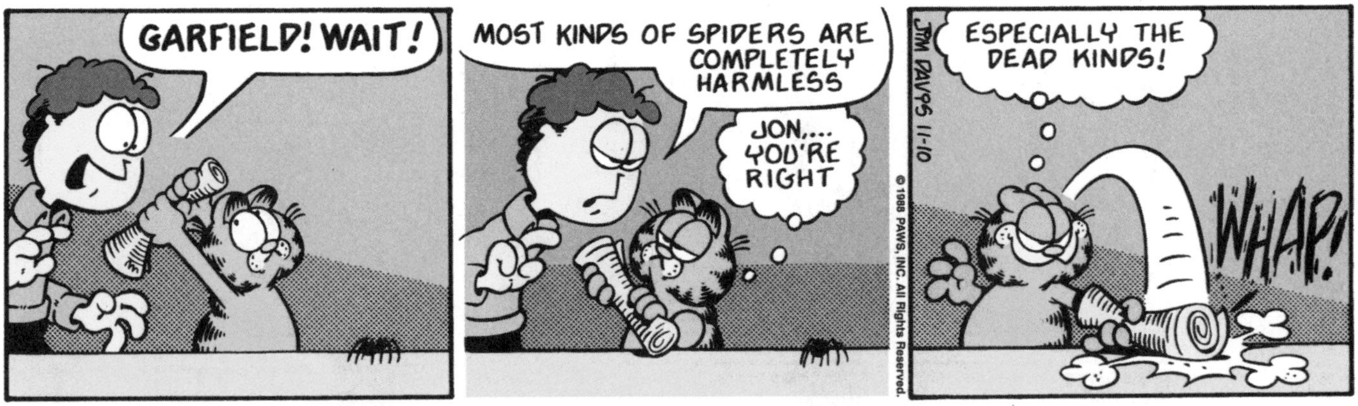
GARFIELD! WAIT!
MOST KINDS OF SPIDERS ARE COMPLETELY HARMLESS
JON,... YOU'RE RIGHT
JIM DAVIS 11-10
© 1988 PAWS, INC. All Rights Reserved.
ESPECIALLY THE DEAD KINDS!
WHAP!

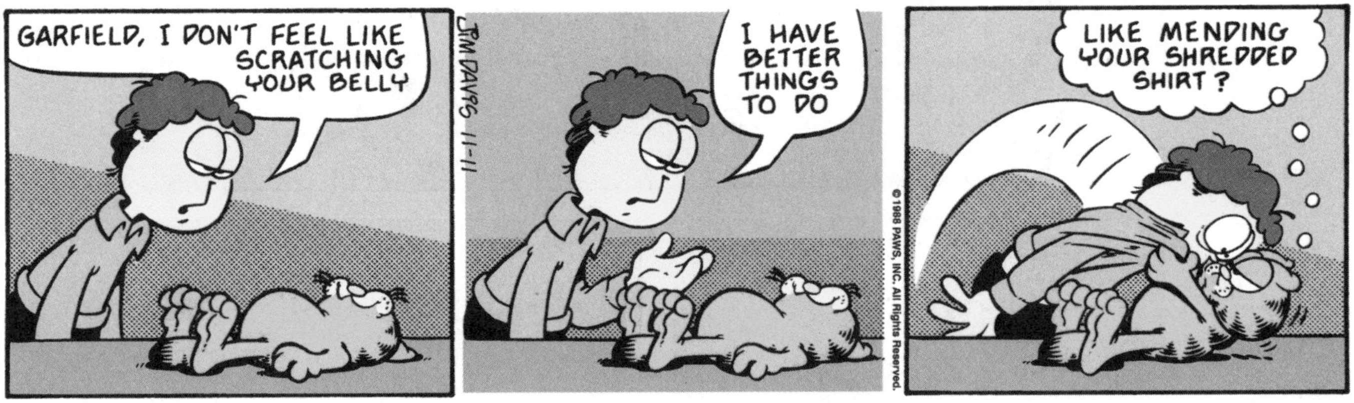
GARFIELD, I DON'T FEEL LIKE SCRATCHING YOUR BELLY
JIM DAVIS 11-11
I HAVE BETTER THINGS TO DO
© 1988 PAWS, INC. All Rights Reserved.
LIKE MENDING YOUR SHREDDED SHIRT?

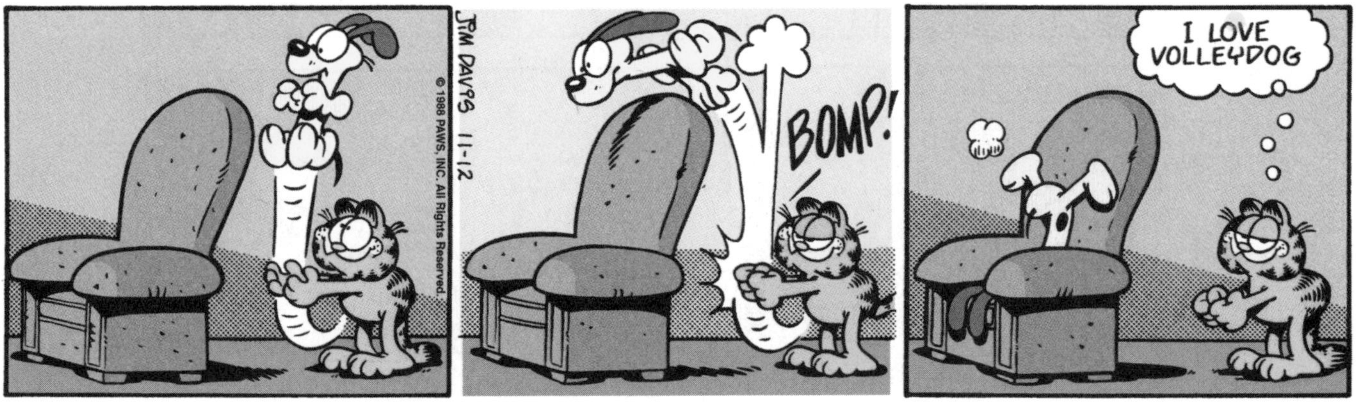
JIM DAVIS 11-12
© 1988 PAWS, INC. All Rights Reserved.
BOMP!
I LOVE VOLLEYDOG

GARFIELD
THAT'S THE LAST TIME I HIDE PET SNACKS ON MY PERSON
SOME PETS ARE WELL BEHAVED, AND THEN THERE ARE MY PETS. I CAN'T LEAVE THEM ALONE FOR A SECOND. WATCH THIS
SO LONG, BOYS! I'LL ONLY BE GONE FOR A SECOND!
JIM DAVIS 11-13
© 1988 PAWS, INC. All Rights Reserved.
ONE
I REST MY CASE

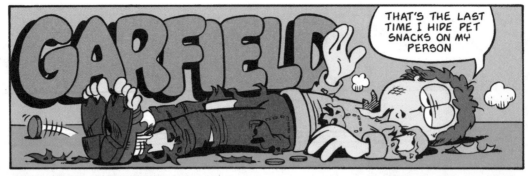

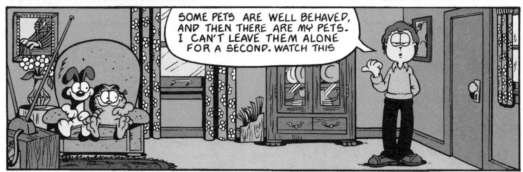

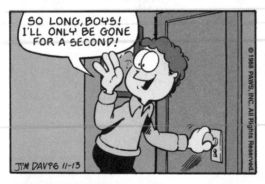

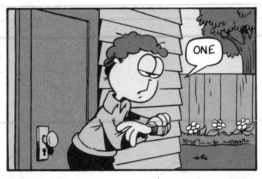

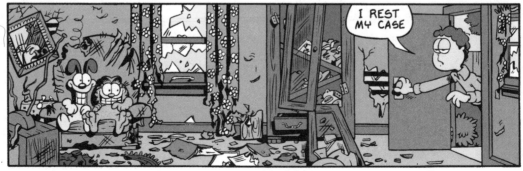

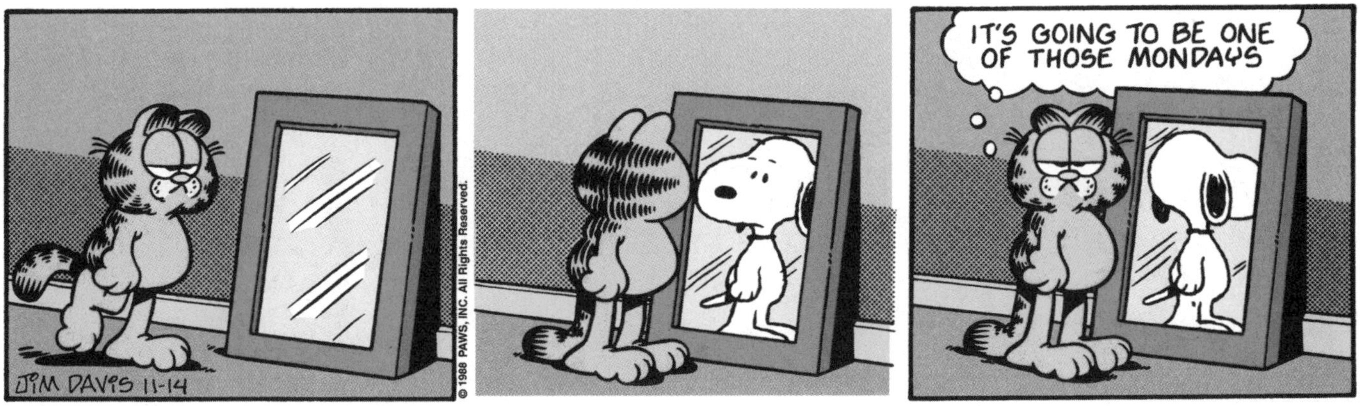
JIM DAVIS 11-14
© 1988 PAWS, INC. All Rights Reserved.
IT'S GOING TO BE ONE OF THOSE MONDAYS

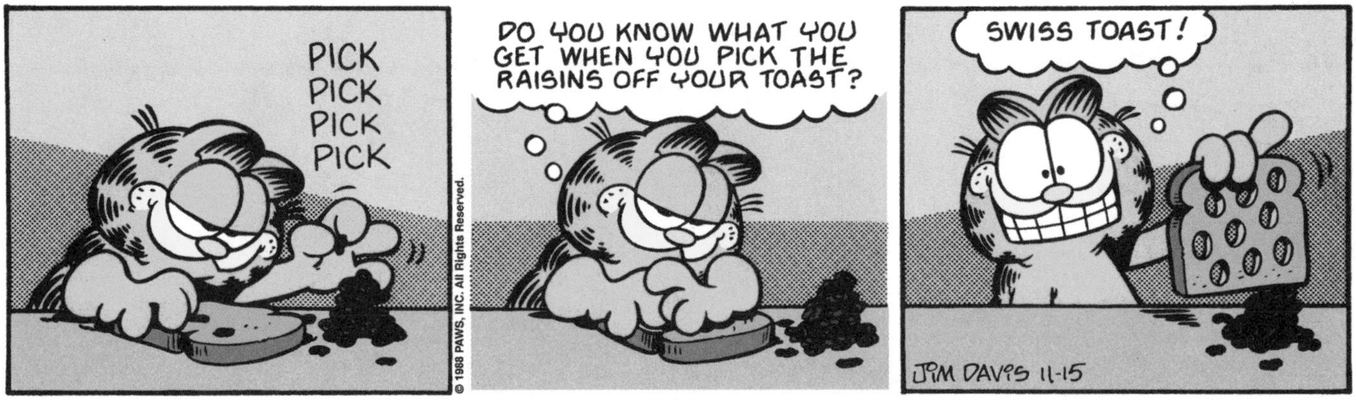
PICK PICK PICK PICK
© 1988 PAWS, INC. All Rights Reserved.
DO YOU KNOW WHAT YOU GET WHEN YOU PICK THE RAISINS OFF YOUR TOAST?
SWISS TOAST!
JIM DAVIS 11-15

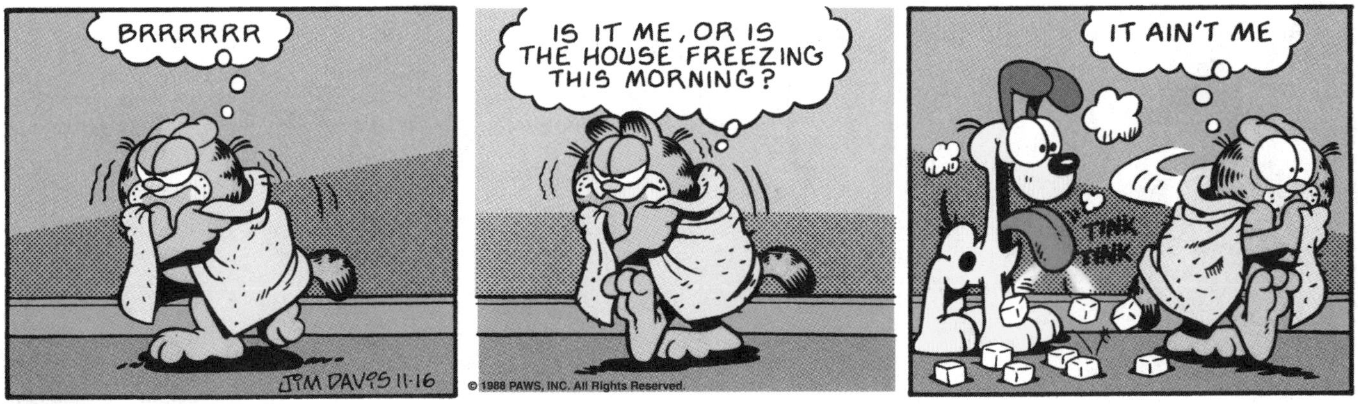
BRRRRRRR
JIM DAVIS 11-16
IS IT ME, OR IS THE HOUSE FREEZING THIS MORNING?
© 1988 PAWS, INC. All Rights Reserved.
IT AIN'T ME
TINK
TINK

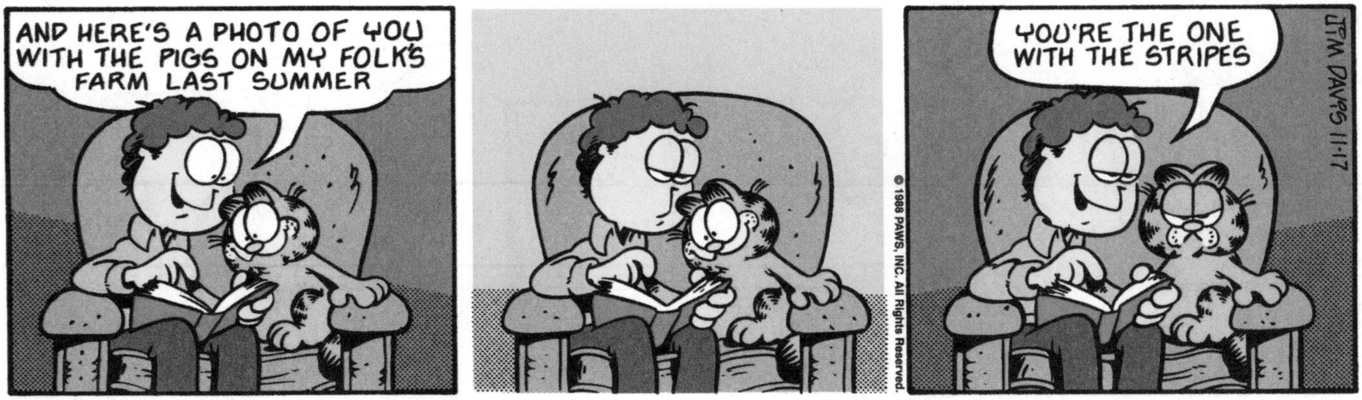
AND HERE'S A PHOTO OF YOU WITH THE PIGS ON MY FOLK'S FARM LAST SUMMER
© 1988 PAWS, INC. All Rights Reserved.
YOU'RE THE ONE WITH THE STRIPES
JIM DAVIS 11-17

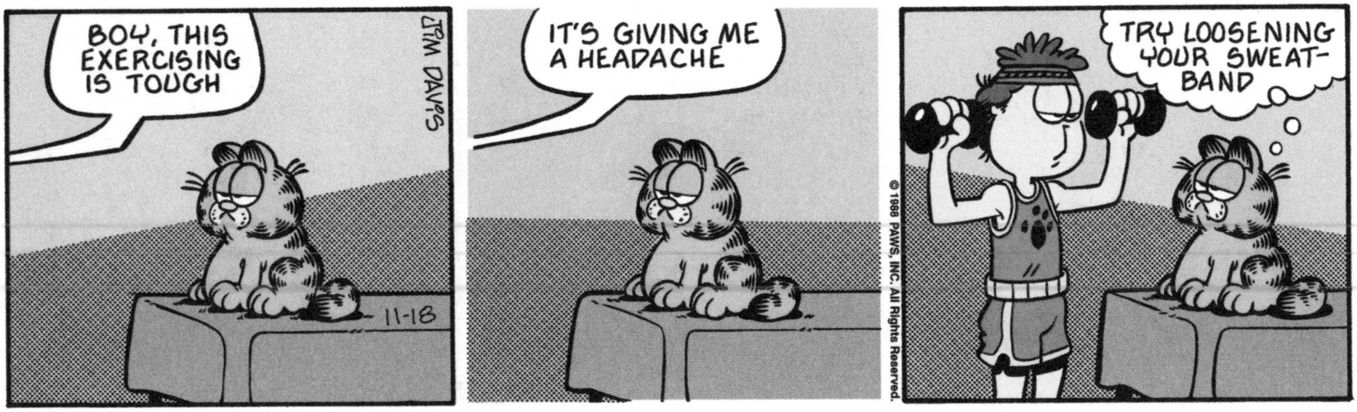
BOY, THIS EXERCISING IS TOUGH
JIM DAVIS
11-18
IT'S GIVING ME A HEADACHE
© 1988 PAWS, INC. All Rights Reserved.
TRY LOOSENING YOUR SWEAT-BAND

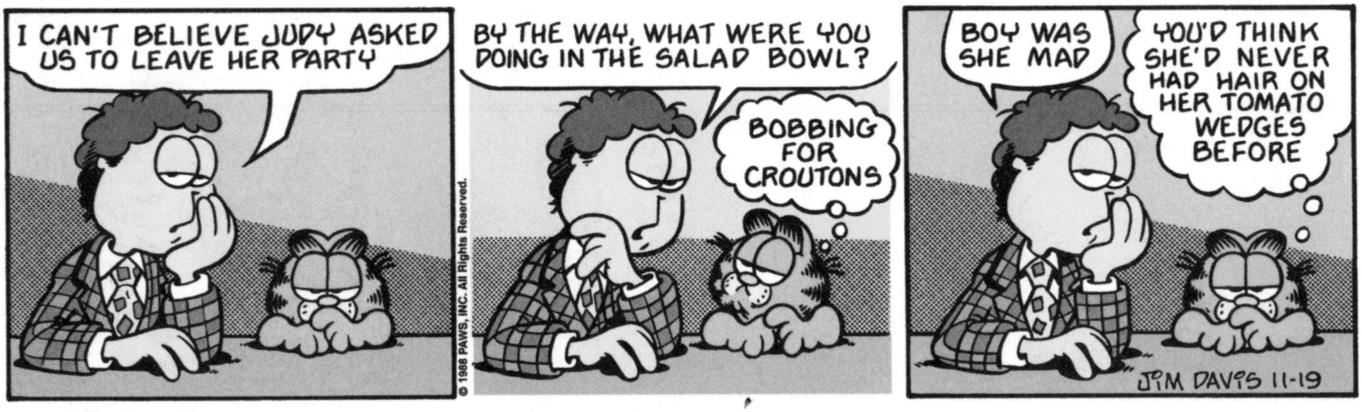
I CAN'T BELIEVE JUDY ASKED US TO LEAVE HER PARTY
© 1988 PAWS, INC. All Rights Reserved.
BY THE WAY, WHAT WERE YOU DOING IN THE SALAD BOWL?
BOBBING FOR CROUTONS
BOY WAS SHE MAD
YOU'D THINK SHE'D NEVER HAD HAIR ON HER TOMATO WEDGES BEFORE
JIM DAVIS 11-19

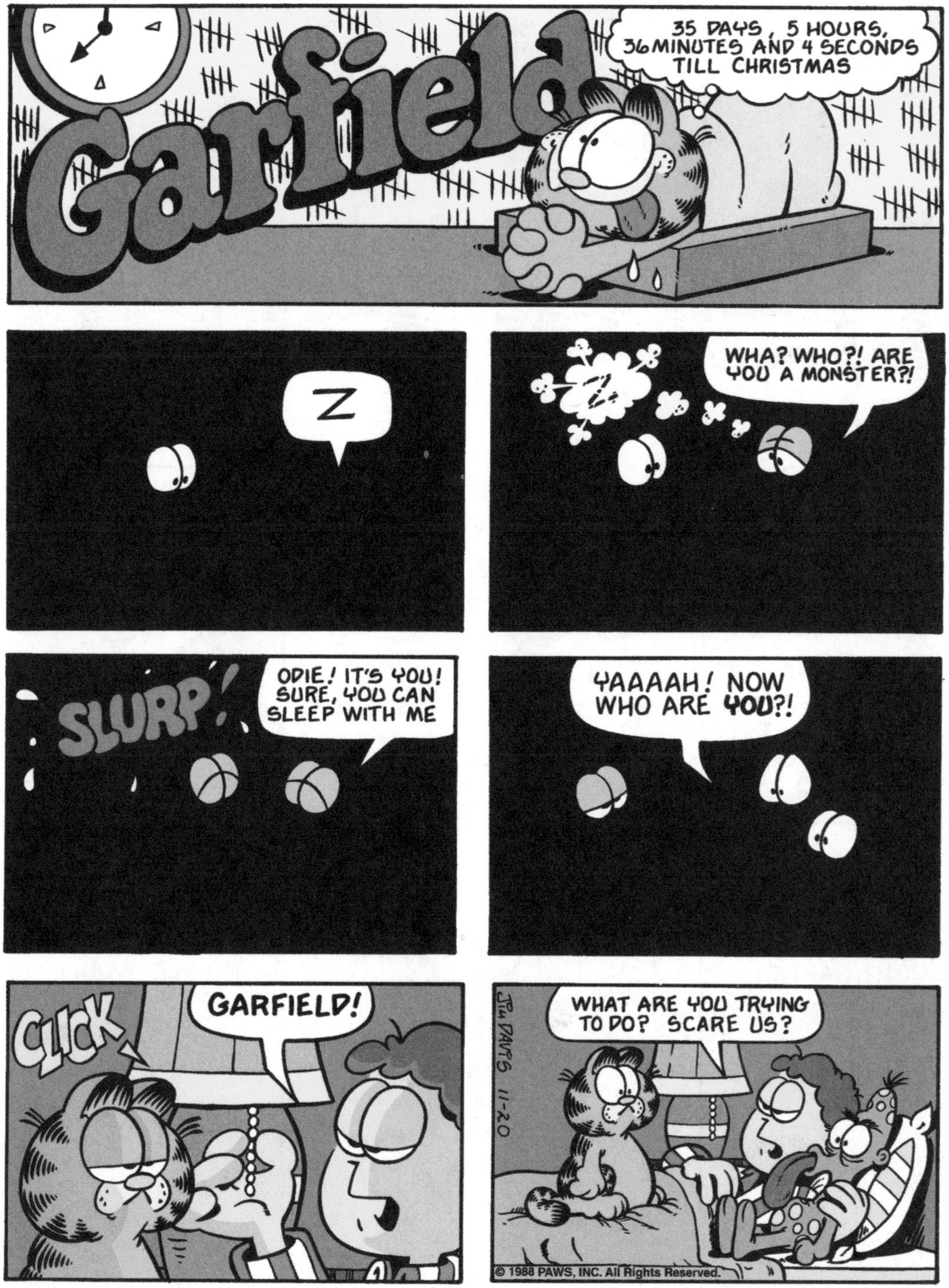
Garfield
35 DAYS, 5 HOURS, 36 MINUTES AND 4 SECONDS TILL CHRISTMAS
Z
WHA? WHO?! ARE YOU A MONSTER?!
SLURP!
ODIE! IT'S YOU! SURE, YOU CAN SLEEP WITH ME
YAAAAH! NOW WHO ARE **YOU**?!
CLICK
GARFIELD!
JIM DAVIS 11-20
WHAT ARE YOU TRYING TO DO? SCARE US?
© 1988 PAWS, INC. All Rights Reserved.

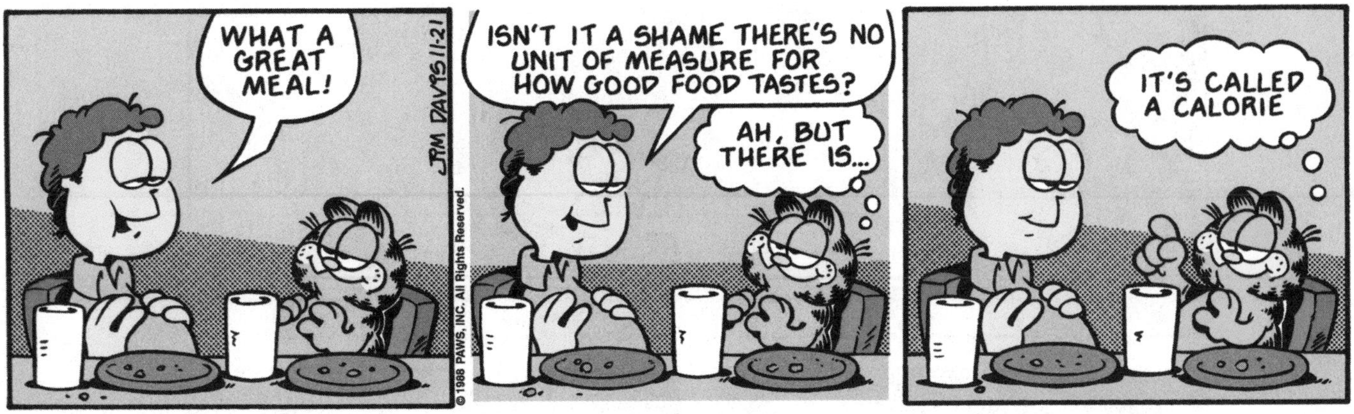
WHAT A GREAT MEAL!
JIM DAVIS 11-21
© 1988 PAWS, INC. All Rights Reserved.
ISN'T IT A SHAME THERE'S NO UNIT OF MEASURE FOR HOW GOOD FOOD TASTES?
AH, BUT THERE IS...
IT'S CALLED A CALORIE

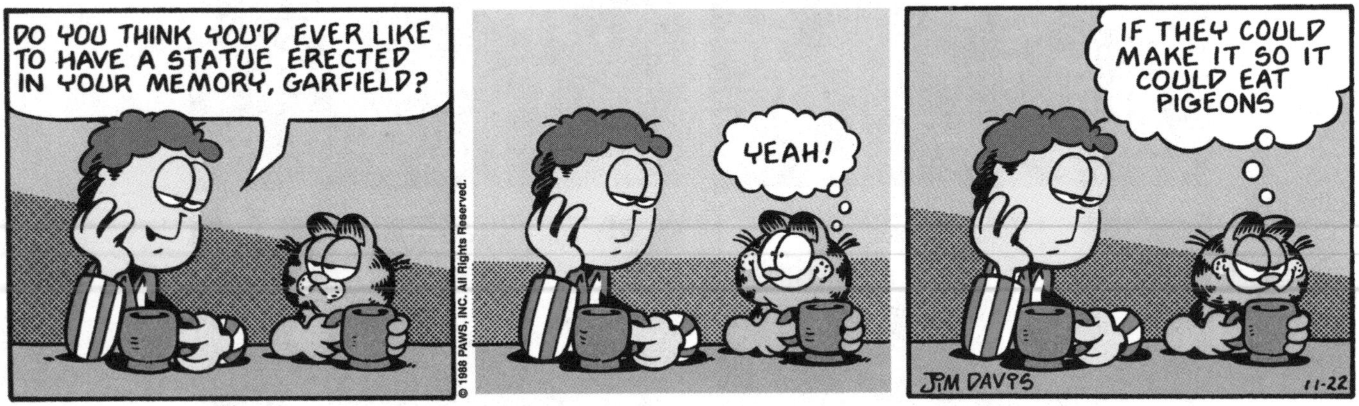
DO YOU THINK YOU'D EVER LIKE TO HAVE A STATUE ERECTED IN YOUR MEMORY, GARFIELD?
© 1988 PAWS, INC. All Rights Reserved.
YEAH!
IF THEY COULD MAKE IT SO IT COULD EAT PIGEONS
JIM DAVIS
11-22

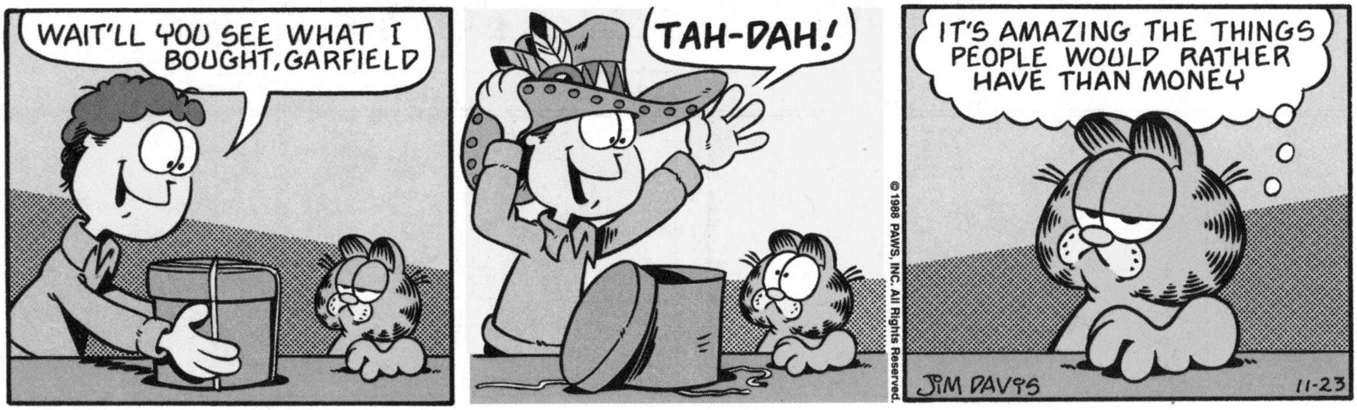
WAIT'LL YOU SEE WHAT I BOUGHT, GARFIELD
TAH-DAH!
© 1988 PAWS, INC. All Rights Reserved.
IT'S AMAZING THE THINGS PEOPLE WOULD RATHER HAVE THAN MONEY
JIM DAVIS
11-23

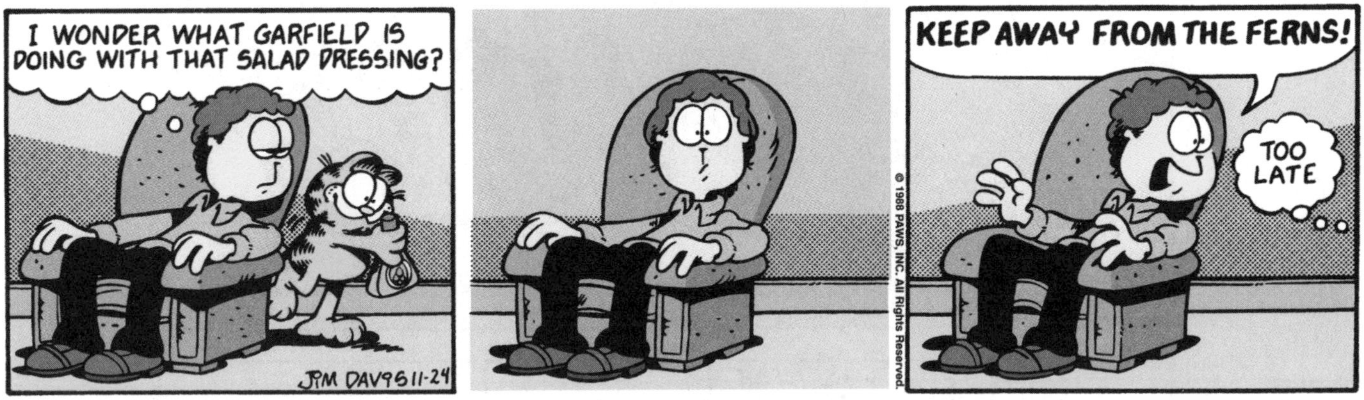
I WONDER WHAT GARFIELD IS DOING WITH THAT SALAD DRESSING?
JIM DAVIS 11-24
KEEP AWAY FROM THE FERNS!
TOO LATE
© 1988 PAWS, INC. All Rights Reserved.

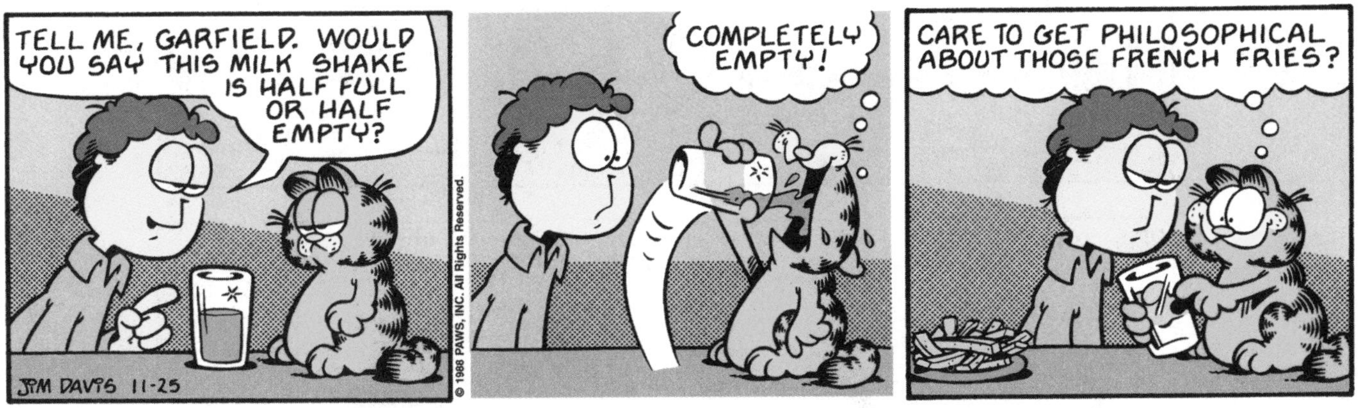
TELL ME, GARFIELD. WOULD YOU SAY THIS MILK SHAKE IS HALF FULL OR HALF EMPTY?
JIM DAVIS 11-25
© 1988 PAWS, INC. All Rights Reserved.
COMPLETELY EMPTY!
CARE TO GET PHILOSOPHICAL ABOUT THOSE FRENCH FRIES?

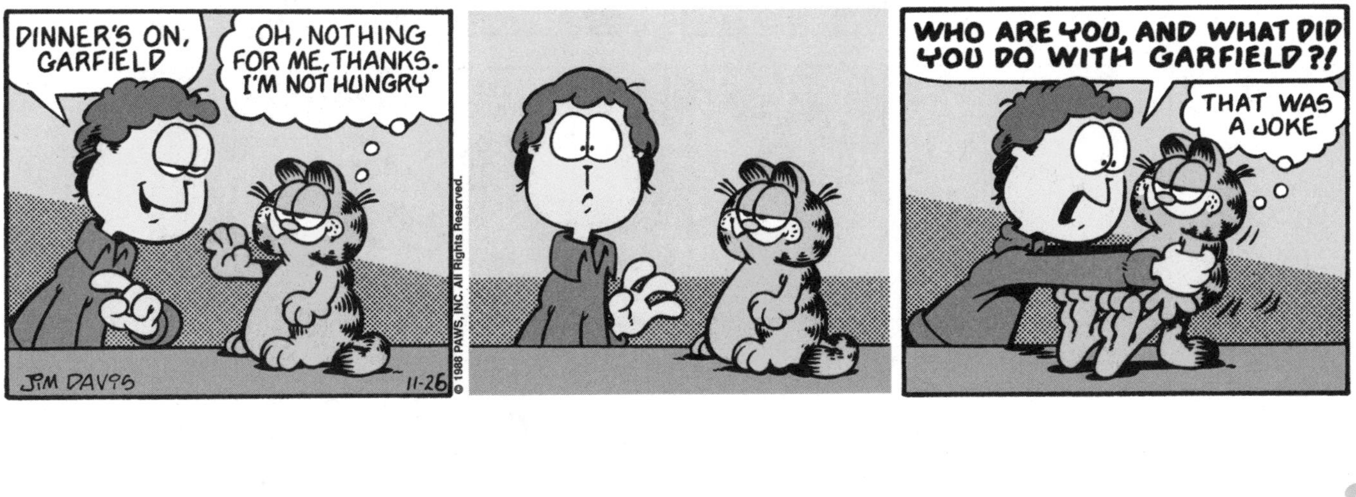
DINNER'S ON, GARFIELD
OH, NOTHING FOR ME, THANKS. I'M NOT HUNGRY
JIM DAVIS 11-26
© 1988 PAWS, INC. All Rights Reserved.
WHO ARE YOU, AND WHAT DID YOU DO WITH GARFIELD?!
THAT WAS A JOKE

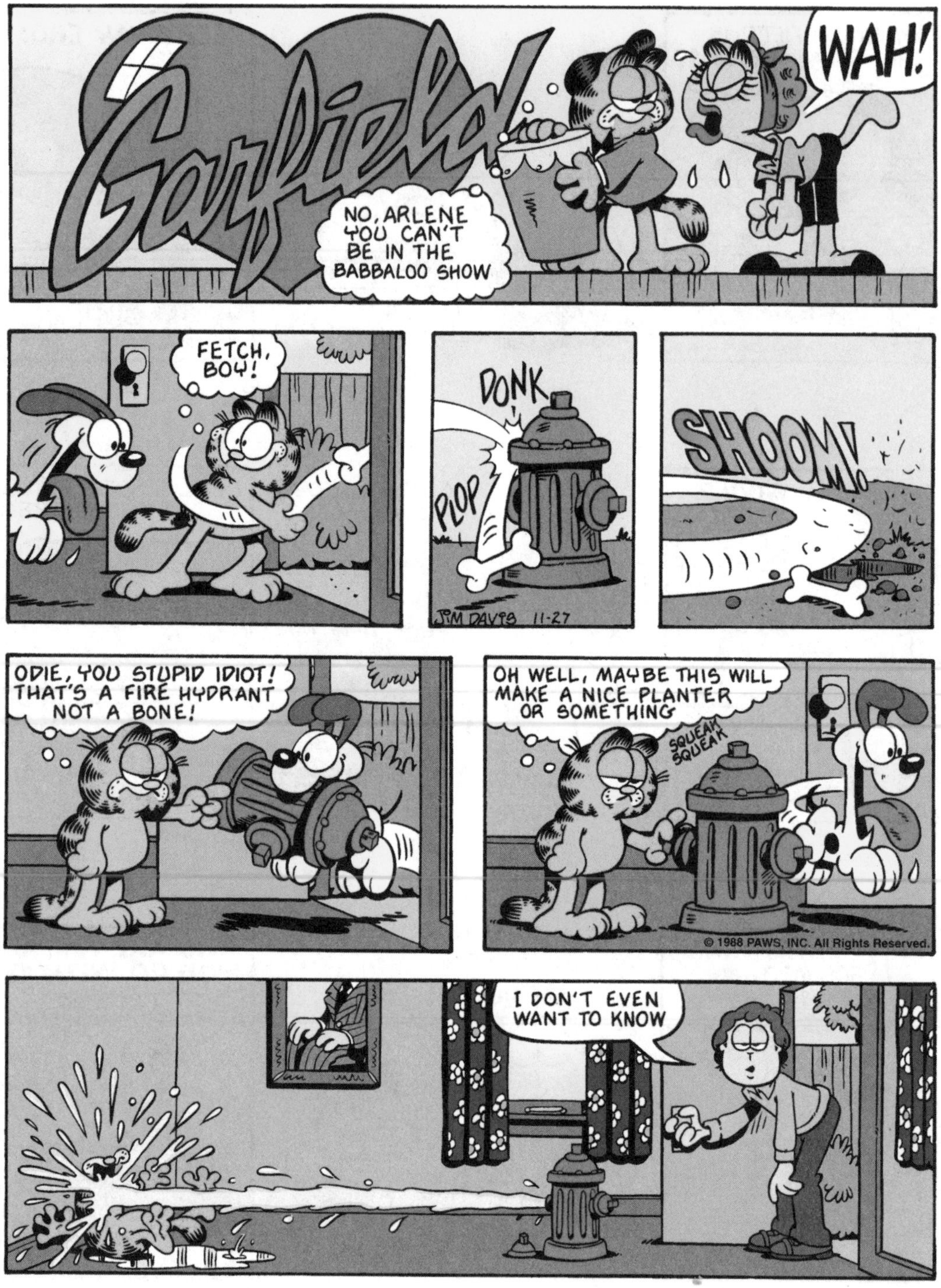
Garfield
WAH!
NO, ARLENE YOU CAN'T BE IN THE BABBALOO SHOW
FETCH, BOY!
DONK
PLOP
SHOOM!
JIM DAVIS 11-27
ODIE, YOU STUPID IDIOT! THAT'S A FIRE HYDRANT NOT A BONE!
OH WELL, MAYBE THIS WILL MAKE A NICE PLANTER OR SOMETHING
SQUEAK SQUEAK
© 1988 PAWS, INC. All Rights Reserved.
I DON'T EVEN WANT TO KNOW

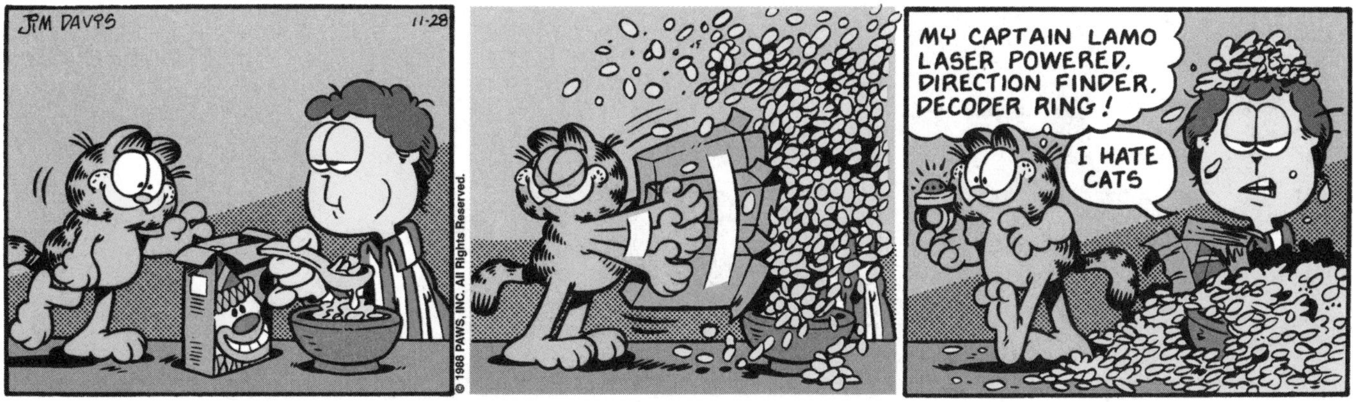
JIM DAVIS
11-28
© 1988 PAWS, INC. All Rights Reserved.
MY CAPTAIN LAMO LASER POWERED, DIRECTION FINDER, DECODER RING!
I HATE CATS

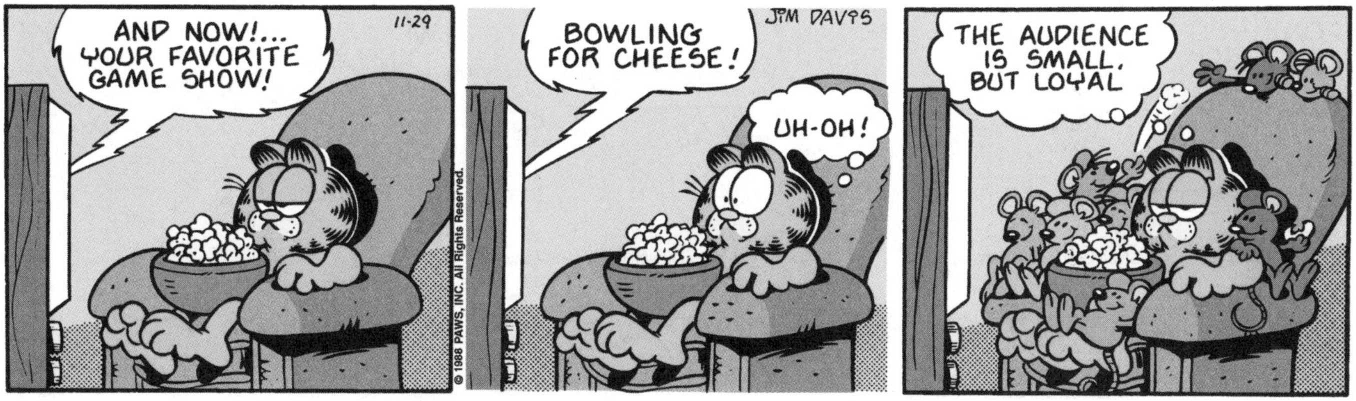
11-29
AND NOW!... YOUR FAVORITE GAME SHOW!
© 1988 PAWS, INC. All Rights Reserved.
JIM DAVIS
BOWLING FOR CHEESE!
UH-OH!
THE AUDIENCE IS SMALL, BUT LOYAL

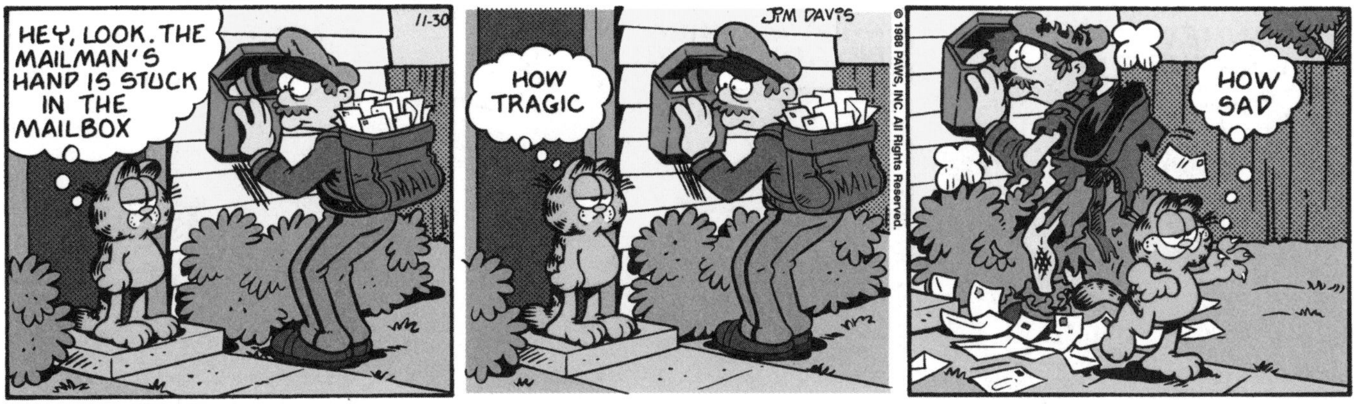
11-30
HEY, LOOK. THE MAILMAN'S HAND IS STUCK IN THE MAILBOX
MAIL
JIM DAVIS
HOW TRAGIC
© 1988 PAWS, INC. All Rights Reserved.
HOW SAD

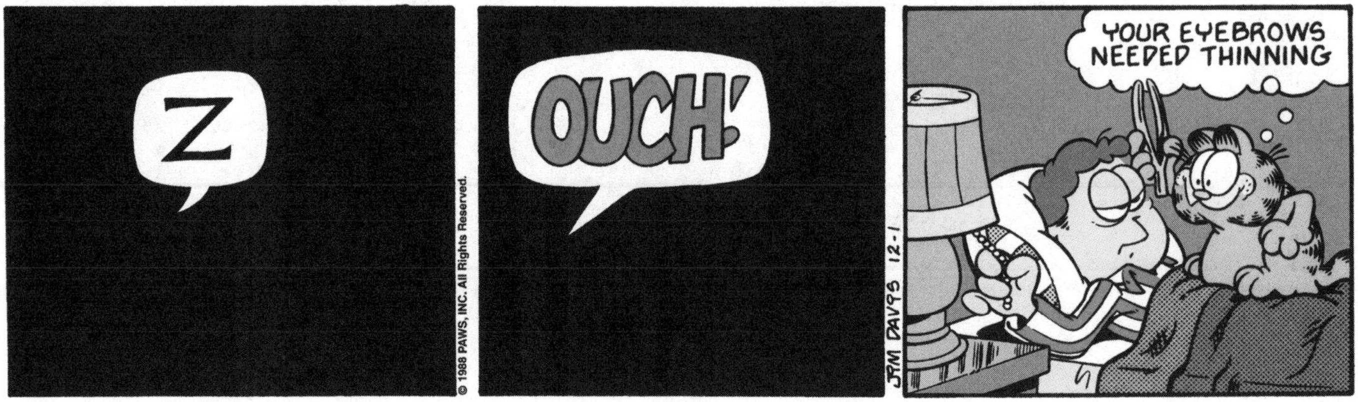
Z
OUCH!
© 1988 PAWS, INC. All Rights Reserved.
JIM DAVIS 12-1
YOUR EYEBROWS NEEDED THINNING

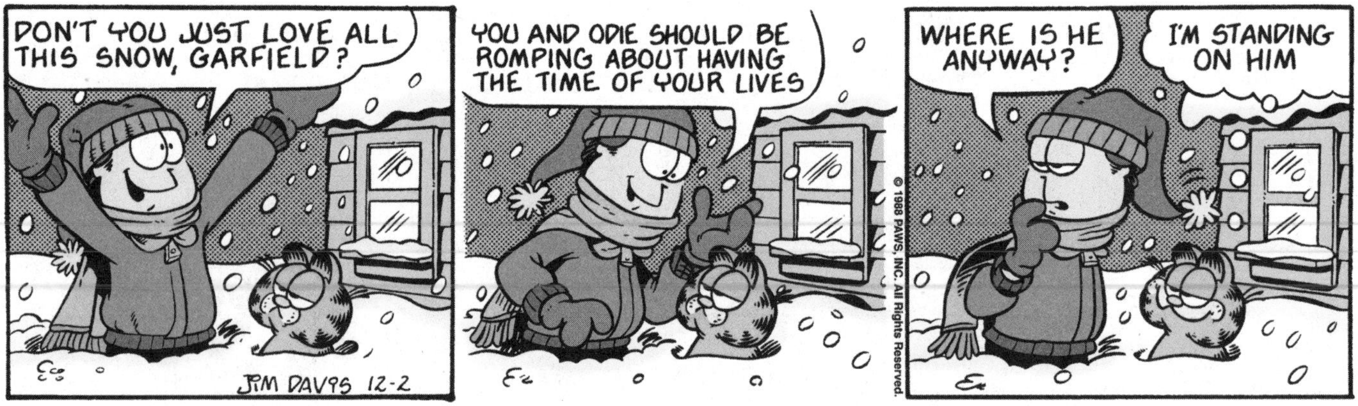
DON'T YOU JUST LOVE ALL THIS SNOW, GARFIELD?
JIM DAVIS 12-2
YOU AND ODIE SHOULD BE ROMPING ABOUT HAVING THE TIME OF YOUR LIVES
© 1988 PAWS, INC. All Rights Reserved.
WHERE IS HE ANYWAY?
I'M STANDING ON HIM

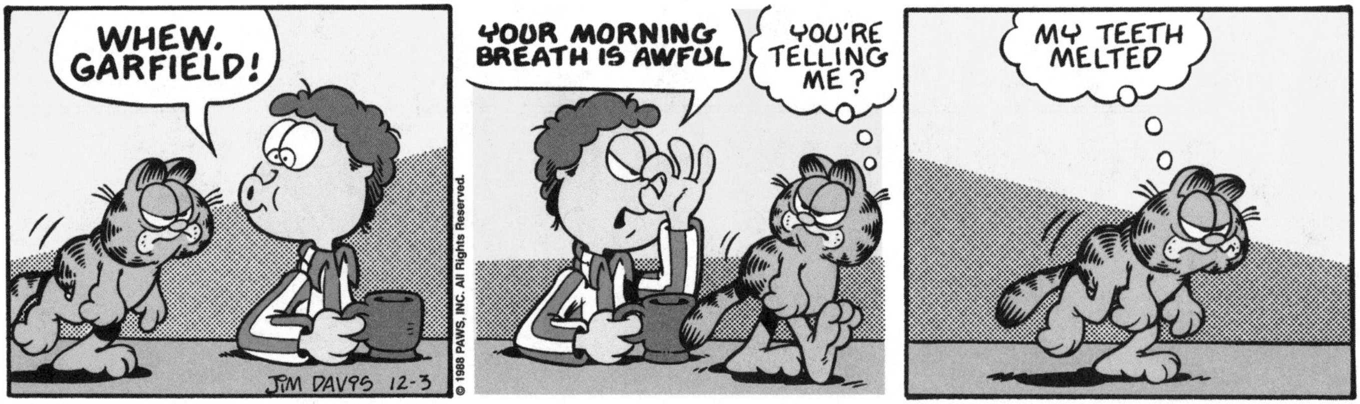
WHEW. GARFIELD!
JIM DAVIS 12-3
© 1988 PAWS, INC. All Rights Reserved.
YOUR MORNING BREATH IS AWFUL
YOU'RE TELLING ME?
MY TEETH MELTED

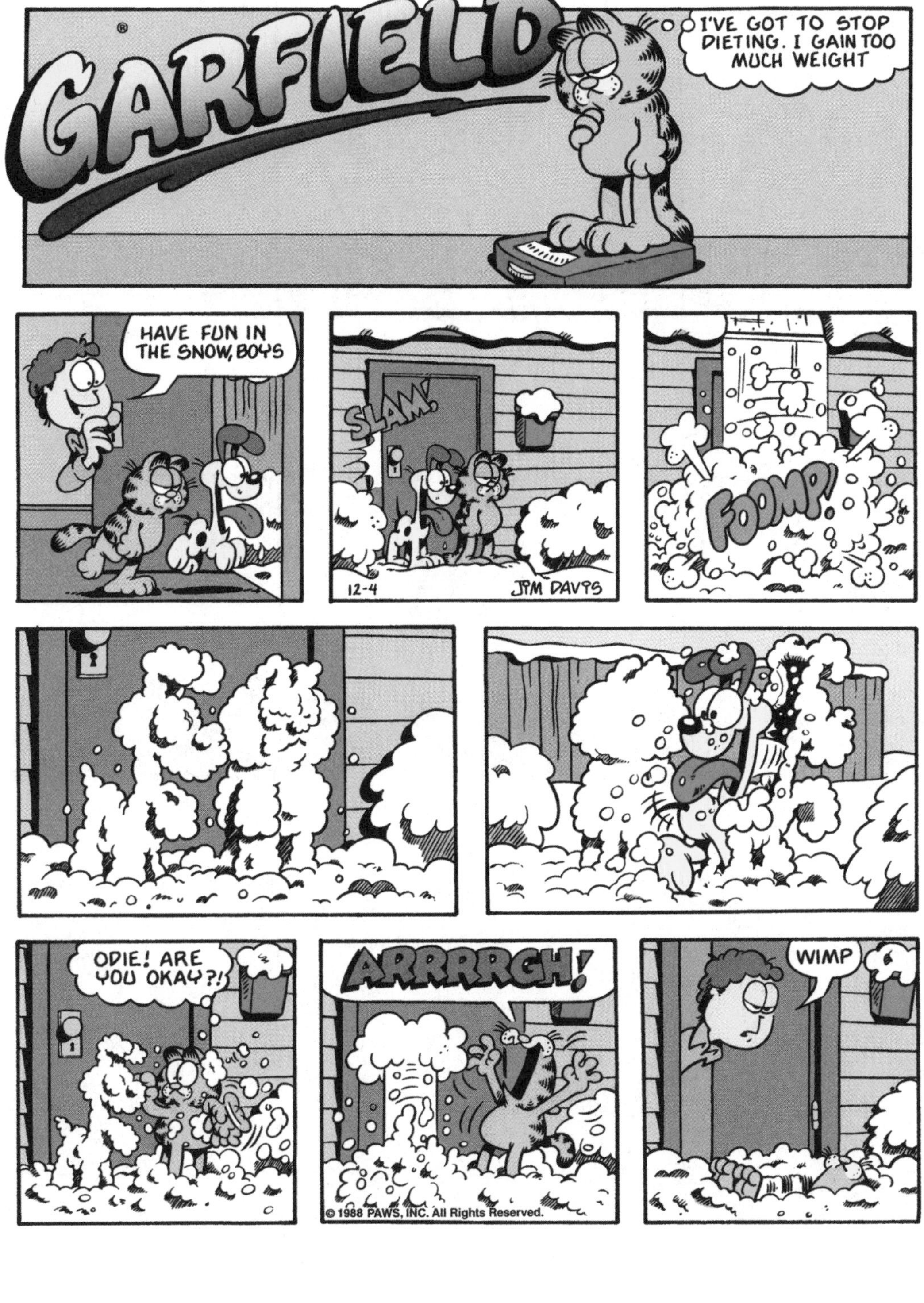
GARFIELD
I'VE GOT TO STOP DIETING. I GAIN TOO MUCH WEIGHT
HAVE FUN IN THE SNOW, BOYS
SLAM!
12-4
JIM DAVIS
FOOMP!
ODIE! ARE YOU OKAY?!
ARRRRGH!
© 1988 PAWS, INC. All Rights Reserved.
WIMP

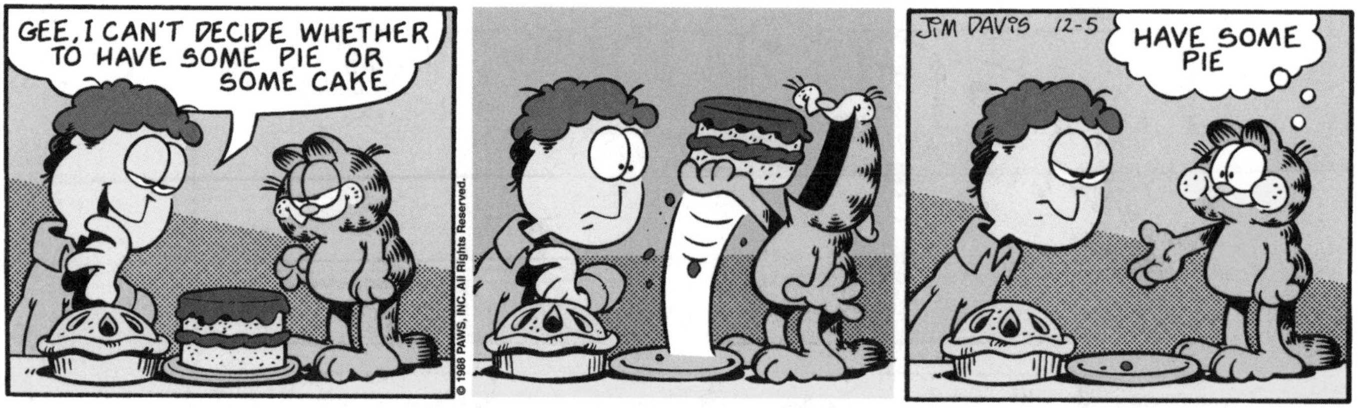
GEE, I CAN'T DECIDE WHETHER TO HAVE SOME PIE OR SOME CAKE
© 1988 PAWS, INC. All Rights Reserved.
JIM DAVIS 12-5
HAVE SOME PIE

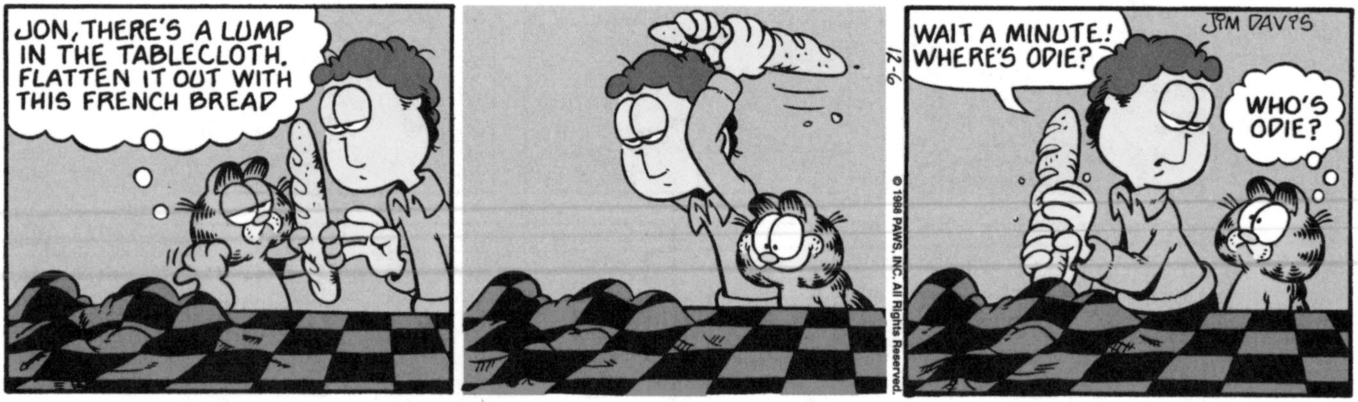
JON, THERE'S A LUMP IN THE TABLECLOTH. FLATTEN IT OUT WITH THIS FRENCH BREAD
12-6
© 1988 PAWS, INC. All Rights Reserved.
WAIT A MINUTE! WHERE'S ODIE?
JIM DAVIS
WHO'S ODIE?

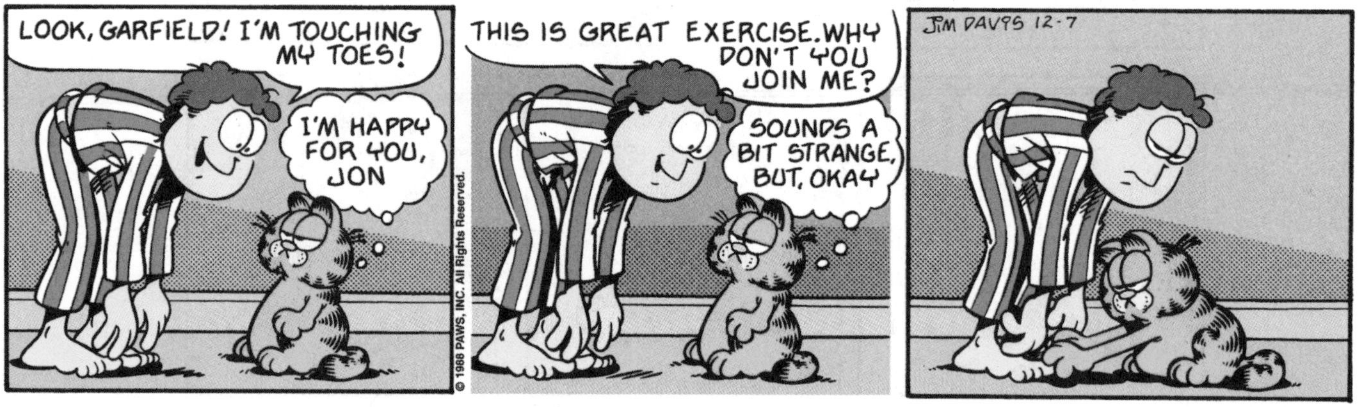
LOOK, GARFIELD! I'M TOUCHING MY TOES!
I'M HAPPY FOR YOU, JON
© 1988 PAWS, INC. All Rights Reserved.
THIS IS GREAT EXERCISE. WHY DON'T YOU JOIN ME?
SOUNDS A BIT STRANGE, BUT, OKAY
JIM DAVIS 12-7

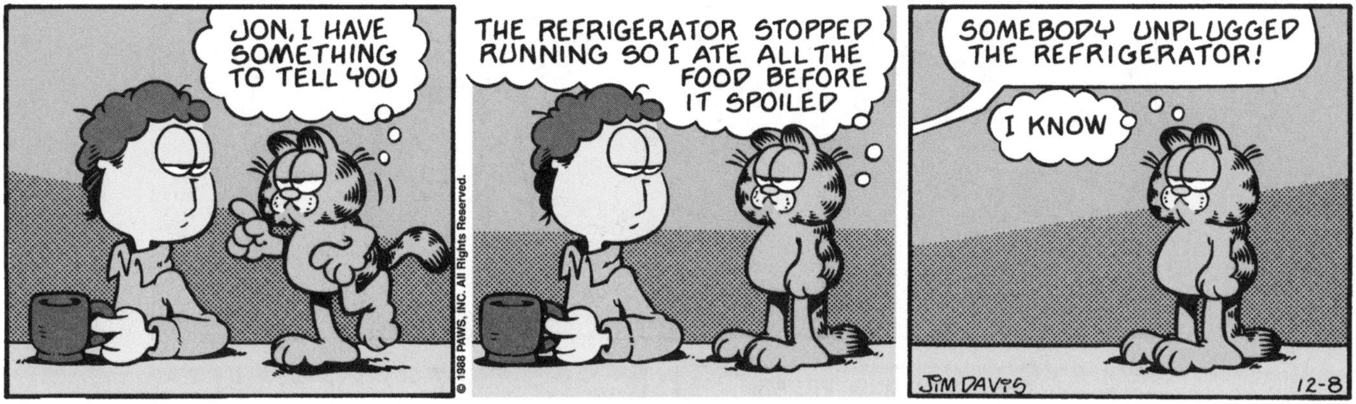
JON, I HAVE SOMETHING TO TELL YOU
© 1988 PAWS, INC. All Rights Reserved.
THE REFRIGERATOR STOPPED RUNNING SO I ATE ALL THE FOOD BEFORE IT SPOILED
SOMEBODY UNPLUGGED THE REFRIGERATOR!
I KNOW
JIM DAVIS
12-8

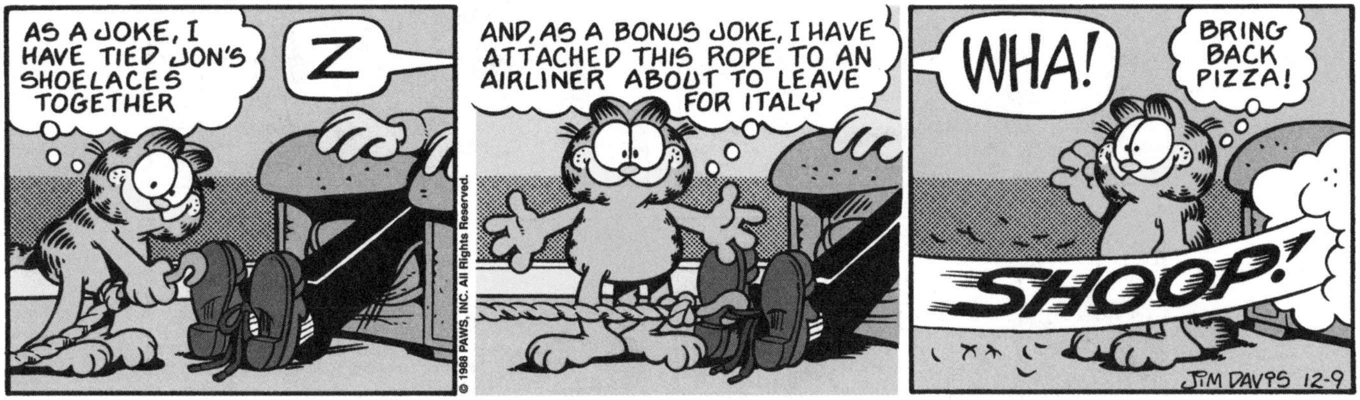
AS A JOKE, I HAVE TIED JON'S SHOELACES TOGETHER
Z
© 1988 PAWS, INC. All Rights Reserved.
AND, AS A BONUS JOKE, I HAVE ATTACHED THIS ROPE TO AN AIRLINER ABOUT TO LEAVE FOR ITALY
WHA!
BRING BACK PIZZA!
SHOOP!
JIM DAVIS 12-9

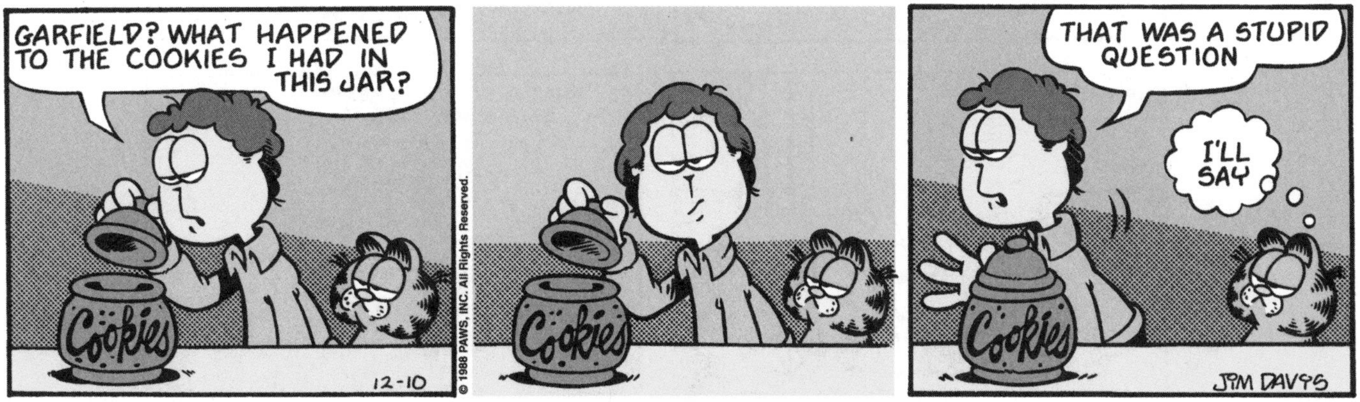
GARFIELD? WHAT HAPPENED TO THE COOKIES I HAD IN THIS JAR?
Cookies
12-10
© 1988 PAWS, INC. All Rights Reserved.
Cookies
THAT WAS A STUPID QUESTION
I'LL SAY
Cookies
JIM DAVIS

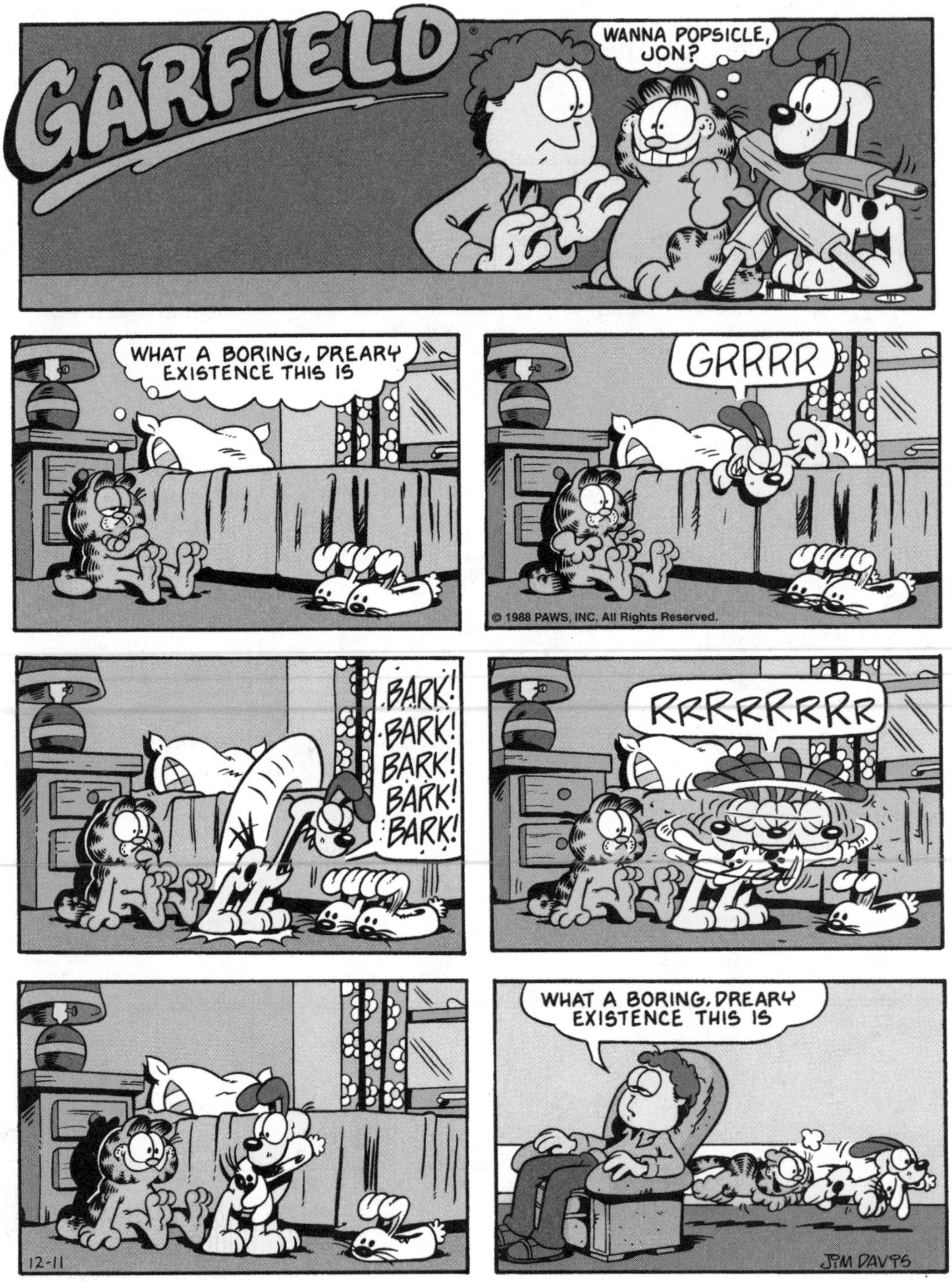
GARFIELD
WANNA POPSICLE, JON?
WHAT A BORING, DREARY EXISTENCE THIS IS
GRRRR
© 1988 PAWS, INC. All Rights Reserved.
BARK! BARK! BARK! BARK! BARK!
RRRRRRRR
12-11
WHAT A BORING, DREARY EXISTENCE THIS IS
JIM DAVIS

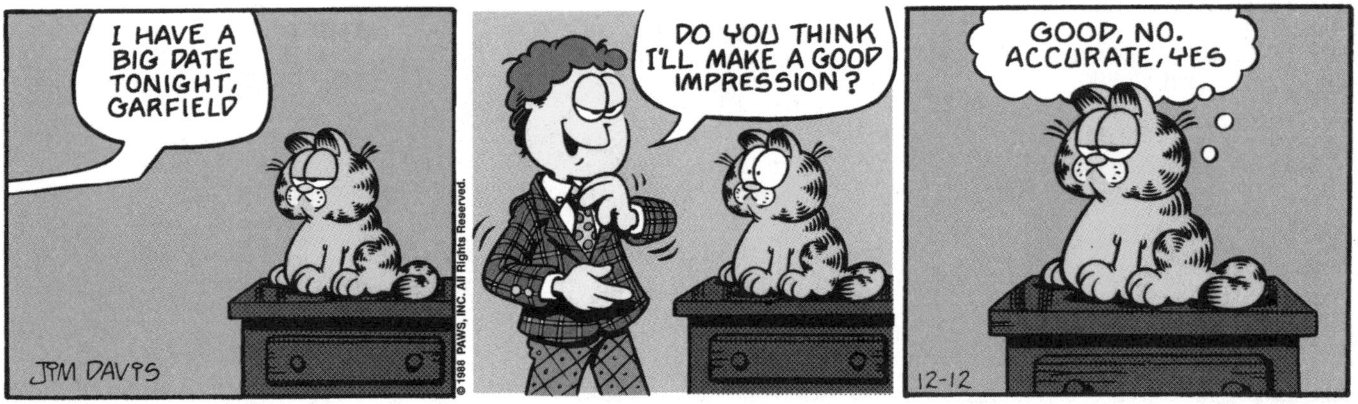
I HAVE A BIG DATE TONIGHT, GARFIELD
JIM DAVIS
© 1988 PAWS, INC. All Rights Reserved.
DO YOU THINK I'LL MAKE A GOOD IMPRESSION?
GOOD, NO. ACCURATE, YES
12-12

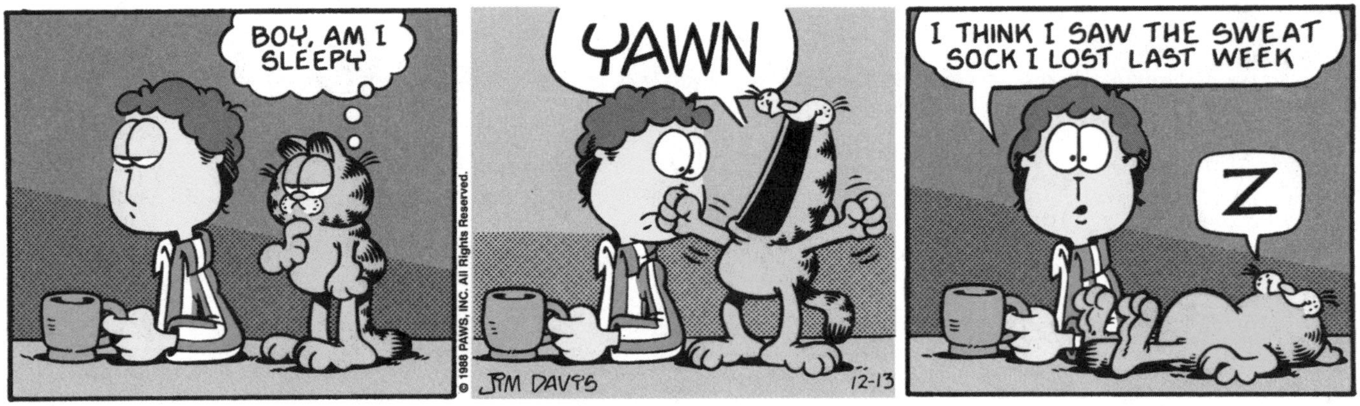
BOY, AM I SLEEPY
© 1988 PAWS, INC. All Rights Reserved.
YAWN
JIM DAVIS
12-13
I THINK I SAW THE SWEAT SOCK I LOST LAST WEEK
Z

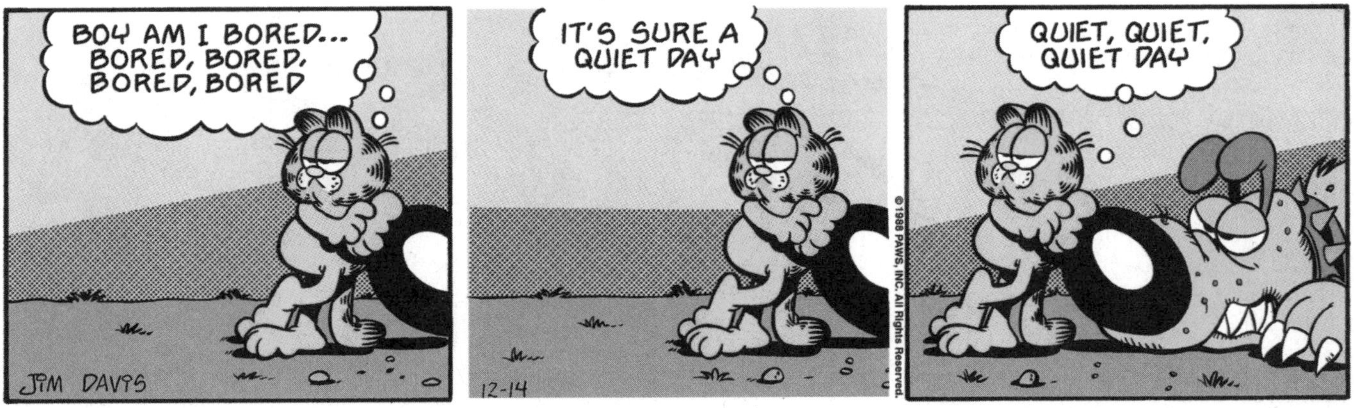
BOY AM I BORED... BORED, BORED, BORED, BORED
JIM DAVIS
IT'S SURE A QUIET DAY
12-14
© 1988 PAWS, INC. All Rights Reserved.
QUIET, QUIET, QUIET DAY

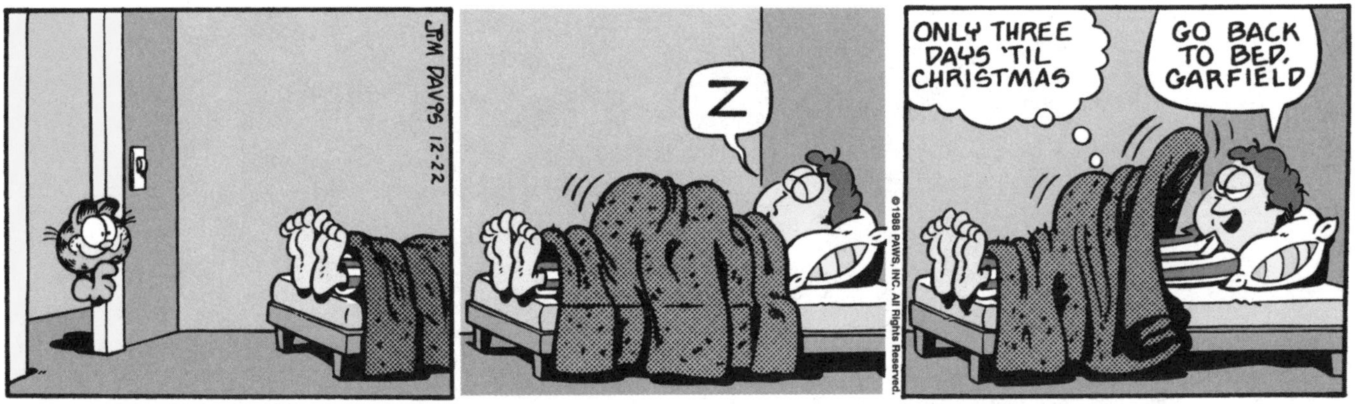
JIM DAVIS 12-22
Z
© 1988 PAWS, INC. All Rights Reserved.
ONLY THREE DAYS 'TIL CHRISTMAS
GO BACK TO BED, GARFIELD

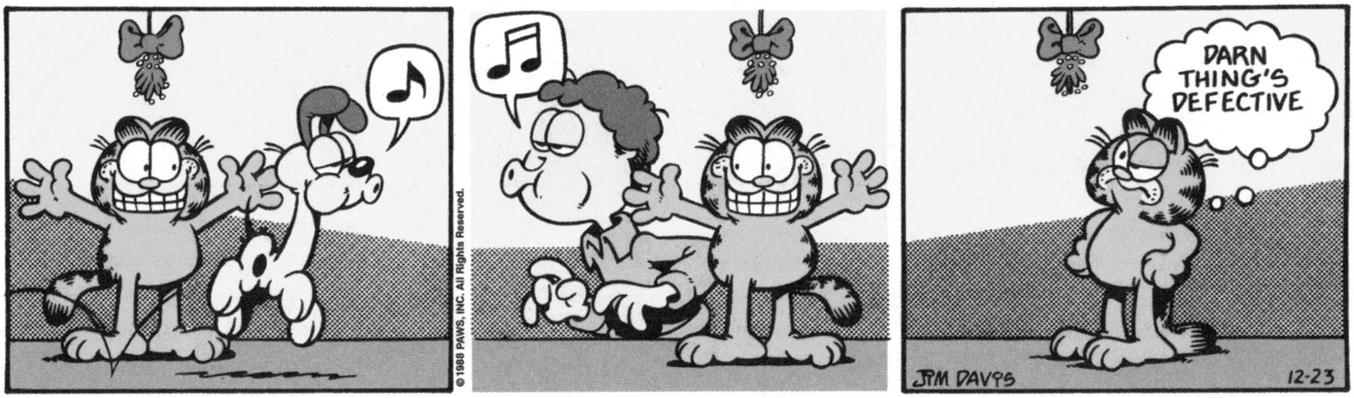
© 1988 PAWS, INC. All Rights Reserved.
DARN THING'S DEFECTIVE
JIM DAVIS
12-23

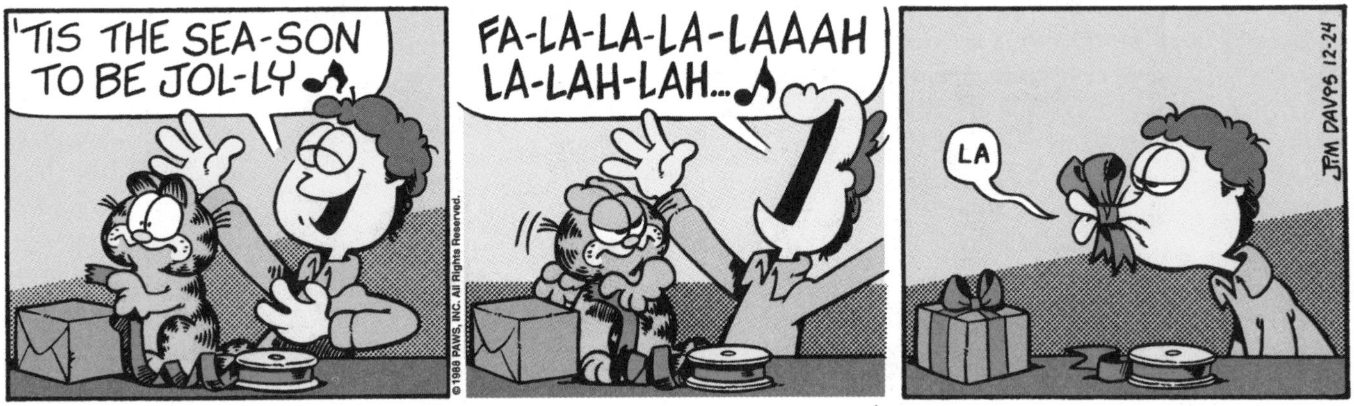
'TIS THE SEA-SON TO BE JOL-LY
© 1988 PAWS, INC. All Rights Reserved.
FA-LA-LA-LA-LAAAH LA-LAH-LAH...
LA
JIM DAVIS 12-24

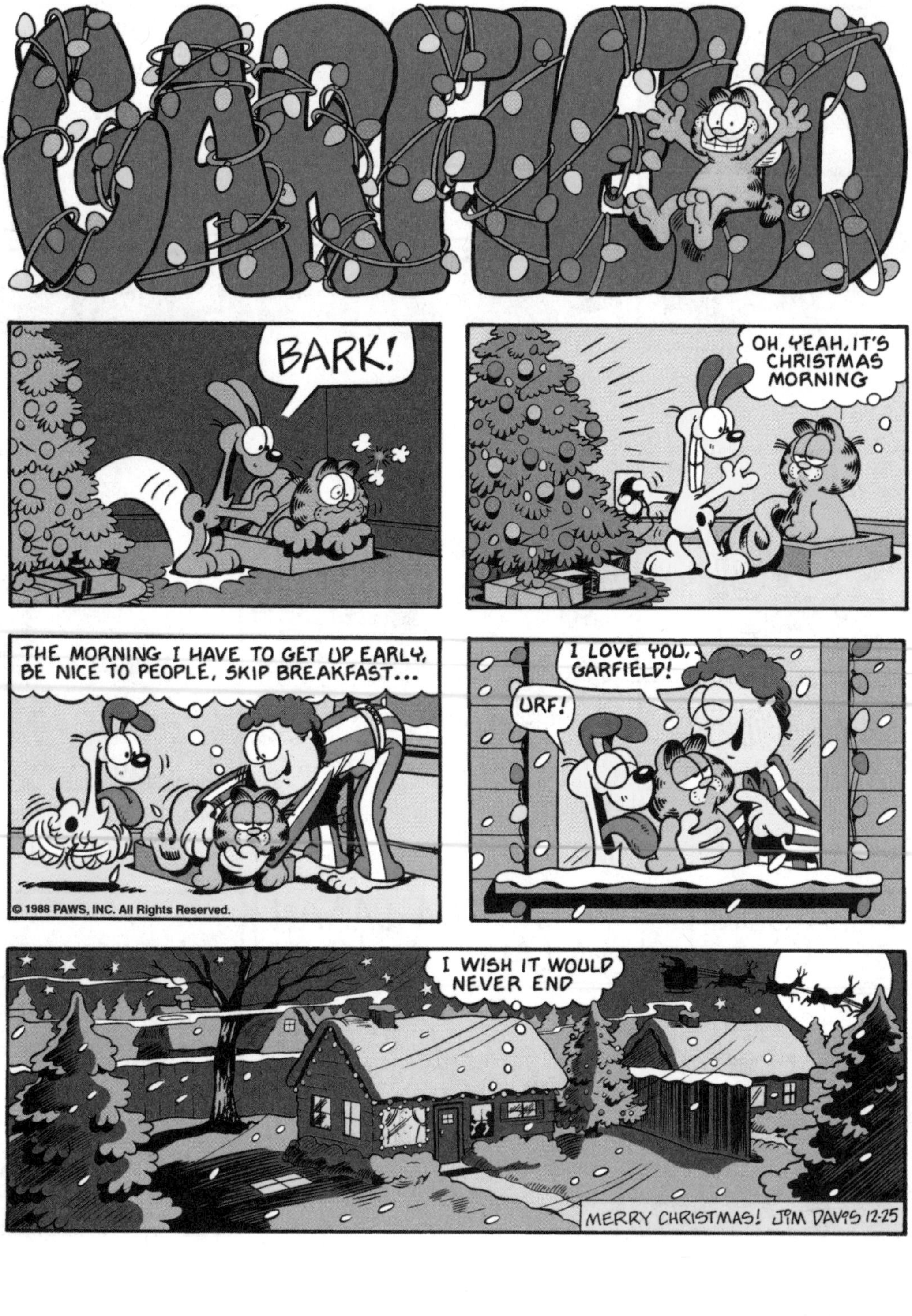
GARFIELD
BARK!
OH, YEAH, IT'S CHRISTMAS MORNING
THE MORNING I HAVE TO GET UP EARLY, BE NICE TO PEOPLE, SKIP BREAKFAST...
© 1988 PAWS, INC. All Rights Reserved.
I LOVE YOU, GARFIELD!
URF!
I WISH IT WOULD NEVER END
MERRY CHRISTMAS! JIM DAVIS 12-25

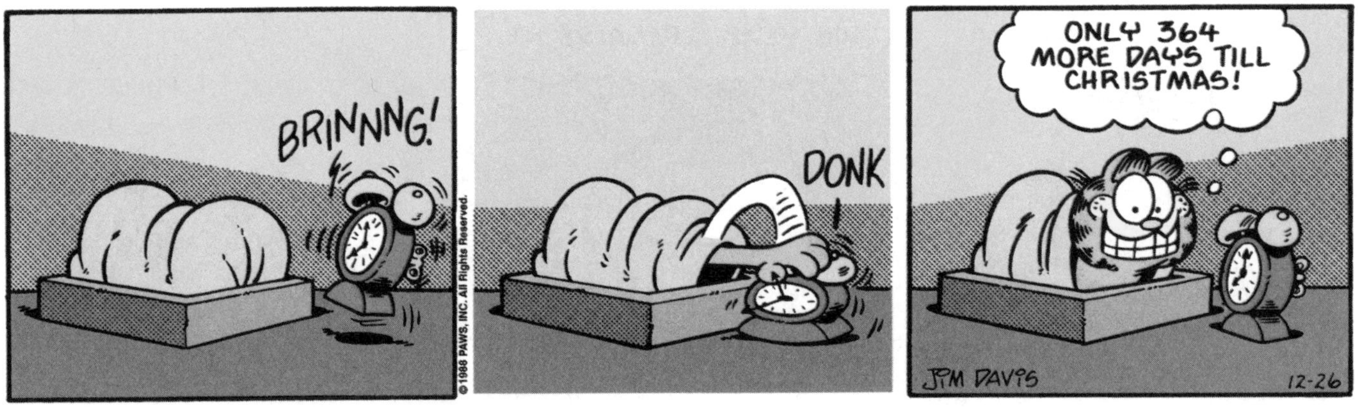
BRINNNG!
DONK
ONLY 364 MORE DAYS TILL CHRISTMAS!
JIM DAVIS
12-26

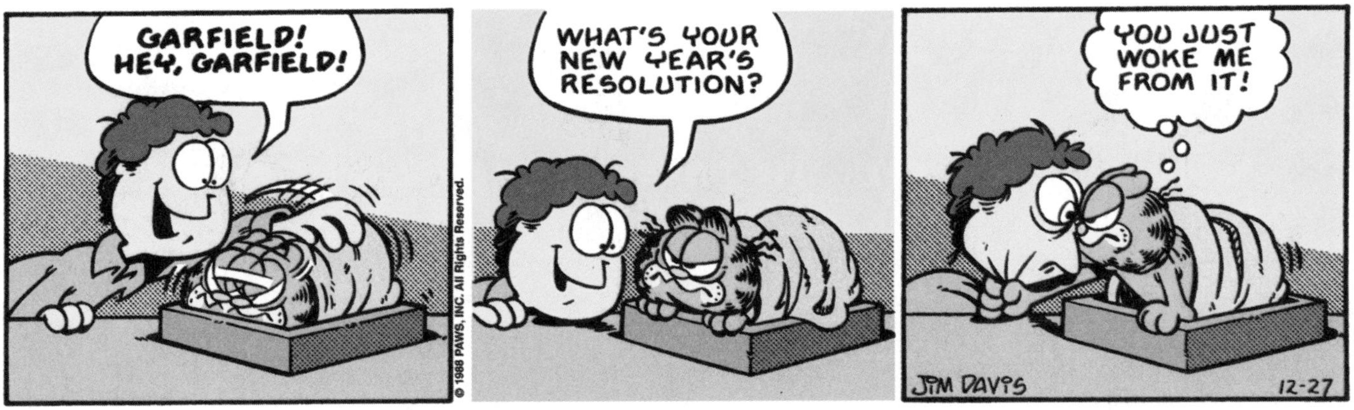
GARFIELD! HEY, GARFIELD!
WHAT'S YOUR NEW YEAR'S RESOLUTION?
YOU JUST WOKE ME FROM IT!
JIM DAVIS
12-27

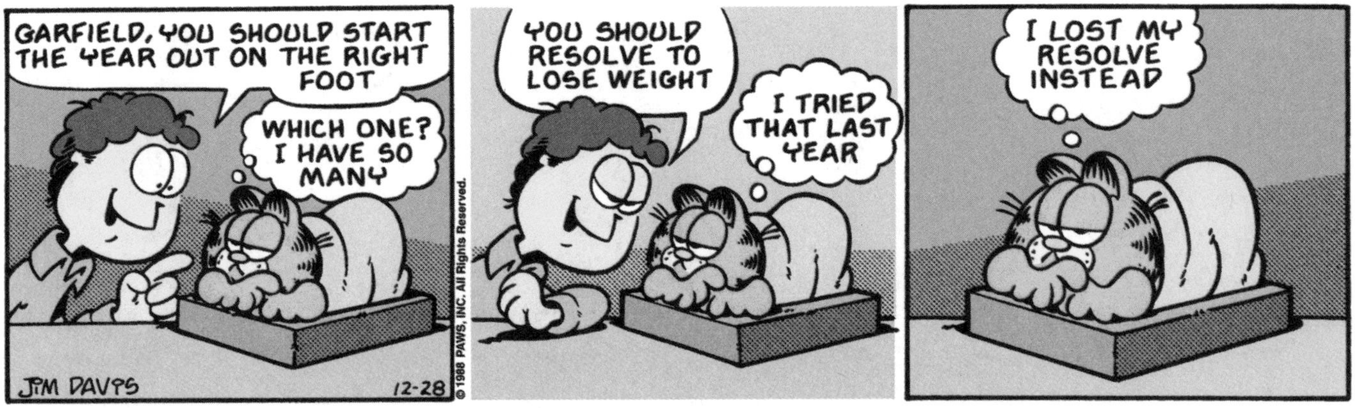
GARFIELD, YOU SHOULD START THE YEAR OUT ON THE RIGHT FOOT
WHICH ONE? I HAVE SO MANY
JIM DAVIS
12-28
YOU SHOULD RESOLVE TO LOSE WEIGHT
I TRIED THAT LAST YEAR
I LOST MY RESOLVE INSTEAD

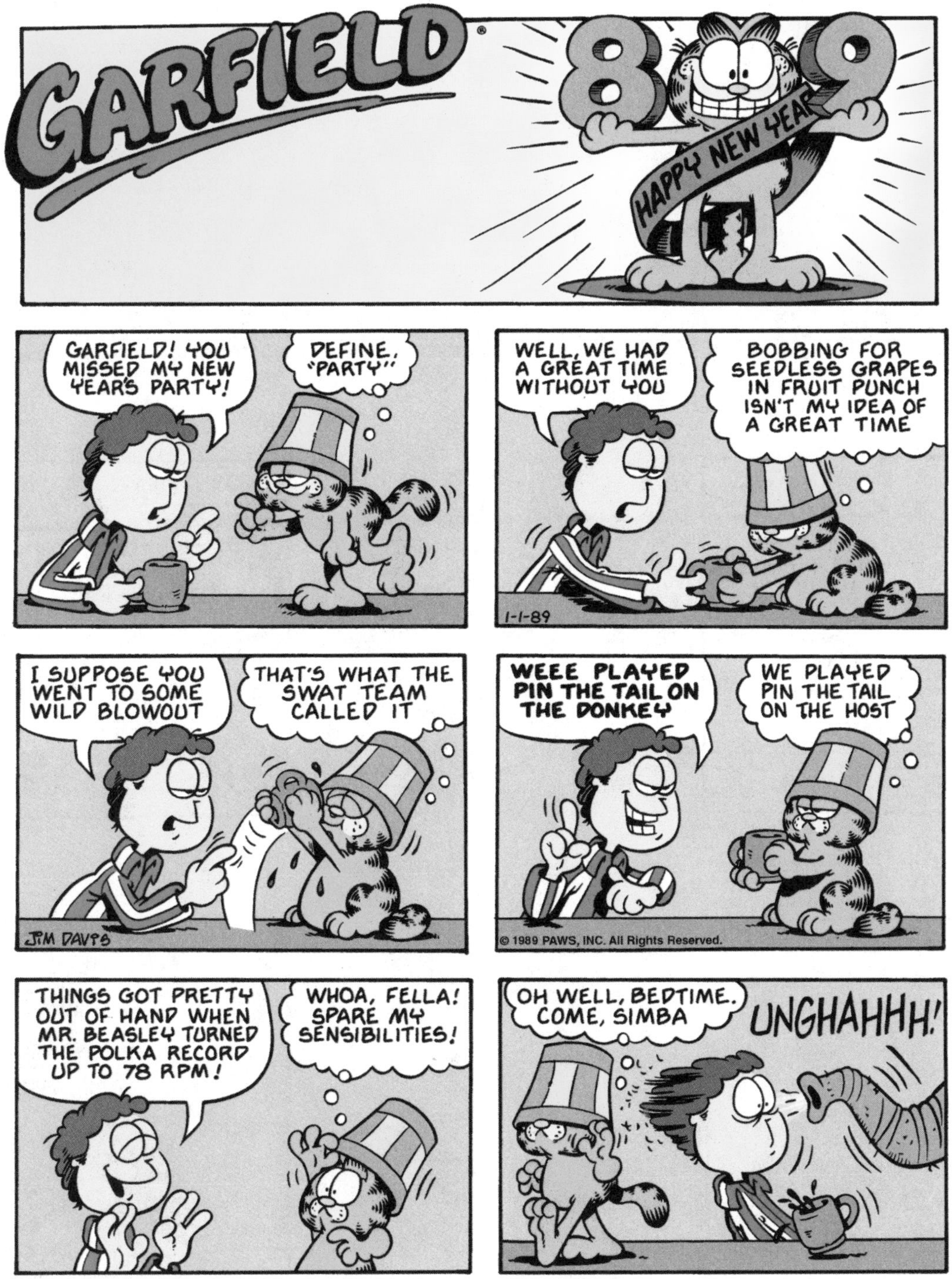
GARFIELD
8 9
HAPPY NEW YEAR
GARFIELD! YOU MISSED MY NEW YEAR'S PARTY!
DEFINE "PARTY"
WELL, WE HAD A GREAT TIME WITHOUT YOU
BOBBING FOR SEEDLESS GRAPES IN FRUIT PUNCH ISN'T MY IDEA OF A GREAT TIME
1-1-89
I SUPPOSE YOU WENT TO SOME WILD BLOWOUT
THAT'S WHAT THE SWAT TEAM CALLED IT
JIM DAVIS
WEEE PLAYED PIN THE TAIL ON THE DONKEY
WE PLAYED PIN THE TAIL ON THE HOST
© 1989 PAWS, INC. All Rights Reserved.
THINGS GOT PRETTY OUT OF HAND WHEN MR. BEASLEY TURNED THE POLKA RECORD UP TO 78 RPM!
WHOA, FELLA! SPARE MY SENSIBILITIES!
OH WELL, BEDTIME. COME, SIMBA
UNGHAHHH!

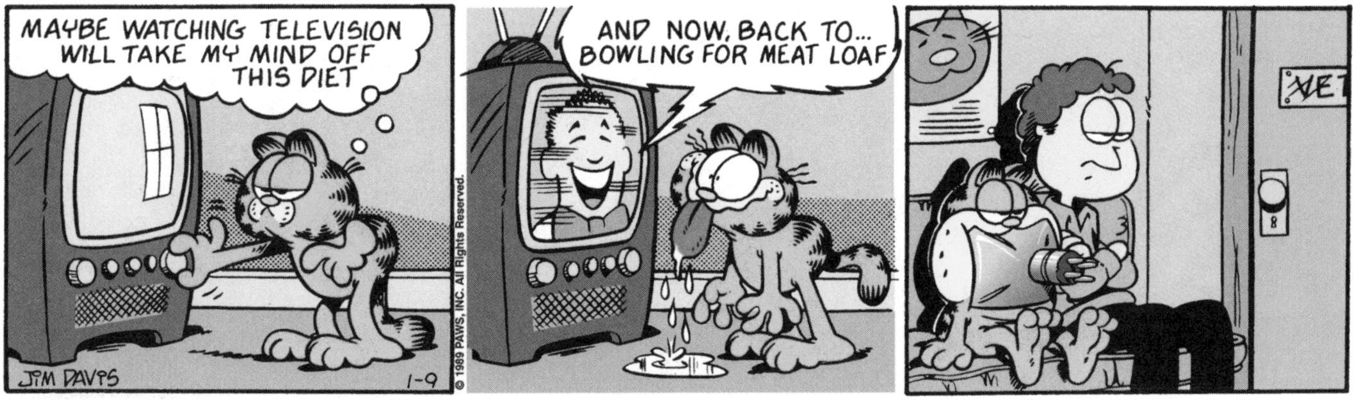
MAYBE WATCHING TELEVISION WILL TAKE MY MIND OFF THIS DIET
AND NOW, BACK TO... BOWLING FOR MEAT LOAF
JIM DAVIS 1-9
© 1989 PAWS, INC. All Rights Reserved.

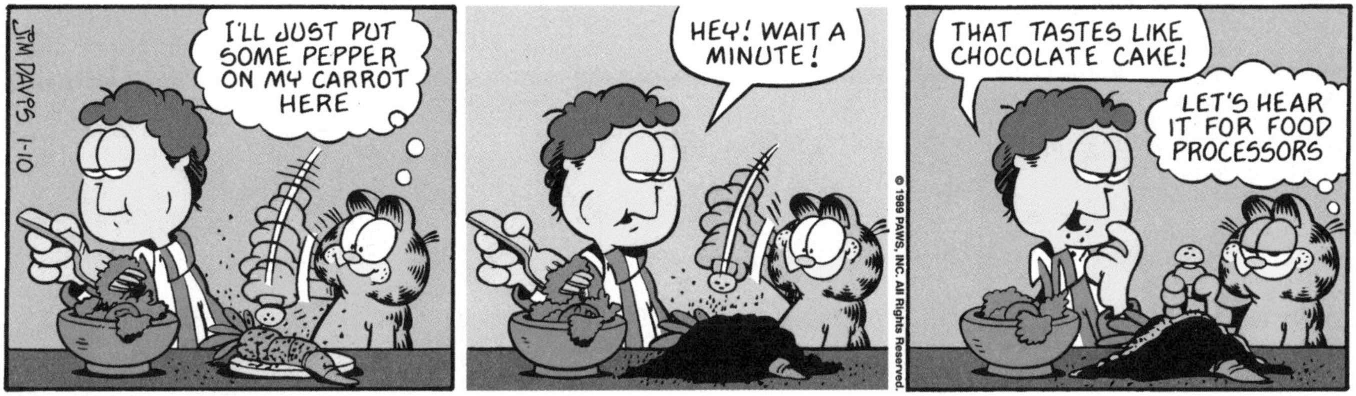
I'LL JUST PUT SOME PEPPER ON MY CARROT HERE
JIM DAVIS 1-10
HEY! WAIT A MINUTE!
THAT TASTES LIKE CHOCOLATE CAKE!
LET'S HEAR IT FOR FOOD PROCESSORS
© 1989 PAWS, INC. All Rights Reserved.

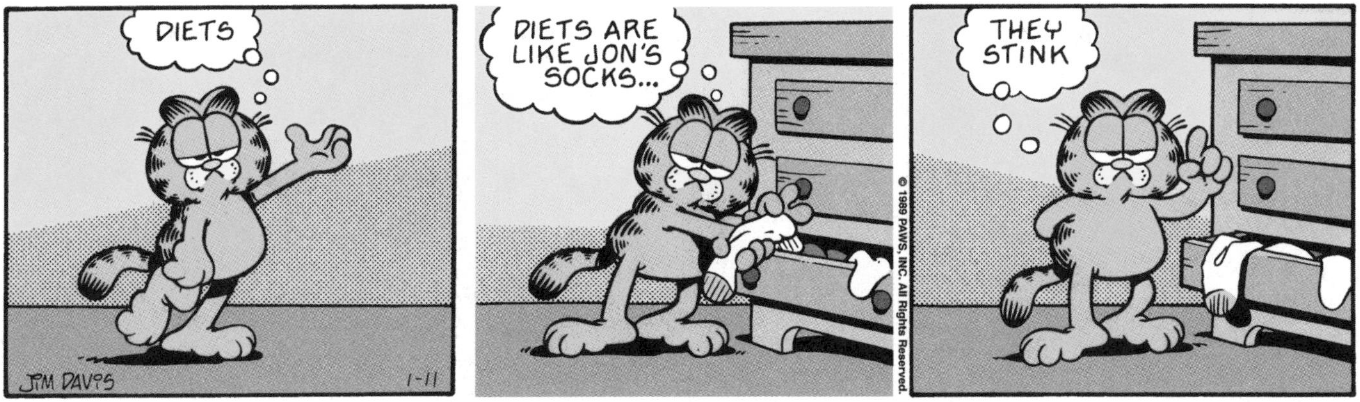
DIETS
JIM DAVIS 1-11
DIETS ARE LIKE JON'S SOCKS...
THEY STINK
© 1989 PAWS, INC. All Rights Reserved.

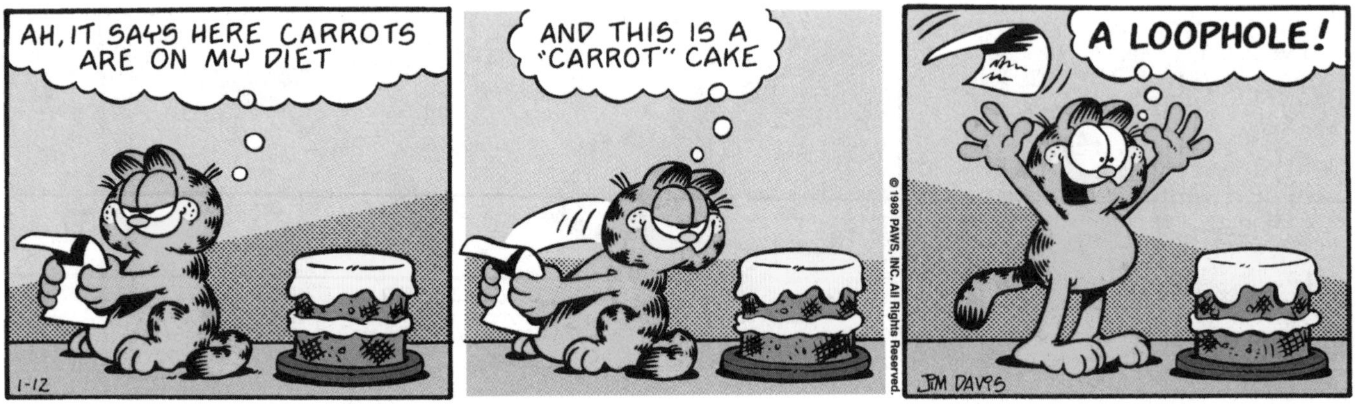
AH, IT SAYS HERE CARROTS ARE ON MY DIET
1-12
AND THIS IS A "CARROT" CAKE
© 1989 PAWS, INC. All Rights Reserved.
A LOOPHOLE!
JIM DAVIS

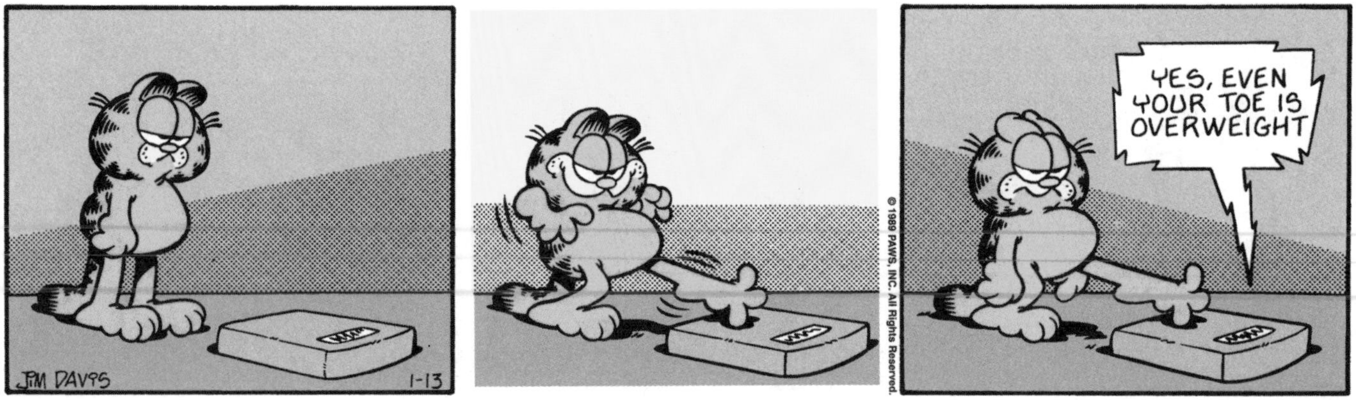
JIM DAVIS
1-13
© 1989 PAWS, INC. All Rights Reserved.
YES, EVEN YOUR TOE IS OVERWEIGHT

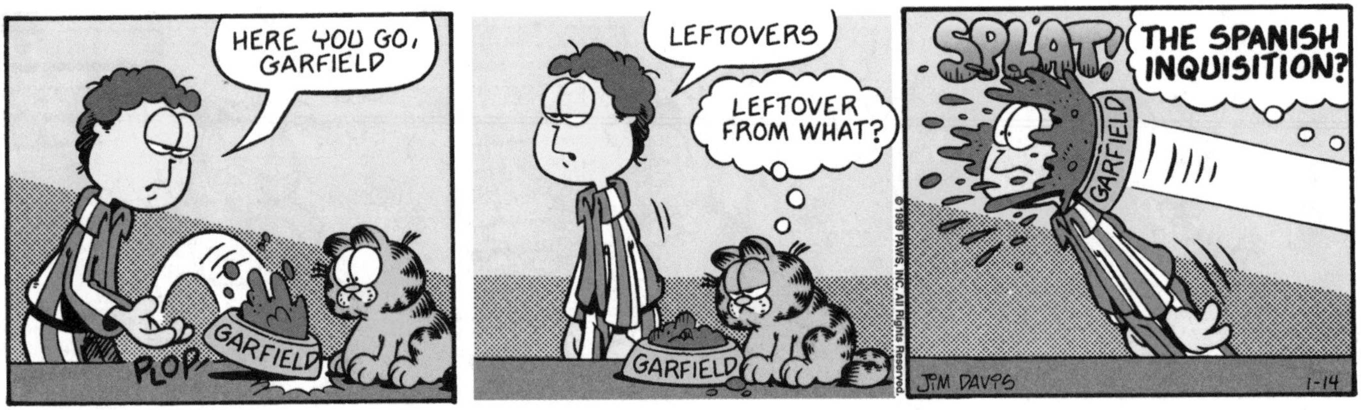
HERE YOU GO, GARFIELD
PLOP
GARFIELD
LEFTOVERS
LEFTOVER FROM WHAT?
GARFIELD
© 1989 PAWS, INC. All Rights Reserved.
SPLAT!
THE SPANISH INQUISITION?
GARFIELD
JIM DAVIS
1-14

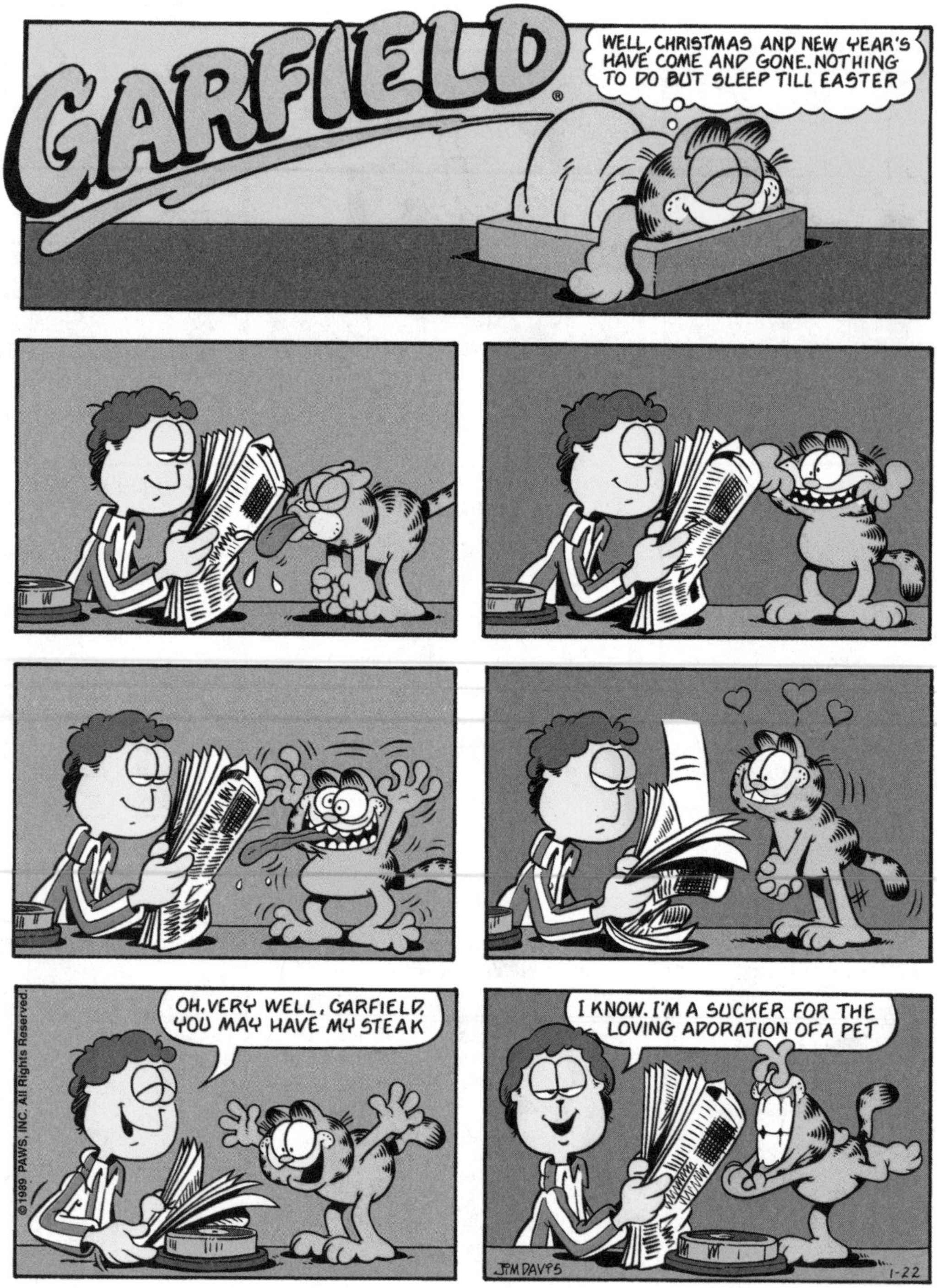
GARFIELD®
WELL, CHRISTMAS AND NEW YEAR'S HAVE COME AND GONE. NOTHING TO DO BUT SLEEP TILL EASTER
OH, VERY WELL, GARFIELD. YOU MAY HAVE MY STEAK
I KNOW. I'M A SUCKER FOR THE LOVING ADORATION OF A PET
© 1989 PAWS, INC. All Rights Reserved.
JIM DAVIS
1-22

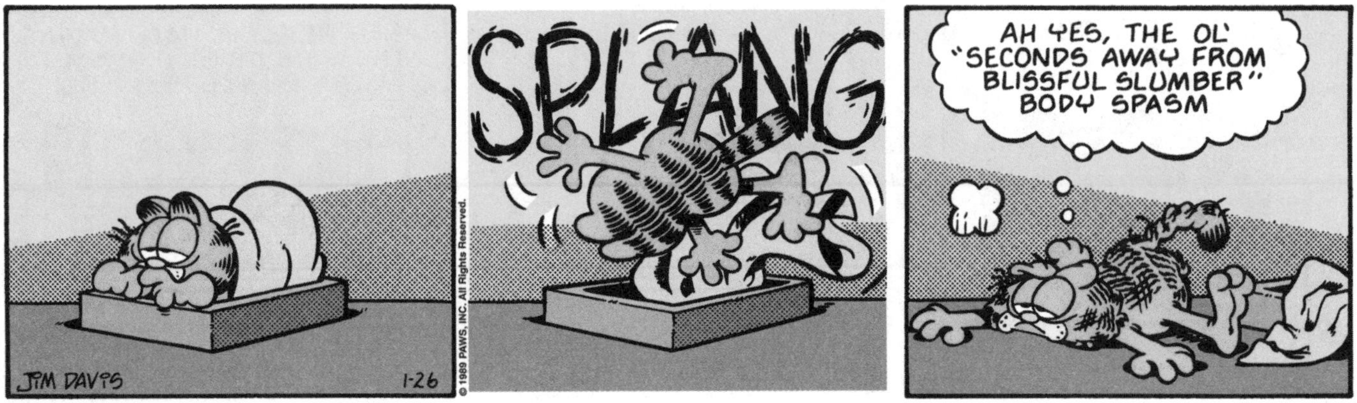
JIM DAVIS
1-26
SPLANG
© 1989 PAWS, INC. All Rights Reserved.
AH YES, THE OL' "SECONDS AWAY FROM BLISSFUL SLUMBER" BODY SPASM

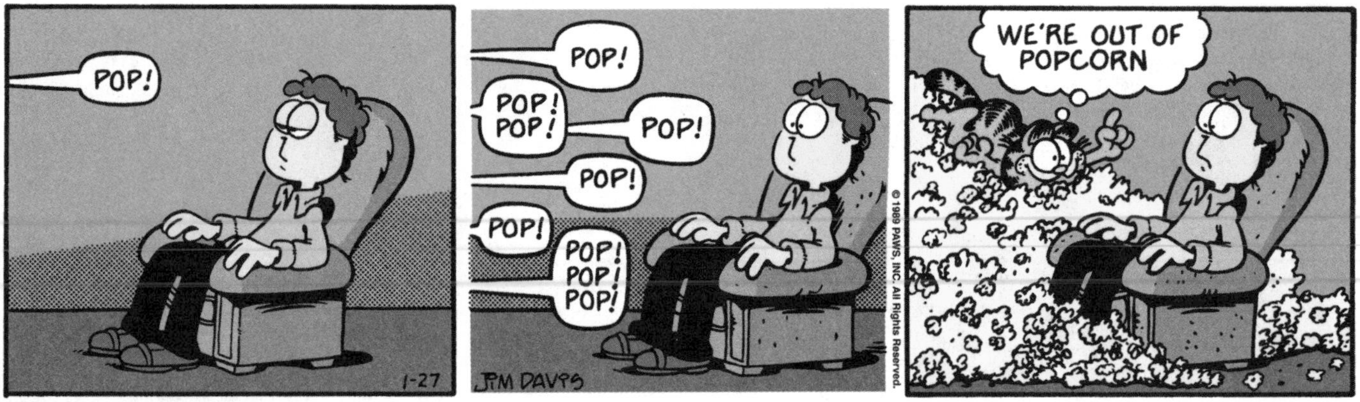
POP!
1-27
POP!
POP! POP!
POP!
POP!
POP!
POP! POP! POP!
JIM DAVIS
© 1989 PAWS, INC. All Rights Reserved.
WE'RE OUT OF POPCORN

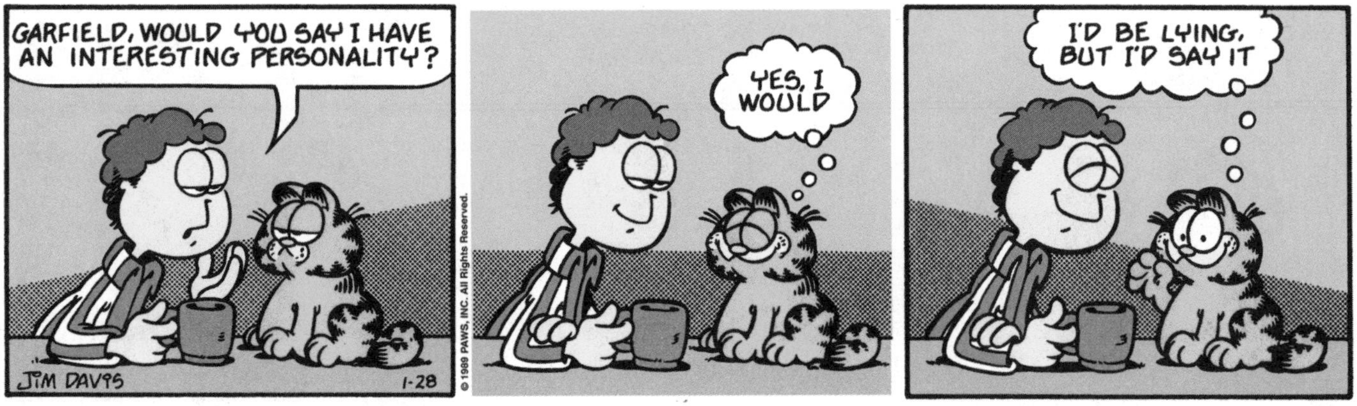
GARFIELD, WOULD YOU SAY I HAVE AN INTERESTING PERSONALITY?
JIM DAVIS
1-28
© 1989 PAWS, INC. All Rights Reserved.
YES, I WOULD
I'D BE LYING, BUT I'D SAY IT

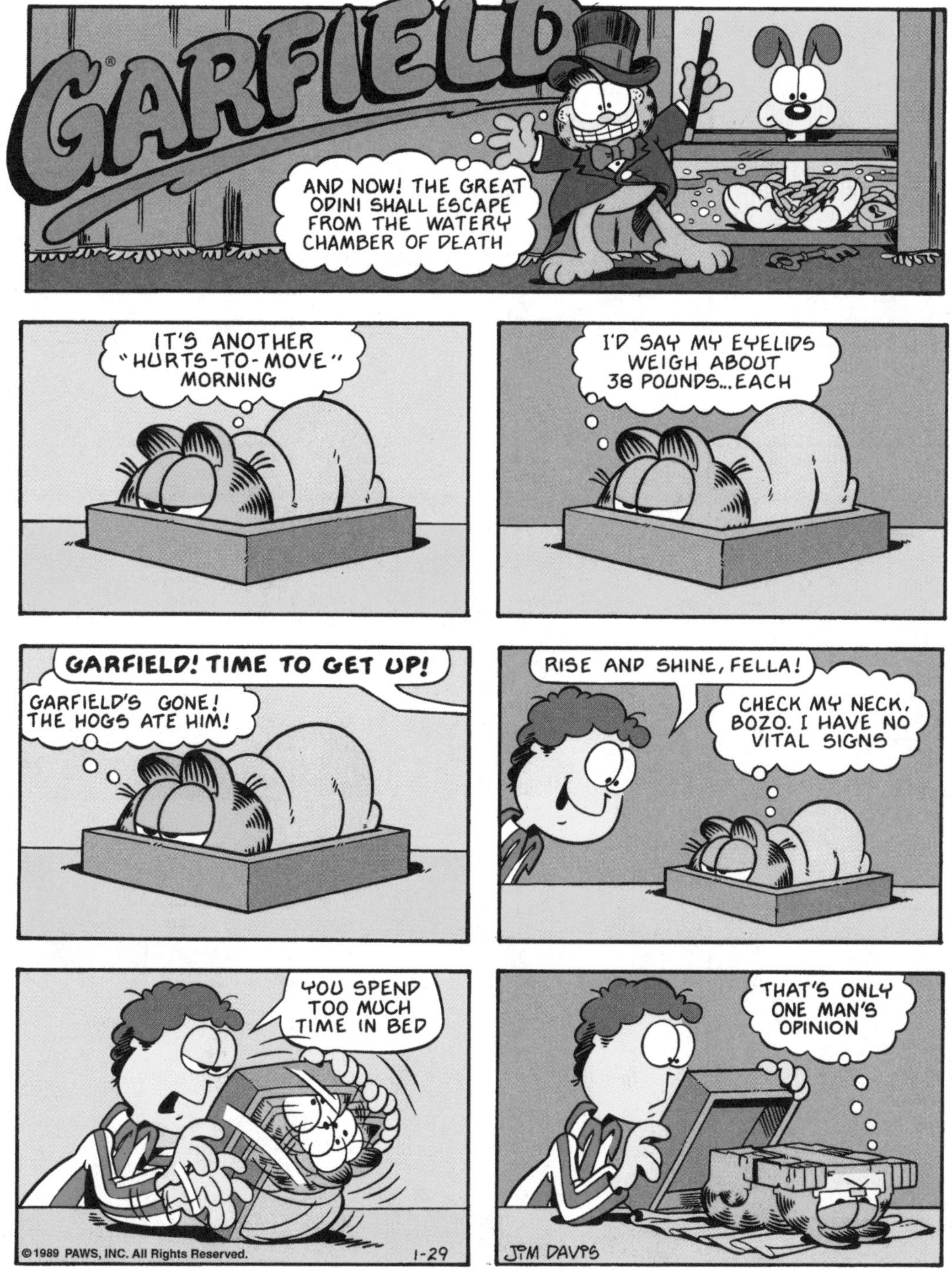
GARFIELD
AND NOW! THE GREAT ODINI SHALL ESCAPE FROM THE WATERY CHAMBER OF DEATH
IT'S ANOTHER "HURTS-TO-MOVE" MORNING
I'D SAY MY EYELIDS WEIGH ABOUT 38 POUNDS...EACH
GARFIELD! TIME TO GET UP!
GARFIELD'S GONE! THE HOGS ATE HIM!
RISE AND SHINE, FELLA!
CHECK MY NECK, BOZO. I HAVE NO VITAL SIGNS
YOU SPEND TOO MUCH TIME IN BED
THAT'S ONLY ONE MAN'S OPINION
1-29
JIM DAVIS

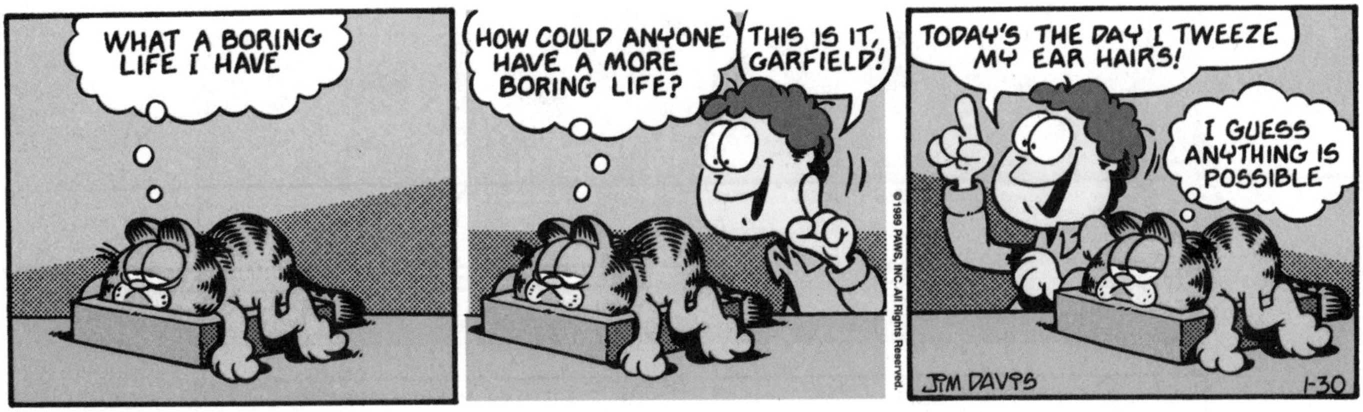
WHAT A BORING LIFE I HAVE
HOW COULD ANYONE HAVE A MORE BORING LIFE?
THIS IS IT, GARFIELD!
TODAY'S THE DAY I TWEEZE MY EAR HAIRS!
I GUESS ANYTHING IS POSSIBLE
JIM DAVIS
1-30
© 1989 PAWS, INC. All Rights Reserved.

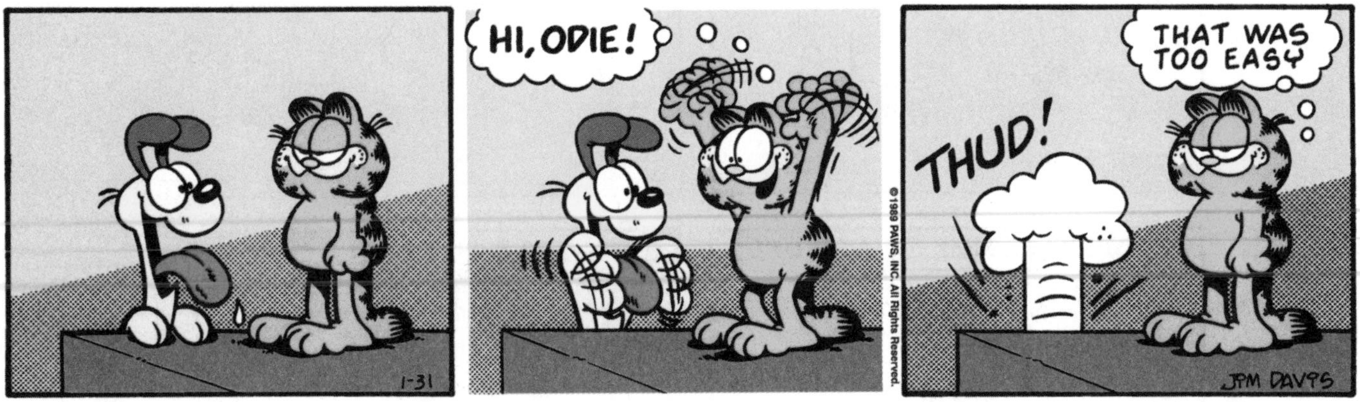
HI, ODIE!
THUD!
THAT WAS TOO EASY
1-31
JIM DAVIS
© 1989 PAWS, INC. All Rights Reserved.

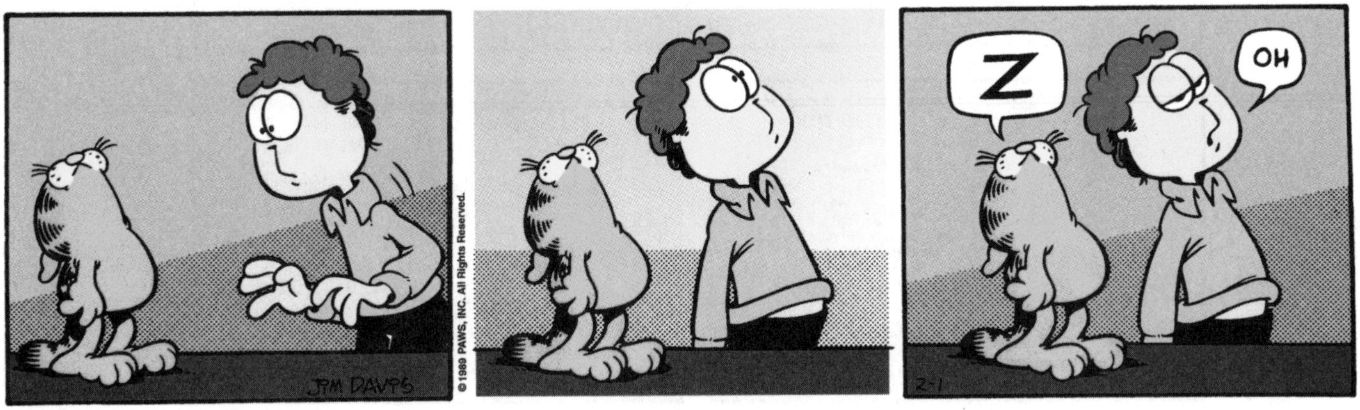
JIM DAVIS
Z
OH
2-1
© 1989 PAWS, INC. All Rights Reserved.

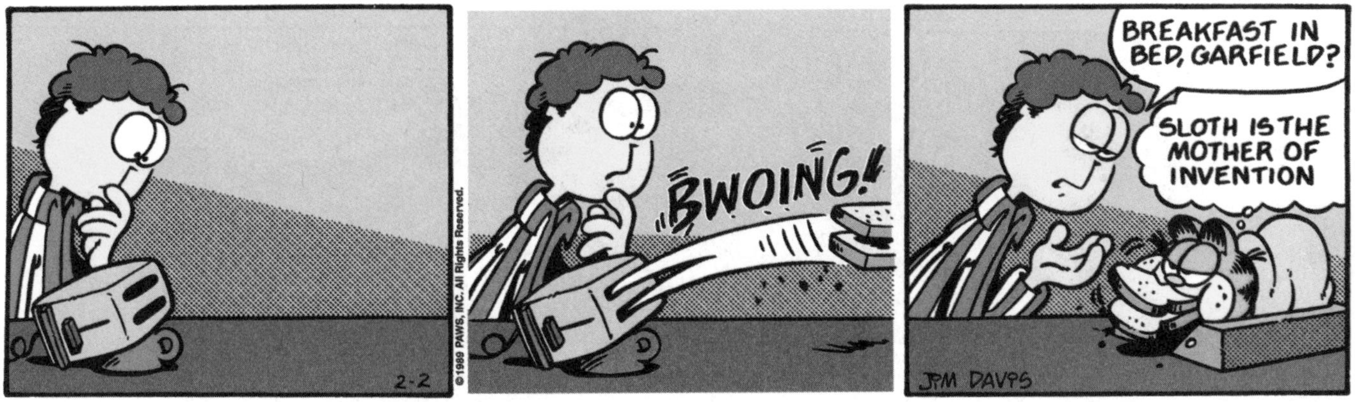
2-2
©1989 PAWS, INC. All Rights Reserved.
BWOING!
BREAKFAST IN BED, GARFIELD?
SLOTH IS THE MOTHER OF INVENTION
JPM DAVPS

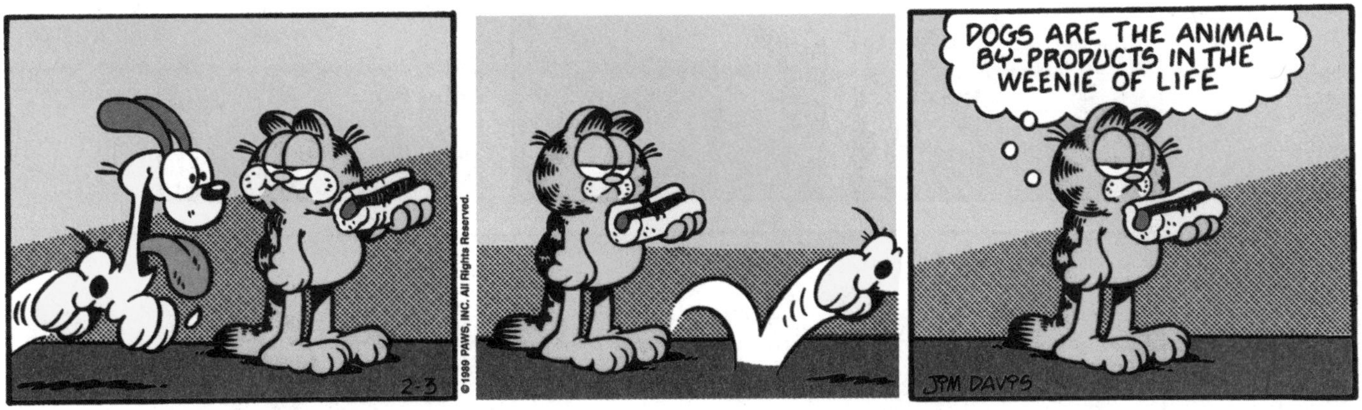
2-3
©1989 PAWS, INC. All Rights Reserved.
DOGS ARE THE ANIMAL BY-PRODUCTS IN THE WEENIE OF LIFE
JPM DAVPS

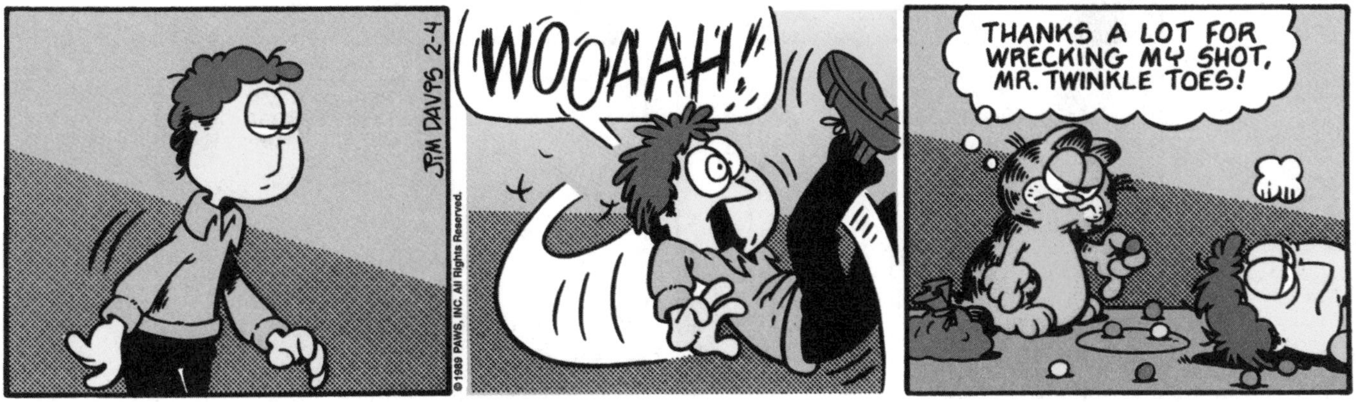
JPM DAVPS 2-4
©1989 PAWS, INC. All Rights Reserved.
WOOAAH!
THANKS A LOT FOR WRECKING MY SHOT, MR. TWINKLE TOES!

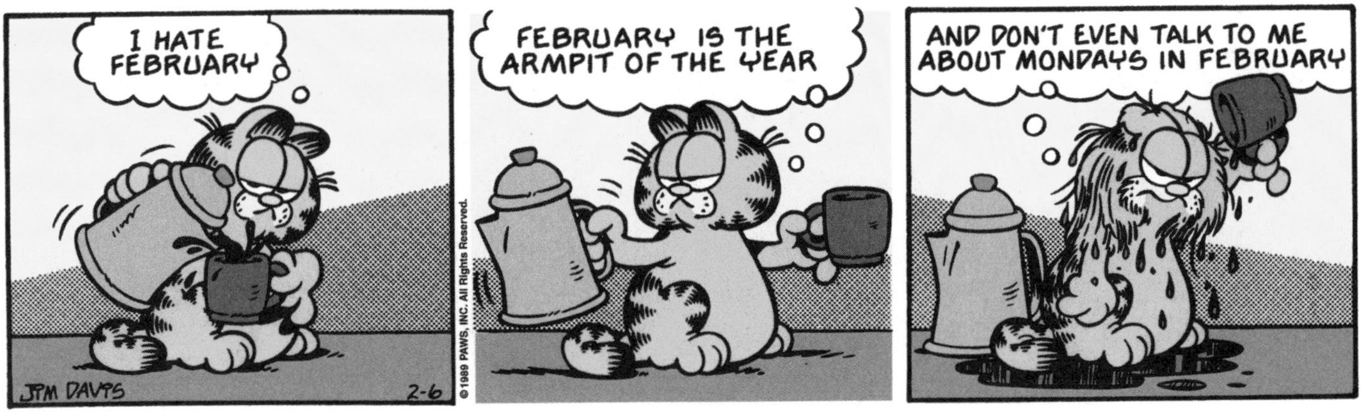
I HATE FEBRUARY
JIM DAVIS 2-6
FEBRUARY IS THE ARMPIT OF THE YEAR
©1989 PAWS, INC. All Rights Reserved.
AND DON'T EVEN TALK TO ME ABOUT MONDAYS IN FEBRUARY

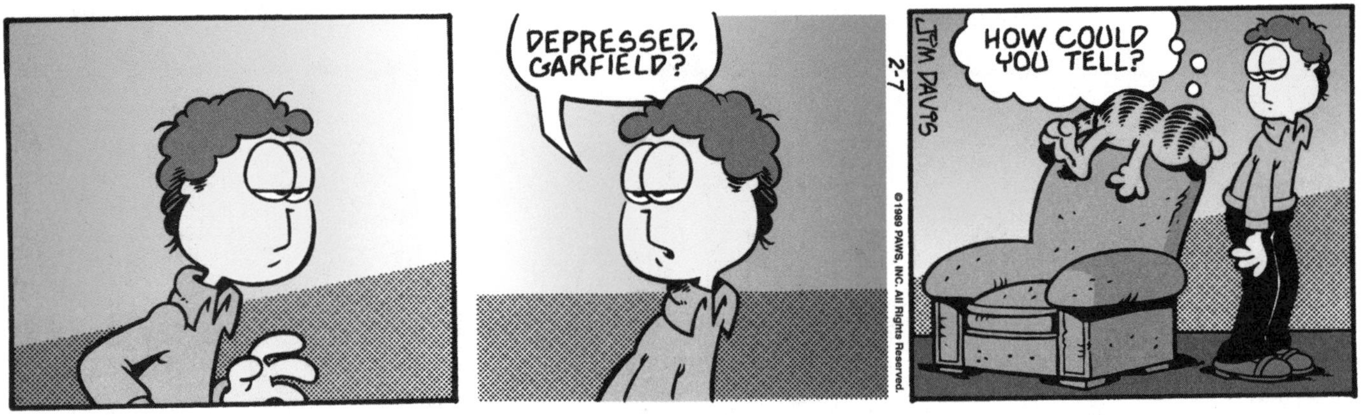
DEPRESSED, GARFIELD?
JIM DAVIS 2-7
©1989 PAWS, INC. All Rights Reserved.
HOW COULD YOU TELL?

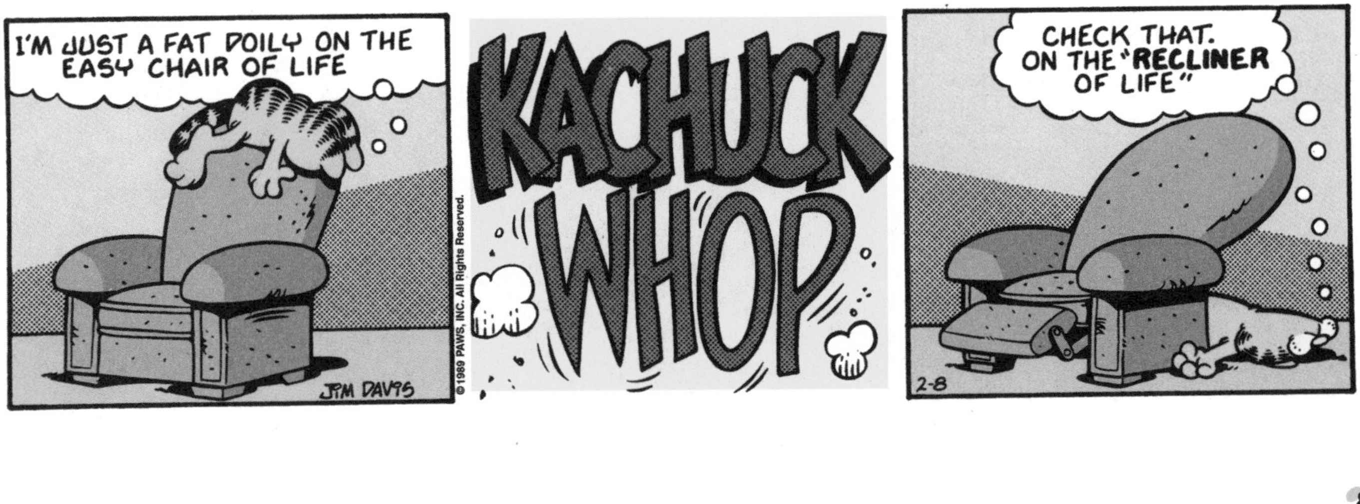
I'M JUST A FAT DOILY ON THE EASY CHAIR OF LIFE
JIM DAVIS
©1989 PAWS, INC. All Rights Reserved.
KACHUCK
WHOP
CHECK THAT. ON THE "RECLINER OF LIFE"
2-8

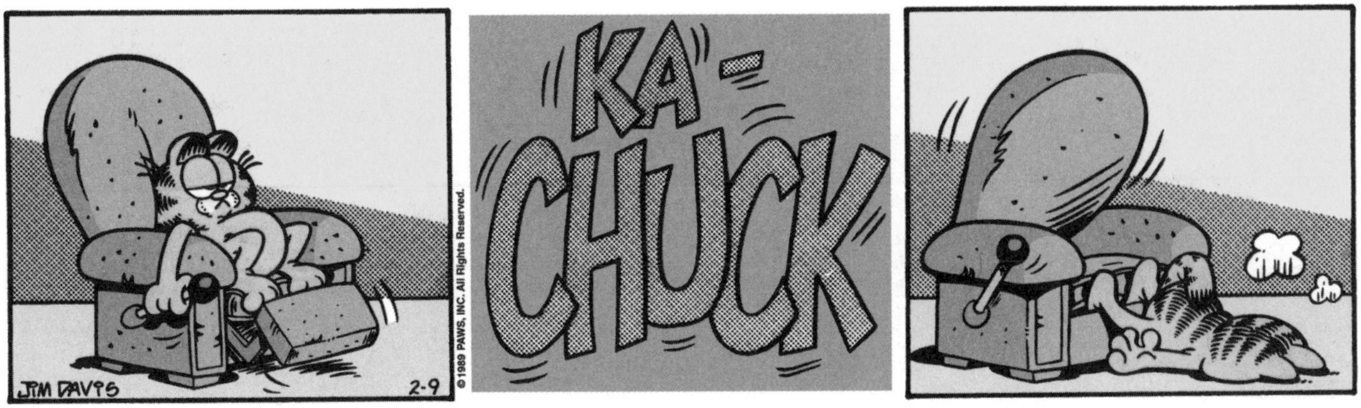
JIM DAVIS
2-9
©1989 PAWS, INC. All Rights Reserved.
KA-
CHUCK

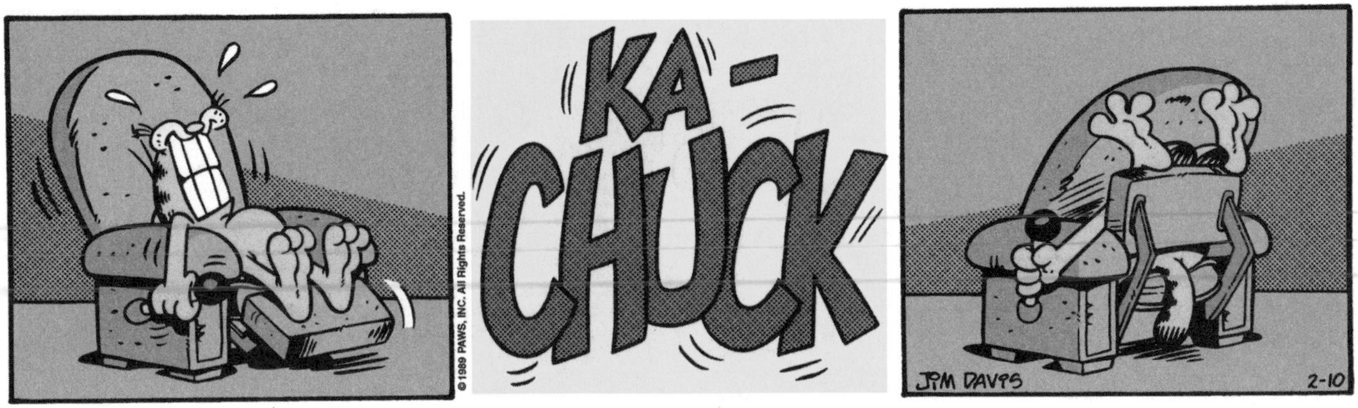
©1989 PAWS, INC. All Rights Reserved.
KA-
CHUCK
JIM DAVIS
2-10

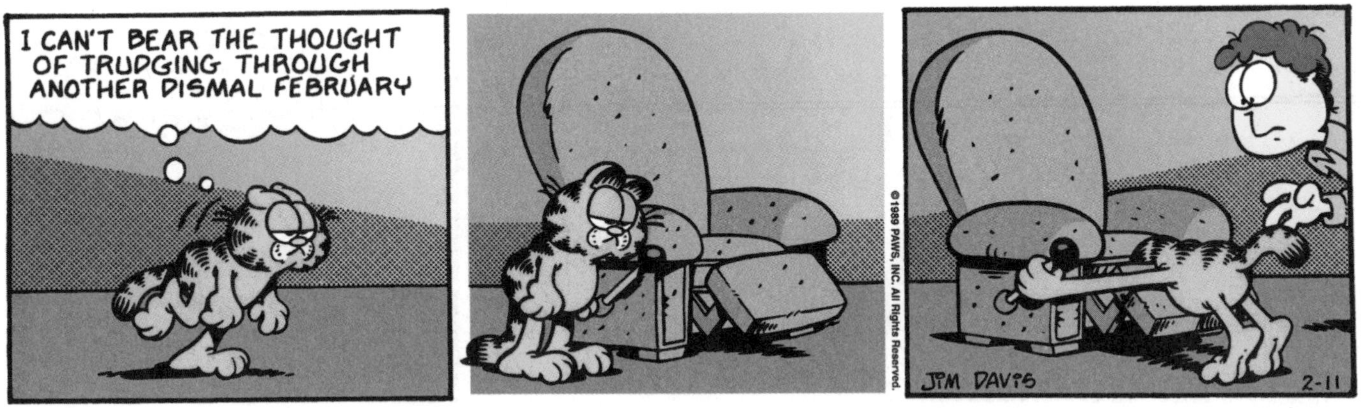
I CAN'T BEAR THE THOUGHT OF TRUDGING THROUGH ANOTHER DISMAL FEBRUARY
©1989 PAWS, INC. All Rights Reserved.
JIM DAVIS
2-11

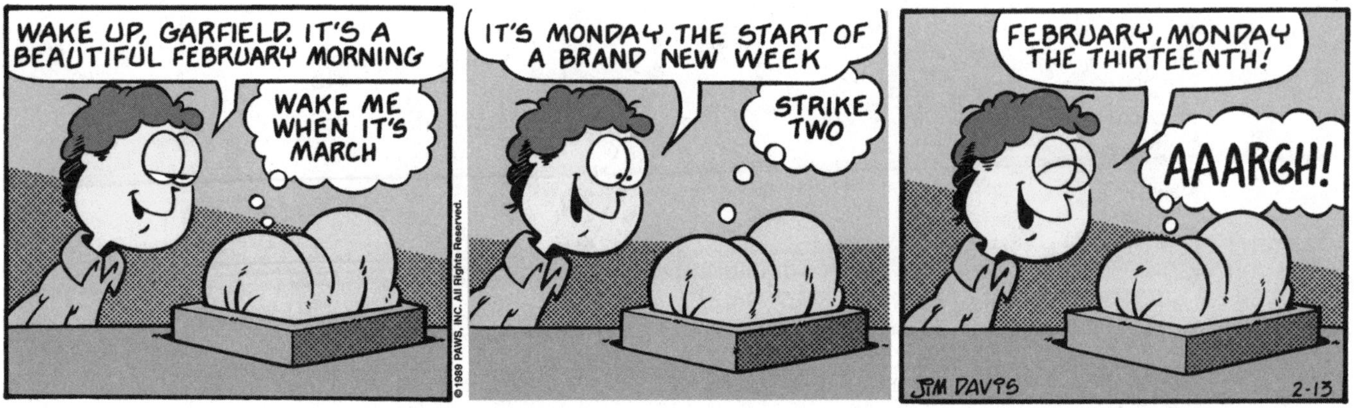
WAKE UP, GARFIELD. IT'S A BEAUTIFUL FEBRUARY MORNING
WAKE ME WHEN IT'S MARCH
IT'S MONDAY, THE START OF A BRAND NEW WEEK
STRIKE TWO
FEBRUARY, MONDAY THE THIRTEENTH!
AAARGH!
© 1989 PAWS, INC. All Rights Reserved.
JIM DAVIS
2-13

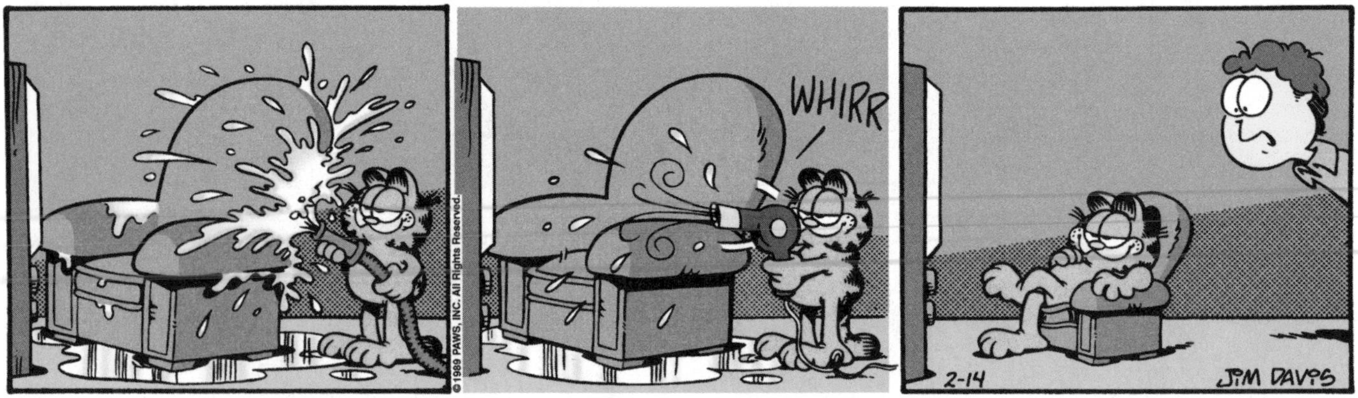
WHIRR
© 1989 PAWS, INC. All Rights Reserved.
2-14
JIM DAVIS

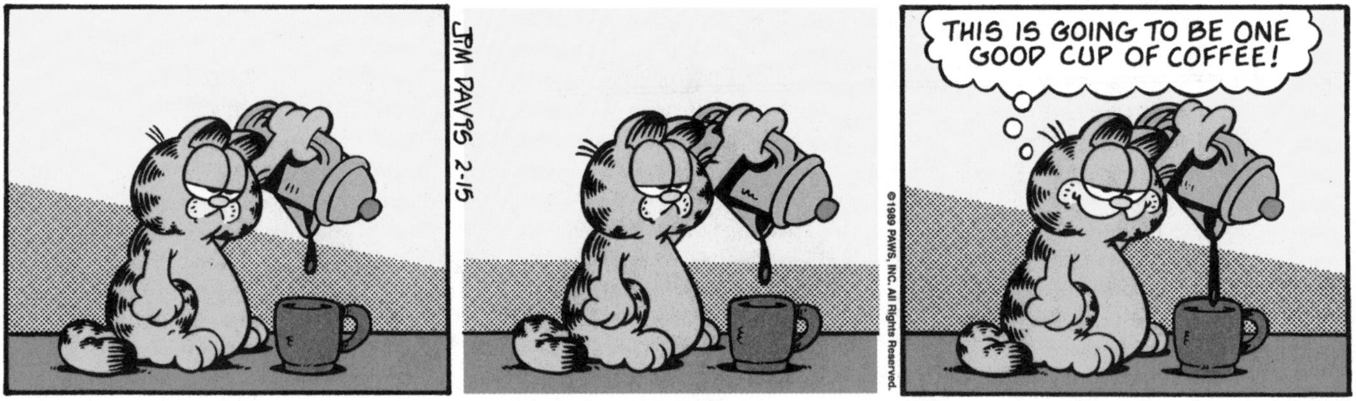
JIM DAVIS 2-15
© 1989 PAWS, INC. All Rights Reserved.
THIS IS GOING TO BE ONE GOOD CUP OF COFFEE!

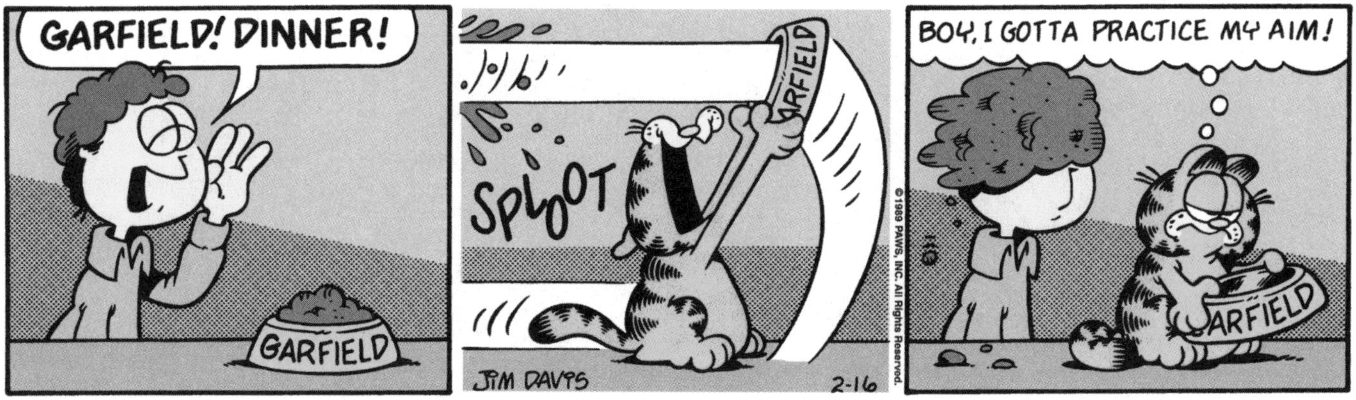
GARFIELD! DINNER!
GARFIELD
SPLOOT
GARFIELD
JIM DAVIS
2-16
© 1989 PAWS, INC. All Rights Reserved.
BOY, I GOTTA PRACTICE MY AIM!
GARFIELD

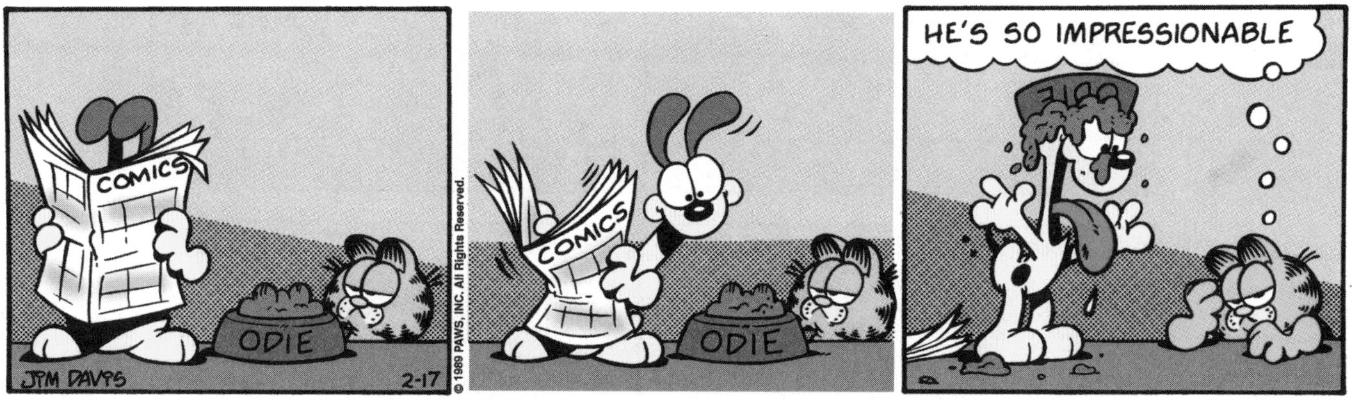
COMICS
ODIE
JIM DAVIS
2-17
© 1989 PAWS, INC. All Rights Reserved.
COMICS
ODIE
HE'S SO IMPRESSIONABLE

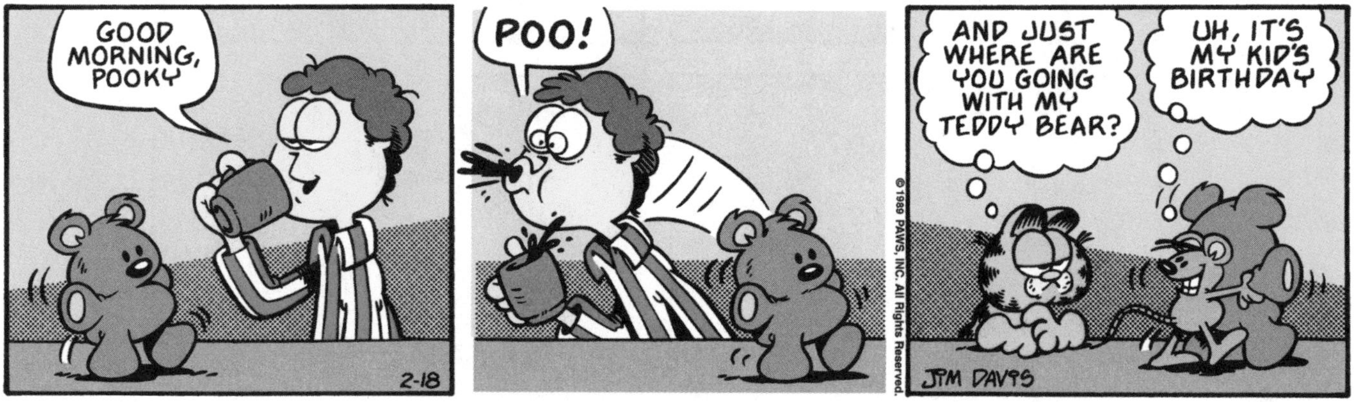
GOOD MORNING, POOKY
2-18
POO!
© 1989 PAWS, INC. All Rights Reserved.
AND JUST WHERE ARE YOU GOING WITH MY TEDDY BEAR?
UH, IT'S MY KID'S BIRTHDAY
JIM DAVIS

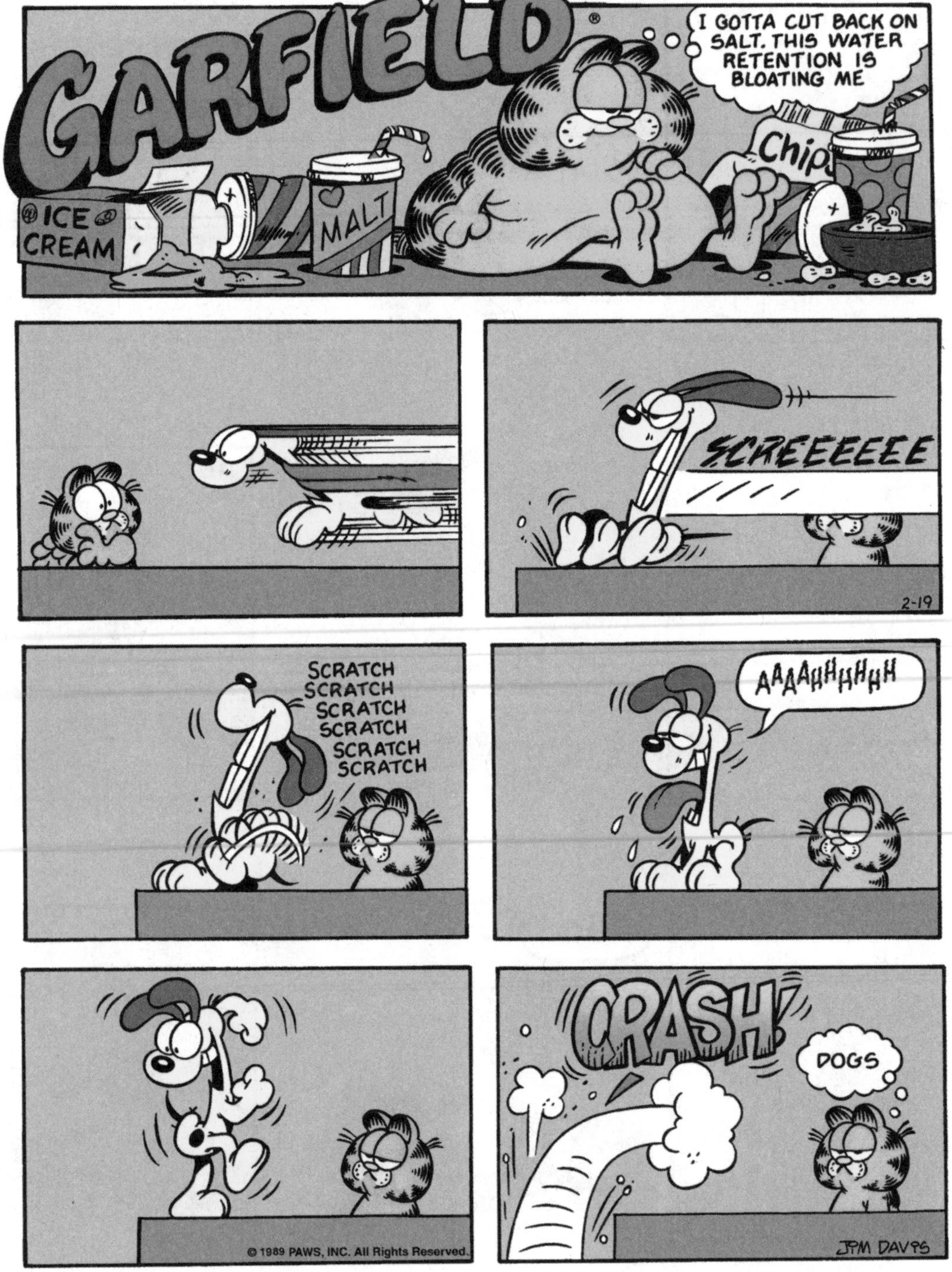
GARFIELD®
I GOTTA CUT BACK ON SALT. THIS WATER RETENTION IS BLOATING ME
ICE CREAM
MALT
Chip
SCREEEEEEE
2-19
SCRATCH SCRATCH SCRATCH SCRATCH SCRATCH SCRATCH
AAAAHHHHHH
© 1989 PAWS, INC. All Rights Reserved.
CRASH
DOGS
JPM DAVPS

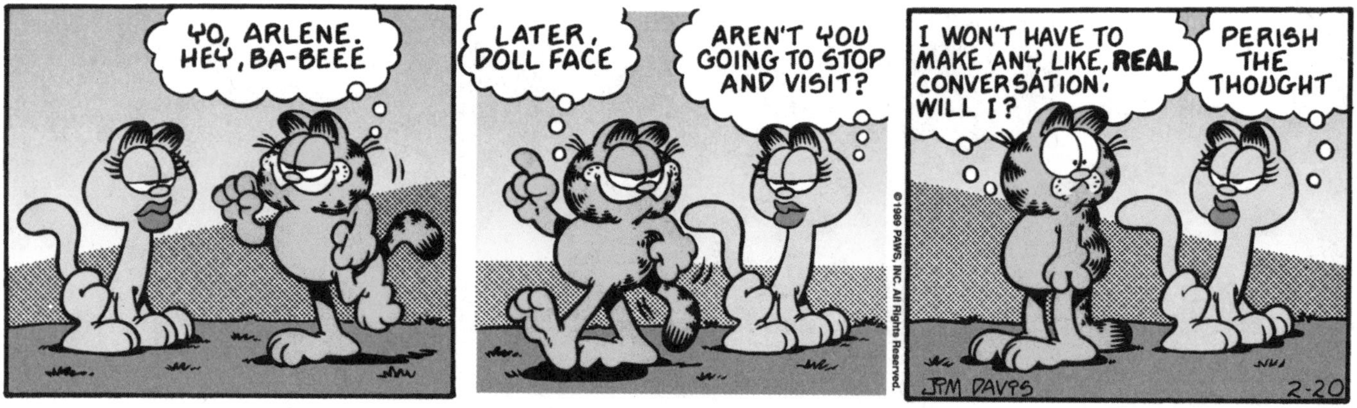
YO, ARLENE. HEY, BA-BEEE
LATER, DOLL FACE
AREN'T YOU GOING TO STOP AND VISIT?
I WON'T HAVE TO MAKE ANY LIKE, REAL CONVERSATION, WILL I?
PERISH THE THOUGHT
© 1989 PAWS, INC. All Rights Reserved.
JIM DAVIS
2-20

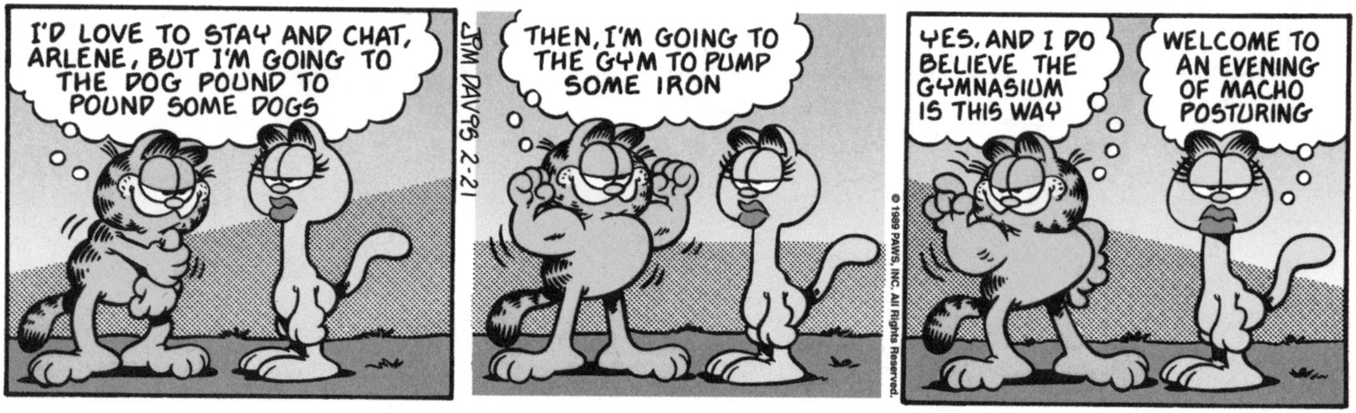
I'D LOVE TO STAY AND CHAT, ARLENE, BUT I'M GOING TO THE DOG POUND TO POUND SOME DOGS
JIM DAVIS 2-21
THEN, I'M GOING TO THE GYM TO PUMP SOME IRON
YES, AND I DO BELIEVE THE GYMNASIUM IS THIS WAY
WELCOME TO AN EVENING OF MACHO POSTURING
© 1989 PAWS, INC. All Rights Reserved.

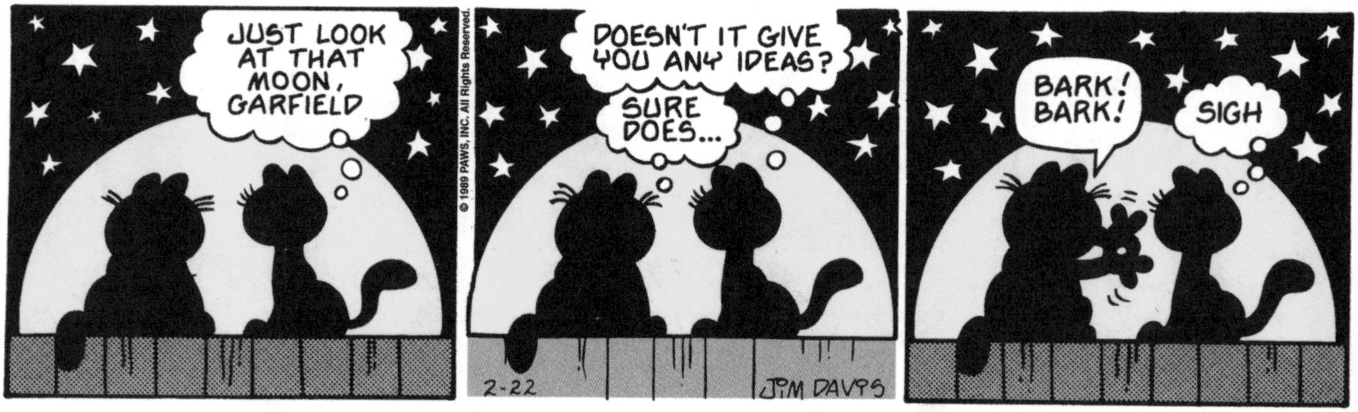
JUST LOOK AT THAT MOON, GARFIELD
© 1989 PAWS, INC. All Rights Reserved.
DOESN'T IT GIVE YOU ANY IDEAS?
SURE DOES...
2-22
JIM DAVIS
BARK! BARK!
SIGH